A WILSON CENTER CONFERENCE REPORT

VIETNAM AS HISTORY

TEN YEARS AFTER THE PARIS PEACE ACCORDS

Peter Braestrup, Editor

JANUARY 1984

UNIVERSITY PRESS OF AMERICA

© 1984 by the Woodrow Wilson International Center for Scholars

Co-published by University Press of America,™ Inc.
P.O.B. 19101, Washington, D.C. 20036

Printed in the United States of America

Library of Congress Cataloging in Publication Data
Main entry under title:

Vietnam as history.

    (A Wilson Center conference report)
    Proceedings of a conference held at the Smithsonian Institution, Jan. 7-8, 1983, under the auspices of the Woodrow Wilson International Center for Scholars's International Security Studies Program and the Wilson Quarterly.
    "January 1984."
    Includes bibliographies.
    1. Vietnamese Conflict, 1961-1975—Congresses. 2. Vietnamese Conflict, 1961-1975—United States—Congresses. I. Braestrup, Peter. II. Woodrow Wilson International Center for Scholars. International Security Studies Program. III. Series.
DS557.7.V562   1984   959.704'3373   83-21748
ISBN 0-8191-3653-0 (alk. paper)
ISBN 0-8191-3654-9 (pbk. : alk. paper)

Illustrations: *cover, Ronald E. Pepin, courtesy of the U.S. Army Center for Military History; drawing in the appendices, from The Reporter, February 20, 1966; maps, courtesy of the U.S. Army Center for Military History; charts, from The Wilson Quarterly, Summer 1983.*

THE WILSON CENTER

Smithsonian Institution Building
Washington D.C. 20560

CONTENTS

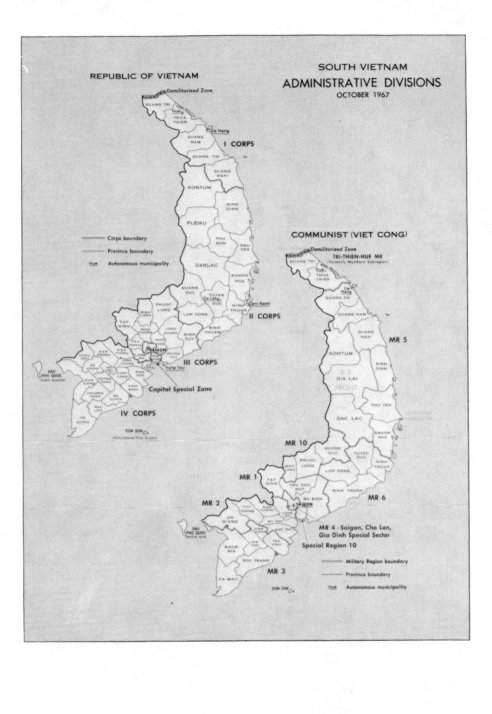

REPUBLIC OF VIETNAM

SOUTH VIETNAM
ADMINISTRATIVE DIVISIONS
OCTOBER 1967

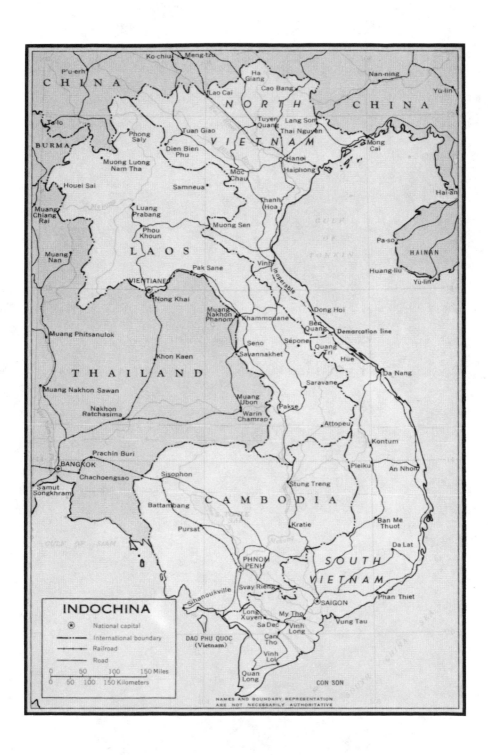

INDOCHINA

⊛ National capital
╌╎╌ International boundary
┼┼┼ Railroad
─── Road

0 — 50 — 100 — 150 Miles
0 — 50 100 — 150 Kilometers

NAMES AND BOUNDARY REPRESENTATION
ARE NOT NECESSARILY AUTHORITATIVE

INTRODUCTION

On January 7–8, 1983, some 50 leading historians and analysts of the United States experience in the Vietnam War, 1964–1973, gathered to discuss a set of ten specially commissioned papers at the Woodrow Wilson International Center for Scholars at the Smithsonian Institution. The meeting was held under the auspices of the Center's International Security Studies Program and *The Wilson Quarterly*.

This conference marked the tenth anniversary of the Paris Peace Agreements (January 27, 1973) and the 15th anniversary of the onset of the Vietnamese Communists' offensive of Tet 1968 (January 30–31). The meeting's chief goal was to discuss what scholars now know (and do not know) about the higher conduct of the war in 1964–1973 by the United States, North Vietnam, and South Vietnam.

A second purpose was to discuss what lessons, if any, this experience, as now perceived, should signal to U.S. civilian and military leaders in the 1980s.

The conference's focus on the "higher conduct" of the war necessarily barred detailed consideration of other key aspects of the long Vietnam conflict, notably the evolution of the formal U.S. commitment to preserve a non-communist South Vietnam that began in 1955; the role of Communist China and the Soviet Union; developments in neighboring Laos and Cambodia; the changes in congressional sentiment as U.S. involvement deepened; the battlefield tactics and the twists and turns of U.S. negotiating policy; and the events in Indochina in 1973–75 after U.S. withdrawal from Vietnam.

As the conference discussions made clear, not all Vietnam scholars and analysts agree on all issues of "fact" or interpretation.

But there was a surprising degree of agreement on the answers to such questions as: Did Hanoi really wage and win a "people's war" in South Vietnam? Was the U.S. commitment to South Vietnam "immoral"? Was Lyndon Johnson eager to put U.S. troops into Vietnam in 1964–65? Was he optimistic about success? Were his professed fears of Chinese or Soviet intervention supported by intelligence estimates of the time? Did he really consider all the alternatives to U.S. troop commitment presented to him? Did he entertain a strategy for "winning"? Did the U.S. military really confront LBJ with its case for a stronger national effort? Did U.S. hopes for a negotiated compromise settlement ever rest on solid grounds? Was the Vietnam War more unpopular in America than was the Korean War? Did the U.S. peace movement shorten the Vietnam War? Did television coverage *per se* shape U.S. opinion? Were the U.S. forces and their South Vietnamese allies unable to cope with Hanoi's troops on the battlefield? Could the North Vietnamese have sustained the war effort in the South without sanctuaries in Laos and Cambodia? Did the Nixon-Kissinger strategy of troop withdrawals and peace negotiations with Hanoi hold any real promise of lasting success?

To each of these questions most of the conferees tended to answer "No," albeit with varying degrees of emphasis. These responses contradict many claims by hawks and doves during the war years, assertions that are still echoed in media retrospectives and in analogies (El Salvador, Afghanistan) drawn by public figures and journalists since the war.

Most of the participants seemed to agree that U.S. military intervention in Vietnam was a mistake. They also tended to agree that in a military sense the war in South Vietnam could have been, and in many ways by 1972 was, "won" against Hanoi's forces. Yet several participants also insisted that, given Hanoi's goals and tenacity, stable non-communist control of South Vietnam would have required the continued presence of a sizable residual U.S. force for perhaps as long as thirty years. Suggesting that such a lengthy military commitment would have proved unacceptable to the Congress and the American people, these scholars and policy analysts debated at some length the question of whether President Lyndon B. Johnson, aware as he was of the dim prospects for clearcut success, could have avoided major U.S. military intervention in 1965. While the participants were divided in their answers to this question, they agreed that whatever type of assistance the U.S. had undertaken, the President should have first determined and then fully explained the goals, prospects for success, and anticipated costs to Congress and the American people, and obtained their approval. And before any future U.S. intervention overseas, many participants agreed, the President should follow a similar procedure. These conclusions were among many that emerged from two days' intense exchange.

As several conferees noted, few academic scholars are now working on the history of the war. It is not a fashionable research topic in universities today although the war is widely taught on campus as history and the mass media fitfully replay old Vietnam clichés. The only specialized academic center for serious reseach on the war (and on other Indochinese matters) is the Indochina Studies Program, Institute of East Asian Studies, University of California at Berkeley (see Background Books Essay). Journalists and the armed services' historians are doing most of the retrospective work, even as the LBJ Library in Austin has begun to release important documents on the Johnson administration's conduct of the war. The Nixon-Ford documents are still largely held secret. Declassification of other wartime documents has slowed, frustrating even the military's own historians. And many questions of "fact" and interpretation remain.

This book represents an edited version of the conference proceedings. It is intended to be useful to teachers, Indochina specialists, journalists, and others as an indication of current thinking by serious scholars on the war and its lessons.

The transcript of the discussions has been edited in the interests of brevity and clarity. The papers of Messrs. Pike and Summers, as revised, appeared in the *Wilson Quarterly* (Summer 1983) and the *WQ* versions are used here. The informal remarks of Messrs. Lichty and Mueller have been reworked for publication herein. A special analysis by Mr. Mueller of public opinion data was prepared for this volume's appendices. Charts from the *WQ* Summer 1983 issue on Vietnam are reproduced herein, as is a bibliographic essay and a report on Vietnam veterans. A brief chronology is also appended.

No such conference report can serve as adequate testimony to the bravery of the Americans and their allies who fought in Vietnam or to the tenacity of their adversaries. It cannot reflect the ordeal of the people of Indochina, or convey the disarray and division that came to afflict America during the war years. Even so, there is value in looking back at the war's conduct in a dispassionate way and seeing what those who have been writing about it have come to think ten years after the United States left South Vietnam.

Samual F. Wells, Jr.
Peter Braestrup, Editor

ACKNOWLEDGEMENTS

This book's preparation was undertaken with the help of Elizabeth Dixon, Wilson Center publications officer; Anne Marie Sherry, the conference coordinator; Helen Loerke, editorial assistant; and Pat Sheridan of the Wilson Center staff.

The conference and this book project were strongly encouraged by the Wilson Center's director, James H. Billington, and its deputy director, Prosser Gifford, and reflected the Center's hospitality since 1970 to serious research by Fellows on the Indochina conflict.

The U.S. Army Center for Military History and the Historical Division, Marine Corps Museum, were particularly helpful in supplying data for the conference and for this book.

The conference discussions excerpted herein may not be directly quoted without permission, except where quotation marks are used in the text. The conference was supported in part by the Xerox Foundation and by the Institute for Educational Affairs. Publication of this volume was made possible by grants from I.E.A. and the Earhart Foundation. We are pleased to have as our publisher University Press of America.

CONFERENCE PARTICIPANTS

DEAN C. ALLARD, director of the U.S. Naval Historical Center's Operational Archives, is the co-editor of *Spencer Fullerton Baird and the U.S. Fish Commission: A Study in the History of American Science* (1978), and co-author of *The United States Navy and the Vietnam Conflict: The Setting of the Stage, Vol. I* (1976).

JAMES AUSTIN, an instructor in the Government Department at the University of Texas (Austin), is the author of "The Psychological Factors in Intelligence Activities" (1982) and is presently completing *Blind Men and Elephants: Strategic Assessment of Vietnam*.

DOROTHY AVERY is the analyst for Vietnam for the Southeast Asia and Pacific Division of the Bureau of Intelligence and Research at the Department of State.

LARRY BERMAN, associate professor of political science at the University of California (Davis), has taught at both American and Princeton Universities. He has written extensively on the Presidency, contributing "Johnson and the White House Staff" to *Exploring the Johnson Years* (1981); his most recent book is *Planning a Tragedy: The Americanization of the War in Vietnam* (1982).

RICHARD BETTS, senior fellow in Foreign Policy Studies, Brookings Institution, is the author of *Soldiers, Statesmen and Cold War Crises* (1977) and *Nonproliferation and U.S. Foreign Policy* (1980), and the editor of *Cruise Missiles: Technology, Strategy, Politics* (1981). With Leslie Gelb, he co-authored *The Irony of Vietnam: The System Worked* (1979), which won the 1980 Woodrow Wilson Prize for best book in political science.

DOUGLAS BLAUFARB, a free-lance consultant and writer on strategic issues in Southeast Asia, is the author of *The Counterinsurgency Era: U.S. Doctrine and Performance* (1977); he contributed to *Lessons From An Un-conventional War* (1982).

JOSEPH A. BOSCO, former legal counsel to the Governor of Massachusetts and special assistant to the Secretary of Transportation, is currently practicing law. He is a contributor to the *St. John's Review*.

PETER BRAESTRUP, editor of *The Wilson Quarterly*, former *Washington Post* and *New York Times* correspondent in Vietnam and a past Wilson Center Fellow, is the author of *Big Story: How the American Press and Television Reported and Interpreted the Crisis of Tet 1968 in Vietnam and Washington* (rev. edition, 1983).

ALLAN W. CAMERON, executive assistant to Senator Denton, formerly of Tuft's Fletcher School of Law and Diplomacy, is the author of *Viet-Nam: A Documentary History, Vol. I, 1940–56* (1971; *Indochina: Prospects After "the End"*

(1976) and "The Soviet Union and the Wars in Indochina" in *Soviet Policy in De-veloping Countries* (rev., 1981).

VINCENT H. DEMMA, historian, Southeast Asia Branch, U.S. Army Center of Military History, is currently preparing *The U.S. Army and the Conflict in Southeast Asia 1961–April 1965* for the U.S. Army's official history of the Vietnam War.

I.M. DESTLER, senior associate and director, Carnegie Endowment Project on Executive—Congressional Relations in Foreign Policy, is the author of *Coping with U.S.—Japanese Economic Conflicts* (1982) and *Making Foreign Economic Policy* (1980).

Ambassador BUI DIEM, executive director of the Indochinese Economic De-velopment Center and former Ambassador of the Republic of Vietnam to the United States, contributed to *The Fall of South Vietnam: Statements by Military and Civilian Leaders* (1979). He is preparing an account of the U.S. experience in Viet-nam as viewed by a Vietnamese participant.

ROBERT J. DONOVAN, formerly with the New York *Herald Tribune* (Wash-ington bureau chief) and the *Los Angeles Times*, is the author of *The Future of the Republican Party and Eisenhower: The Inside Story* (1956) and two volumes covering the Presidency of Harry Truman: *Conflict and Crisis* (1977) and *Tumultuous Years* (1982). He is also a former Wilson Center Fellow.

WILLIAM DUIKER, professor of East Asian History, Pennsylvania State Univer-sity, is the author of *The Rise of Nationalism in Vietnam 1900–1941* (1976), *Vietnam Since The Fall of Saigon* (1981) and *The Communist Road To Power In Vietnam* (1981).

Colonel JAMES W. DUNN, chief, Histories Division, U.S. Army Center of Mili-tary History, contributed "Province Advisors in Vietnam, 1962–1965," to *Lessons From An Unconventional War* (1981).

STANLEY L. FALK, deputy chief historian for Southeast Asia, Southeast Asia Branch, U.S. Army Center of Military History, is also director of the official his-torical series *The U.S. Army in Vietnam* and author of *Bataan: The March of Death* (1962), *Decision at Leyte* (1966), and *Liberation of the Philippines* (1971).

ALFRED GOLDBERG, historian, Office of the Secretary of Defense, is the co-author of *The Army Air Forces in World War II* (1956), and editor of *A History of the U.S. Air Force 1907–1957* (1957) and *The Department of Defense: Documents on Estab-lishment and Organization, 1944–1978* (1979).

ALLAN E. GOODMAN, associate dean and director of the Master of Science in Foreign Service Program at Georgetown University, served as presidential brief-ing coordinator for the director of Central Intelligence and as special assistant to the director of the National Foreign Assessment Center. He is the author of *The Lost Peace: America's Search for a Negotiated Settlement of the Vietnam War* (1978) and *Politics in War: The Bases of Political Community in South Vietnam* (1973).

ALAN L. GROPMAN is the Deputy Director for Doctrine Strategy and Plans Integration at U.S. Air Force Headquarters. He is the former Associate Dean of Faculty and Academic Affairs, and the Director of Research and Elective Studies, at the National War College. Author of *Air Power and the Air Lift Evacuation of Kham Duc* (1979) and a contributor to *Conflict Magazine*, he also directed the National War College's Vietnam Studies Program.

JOHN HENRY, president, Crop Genetics International, is the author of "February 1968: Continuity or Change" (1971) and other articles on Washington decision-making in 1968.

VU THUY HOANG, currently a *Washington Post* researcher, is a veteran of the *Washington Post* Saigon bureau. The former managing editor of the government-run daily *Dan-Chu* and former foreign editor of the influential *Chinh Luan*, he is the author of over a dozen articles on Vietnamese refugees for the *Post* and of *Rong Vang Vuot Bien*, an account of the Vietnamese Boat People.

GEORGE C. HERRING, editor of *Diplomatic History* and professor of history at the University of Kentucky, is the author of *Aid to Russia, 1941–1946: Strategy, Diplomacy, and the Origins of the Cold War* (1973), *The Diaries of Edward R. Stettinius, Jr., 1943–46* (1975) and *America's Longest War: The United States and Vietnam 1950–1975* (1979). He is currently working on an edition of the four previously unpublished volumes of the *Pentagon Papers*.

RICHARD A. HUNT, historian, Southeast Asia Branch, U.S. Army Center of Military History, Department of the Army, is the co-editor of *Lessons from an Unconventional War* (1982) and a contributor to *The Vietnam War* (1979). He is presently preparing a two-volume history of the pacification program for CMH.

ARNOLD R. ISAACS, author of *Without Honor* (1983), a study of the fall or South Vietnam, has served as bureau chief of the *Baltimore Sun* in Saigon and Hong Kong.

WILLIAM JAYNE is with the Vietnam Veterans Leadership Program.

STANLEY KARNOW, editor-in-chief, International Writers Service, is a former correspondent in Southeast Asia and author of *Southeast Asia* (1963) and *Mao and China: From Revolution to Revolution* (1972). He worked on a 13-part television series for public television entitled "Vietnam: A Television History," and is the author of a companion book, *Vietnam: A History* (1983).

DOUGLAS KINNARD, Brigadier General, USA (Ret.), professor of political science, University of Vermont, is the author of *The Secretary of Defense* (1980), *The War Managers* (1977), and *President Eisenhower and Strategy Management: A Study in Defense Politics* (1977).

ALLEN H. KITCHENS is the chief of the Southeast Asia and Pacific Division of the Bureau of Intelligence and Research at the Department of State and co-editor of *Foreign Relations of the United States: The Geneva Conference* (1981).

RICHARD KOHN, chief, Office of Air Force History, is a former professor of history at Rutgers University and the author of *Eagle and Sword: The Federalists and the Creation of the Military Establishment in America 1783–1802* (1975). He is also a contributor to *Military Review*, U.S. Naval Institute *Proceedings*, and *American Historical Review*.

LAWRENCE W. LICHTY, professor of communication arts at the University of Maryland (College Park), is the co-author of *American Broadcasting* (1975). A former Wilson Center Fellow, he also wrote "Rough Justice on the Saigon Street" (1977). He has acted as a consultant for the public television series "Vietnam: A Television History."

TIMOTHY J. LOMPERIS, assistant professor of political science, Louisiana State University, served as an intelligence liaison officer in Saigon, received the 1981–82 Helen Dwight Reed Award for the Best Dissertation in International Relations (on Vietnam) and is the author of the forthcoming *Vietnam: The War Everyone Lost—and Won*.

Colonel DAVID MacISAAC (USAF, Ret.), a former Wilson Center Fellow, is now Research Fellow at the Air University's Air Power Research Institute. He has published reviews and review essays on Vietnam in *Air University Review* and *Air Force Magzine*.

ROBERT MANNING, editor-in-chief, Boston Publishing Company, and Fellow at the Kennedy Institute of Politics, is the editor of BPC's multivolume series *The Vietnam Experience* and of *Who We Are: An ATLANTIC MONTHLY Chronicle of the United States and Vietnam* (1965).

ERNEST MAY, Charles Warren Professor of History at Harvard and a former Wilson Center Fellow, is the author of *The Ultimate Decision: The President as Commander in Chief* (1960), *Imperial Democracy: The Emergence of America as a Great Power* (1961), *American Imperialism: A Speculative Essay* (1968), and *Lessons of the Past: The Use and Misuse of History in American Foreign Policy* (1973).

Colonel PAUL L. MILES, associate professor of history at the United States Military Academy (West Point), is the author of the forthcoming *American Grand Strategy in the Second World War: The Role of Admiral William D. Leahy*.

JOHN E. MUELLER, professor of political science at the University of Rochester, has written extensively on public opinion *vis à vis* Vietnam and other wars, and is contributing "Viet Nam Revised" to *Armed Forces and Society* (forthcoming). His books include *War, Presidents, and Public Opinion* (1973), and *Deterrence, Numbers, and History* (1968).

JOHN E. MURRAY, Major General, USA (Ret.) is the author of *The Military Mind and the New Mindlessness* (1976), and *War, Transport, and Show Biz* (1981).

DON OBERDORFER, diplomatic correspondent for the *Washington Post*, is the author of *Tet!* (1971, 1984) which was a finalist for the 1971 National Book Award. He has worked with the Council of the Humanities, Princeton University.

ROBERT OSGOOD, Christian A. Herter Professor of American Foreign Policy and director, American Foreign Policy, at the School of Advanced International Studies, The Johns Hopkins University, is also the director, Security Studies Program, The Johns Hopkins Foreign Policy Institute, and the author of *America and The World, Vol. I: From the Truman Doctrine to Vietnam* (1969) and *Limited War Re-Visited* (1979).

NEAL PETERESEN, acting deputy historian, Office of the Historian, U.S. Department of State, has performed internal research on U.S. policy toward Southeast Asia and prepared documentary compilations on Indochinese and Southeast Asian regional security for *Foreign Relations of the United States* (1950–52 and 1954 volumes); he is the co-editor of *Foreign Relations of the United States: The Geneva Conference* (1981).

DOUGLAS PIKE, director of the Indochina Studies Program of the Institute of East Asian Studies at the University of California (Berkeley), is a retired U.S. Foreign Service Officer whose government posts included Saigon, Hong Kong, Taipei and Tokyo. Author of *War, Peace and the Viet Cong* (1969) and *History of Vietnamese Communism 1925–76* (1978), he is now completing two full-length studies entitled *Soviet-Vietnamese Relations 1917–1982: A Geo-Political Study* and *People's Army of Vietnam: The Army that Beat America*.

ROBERT A. POLLARD is a former research associate with the International Security Studies Program at the Wilson Center. He is the author of "The Cuban Missile Crisis: Legacies and Lessons" (1982) and *Economic Growth and the Origins of the Cold War: The Strategic Ends of Truman's Foreign Economic Policy, 1945–50* (forthcoming), and a contributor to *Economics and World Power: An Assessment of American Diplomacy Since 1789* (1983).

SAMUEL POPKIN, associate professor of political science, University of California (San Diego), is the author of *The Rational Peasant: The Political Economy of Rural Society in Vietnam* (1979), and a contributor to *Vietnam: Some Basic Issues and Alternatives* (1969) and *Conflict in World Politics* (1971).

EARL C. RAVENAL, former director of the Defense Department's Asian Division and a past Wilson Center Fellow, is currently an adjunct professor at Georgetown University's School of Foreign Service. He is the author of *Never Again: Learning from America's Foreign Policy Failures* (1978), *NATO's Unremarked Demise* (1979), and co-author of *Peace with China? U.S. Decisions for Asia* (1971).

PETER W. RODMAN, Fellow in Diplomatic Studies at Georgetown University's Center for Strategic and International Studies, is also director of research for Kissinger Associates, Inc., and author of "Norman Podhoretz and the Vietnam War" (1982).

HERBERT SCHANDLER, Colonel, USA (Ret.), former vice-president, American League for Exports and Security Assistance, is the author of *The Unmaking of a President: Lyndon Johnson and Vietnam* (1977, rev. 1983), as well as of numerous reports on national security. He is presently a partner in H & S Associates.

JOHN SCHLIGHT, deputy chief, Office of Air Force History, and author of "Civilian Control of the Military in Southeast Asia" (1980), is presently completing *A History of the United States Air Force in South Vietnam (1965–68)* and *A History of the United States Air Force in South Vietnam (1968–73)*.

VICTORIA SCHUCK, former chairman of Mount Holyoke College's political science department and past president of Mount Vernon College, is presently researching and writing on the Vietnamese constitution of 1967–75.

NEIL SHEEHAN, past Wilson Center Fellow and former UPI and *New York Times* journalist in Vietnam, is currently writing a new book on John Paul Vann and the American experience in Vietnam. He is also the author of *The Pentagon Papers* (1971) and *The Arnheiter Affair* (1972).

Brigadier General EDWIN H. SIMMONS, director of Marine Corps History and Museums and president of the American Military Institute, is the author of *The United States Marines 1775–1975* (1976), and *Marine Corps Operations in Vietnam 1965–1972* (1973). He is presently supervising the preparation of the Marine Corps ten-volume official history, *U.S. Marines in Vietnam*.

JED C. SNYDER, research associate, International Security Studies Program, the Wilson Center, also holds an appointment as Guest Scholar at the Foreign Policy Institute, School of Advanced International Studies, Johns Hopkins University. He has published research on arms control and Middle Eastern security issues.

RONALD SPECTOR, acting chief, Southeast Asia Branch, U.S. Army Center of Military History, has contributed to *Pacific Historical Review* and *Military Affairs* and is the author of the forthcoming *United States Army in Vietnam: The Early Years*.

Colonel HARRY G. SUMMERS, JR., an infantry veteran of the Korean and Vietnam wars, now on the faculty of the Army War College, is the author of *On Strategy: A Critical Analysis of the Vietnam War* (1982). His articles on military strategy have appeared in *Army*, *Military Review*, the U.S. Naval Institute's *Proceedings*, *Parameters*, *The New Republic*, the *Wall Street Journal*, *Los Angeles Times* and *USA Today*.

DAVID F. TRASK, director, U.S. Army Center of Military History, is the author of *Victory Without Peace: American Foreign Relations During the Twentieth Century* (1968), and co-author of *The Ordeal of World Power: American Diplomacy Since 1900* (1975).

JAMES H. WEBB, served with the U.S. Marines in Vietnam and is the author of *Fields of Fire* (1978), as well as of *A Sense of Honor* (1981).

WILLARD J. WEBB, chief of the Special Projects Branch, Joint Chiefs of Staff Historical Division, has published two volumes of JCS history on the Vietnam War (covering from 1969–1973).

RUSSELL F. WEIGLEY, professor of history at Temple University, has authored *The American Way of War: A History of the United States Military Strategy and Policy* (1973) and *History of the United States Army* (1973). His book *Eisenhower's Lieutenants: The Campaign of France and Germany, 1944–1945* (1981), was nominated for the 1982 American Book Award in History.

SAMUEL F. WELLS, JR., secretary of the Wilson Center's International Security Studies Program, has written extensively for *The Wilson Quarterly* and several leading foreign affairs journals. Co-author of *The Ordeal of World Power: American Diplomacy Since 1900* (1975), he also contributed to *Economics and World Power: An Assessment of American Diplomacy Since 1789* (1983).

BARRY ZORTHIAN, senior vice-president, Gray and Company, is the former U.S. government chief of press relations and psychological operations in Vietnam.

HARRY ZUBKOFF is the chief of Research and Analysis Division, Office of the Secretary of the Air Force.

Note: Affiliations and publications of participants are those listed as of January 1983.

EXCERPTS
FROM CONFERENCE PAPERS AND PROCEEDINGS

THE U.S. CONDUCT OF THE WAR

"Kennedy was less willing to consider disengagement than later apologists suggested, and Johnson was less anxious to escalate than later detractors believed . . . .
"[In the 1960s] the Presidents and their aides knew, at critical junctures, that expanding commitment offered no assurance of success. Yet at each juncture they saw no acceptable alternative to pressing on."

Richard Betts

"The United States did not stumble into Vietnam. Each step was a deliberate choice by a careful President who weighed the alternatives as he saw them, limited each response, and took into account the opinion of the public. . . .
"The Joint Chiefs felt that a more ambitious objective was necessary, that of defeating the enemy both in North and South Vietnam. . . . [But] fundamental differences between military and civilians at the national level concerning the war in Indochina were never resolved. There was no agreed coherent strategy to achieve American military and political objectives, and, indeed, no agreement as to those objectives. . . . Surprisingly enough, however, it does not appear from the available documents that any of the senior military leaders threatened or even contemplated resigning to dramatize their opposition to the limitations on the conduct of the war. . . ."

Herbert Schandler

"Why did it happen? Because Lyndon Johnson dreamed of a Great Society and not of Asian real estate. . . . In the end, the [White House] advisory process mattered only incidentally. Lyndon Johnson mattered a great deal."

Larry Berman

"The military chiefs were sheltered from exposure to hard ethical choices by the umbrella of civilian control. It was one of the distortions of the Vietnam War that civilian control of the military became civilian direction and management, and that military leadership at all levels of command used 'civilian control' as an exoneration from moral responsibility. . . . The war—or the non-war—was fought by the regulars, the 'professionals,' and these 'professionals' were more than willing to accept the role of automatons controlled by their civilian masters."

Brig. Gen. Edwin Simmons

"It should be apparent by now to all but the most inveterate Nixon-haters that his administration inherited an enormously complex, perhaps intractable problem in Vietnam.
"By 1969, extreme measures of one kind or the other may have been required for America to end the war. The available evidence suggests that the new administration rejected the extreme options out of hand . . . because they thought such measures unnecessary."

George Herring

"I think the centralized presidential decision-making under Nixon and Kissinger was probably the most coherent policy-making we are ever going to get, whether you like the content of it or not. . . . Of all the administrations that wrestled with this [Vietnam] problem, Nixon had the least freedom of maneuver."

Peter Rodman

"The apparent early success of Vietnamization, as well as real progress in the pacification program . . . was part of the reason behind the Cambodian incursion."

Stanley Falk

"The military were not really pushing for a Cambodian bombing at the beginning of 1969. It really was the President who seized on this as a way of retaliating for the wave of attacks by the North Vietnamese in February 1969 which was in violation of the bombing halt understanding and we were looking for something to do other than resuming the bombing of the North. . . .
"What happened was that by the end of March and the beginning of April [1970], the North Vietnamese started expanding all over eastern Cambodia, and we were faced with a decision that could not be avoided. If we did nothing . . . we would have been faced by . . . all of eastern Cambodia's being a [North Vietnamese] base area. . . . Our Vietnamization strategy would have been totally unviable at that point."

Peter Rodman

THE NORTH VIETNAMESE AND THE SOUTH VIETNAMESE

"In my view, this sequence [the 1972 U.S. Christmas bombing of Hanoi and the signing of the Paris accords three weeks later] suggests that a similar "all-out" bombing effort in early 1965 could well have prompted Hanoi's leaders to negotiate an agreement, then sought by Lyndon Johnson, providing for a cease-fire and mutual withdrawal of Northern forces and U.S. troops from South Vietnam. Such an accord, of course, would not have ended Hanoi's quest for unification; it would simply have brought a change in tactics and a new timetable."

Douglas Pike

"The idea that North Vietnam could not have been bombed out of the war because of its fanaticism is folly. Japan was much more fanatic. The 1965 bombing was nothing like what had been recommended by the Air Force. Had it been carried out before the radar and the SAMs . . . [were in place in the North], it would have been cheap, relatively, [to the U.S.]."

Alan Gropman

"In contrast to the 'living room war' image of the South Vietnamese soldier as cowardly and bumbling, ARVN . . . paid dearly (nearly 200,000 dead, plus a half million wounded) for its campaign against the regular and guerrilla Communist forces."

Allan Goodman

"We Americans do not have a revolutionary vision for agrarian societies. . . . I am inclined to doubt that there were 'lost opportunities' for the South Vietnamese to have saved themselves—at least not without an interminable American presence."

Stanley Karnow

"Post-mortems on the fall of the GVN generally stress the impact of Communist violations of the Paris Agreement in 1973 and 1974 . . . and the waning political will in the United States to counter these violations.
"Such assessments obscure the fact that the GVN collapsed from within despite nearly two decades of massive American support and the steady erosion of Viet Cong control over and support in the countryside."

Allan Goodman

"To the end, the Republic of Vietnam was too much the creation of the Americans . . . ."

Russell Weigley

LESSONS AND NON-LESSONS OF THE U.S. EXPERIENCE IN VIETNAM

"War may be too serious a matter to leave solely to military professionals, but it is also too serious a matter to leave only to civilian amateurs. Never again must the president commit American men to combat without first fully defining the nation's aims and then rallying Congress and the nation for war. Otherwise, the courageous Americans who fought and died in the defense of South Vietnam will truly have done so in vain."

Col. Harry Summers

"The United States might be able to fight a limited war again, but only if it is not long and inconclusive. . . ."

Richard Betts

"You know what Napoleon said: 'God is on the side of the biggest battalions. . . .' And right about then [1974], God was on the side of the Communists; they were bigger, they were stronger. That's why we lost the war.
"The best choice was that of . . . Maxwell Taylor. He believed in 1965 that we should not support the Vietnamese except logistically. . . . The next war we fight, we ought to do it like the Mafia: contract it out."

John Murray

"We [small nations] end up losing higher stakes than the United States itself because the Americans, they can turn the page and say it is an unhappy chapter of U.S. history, but that is not the same for the South Vietnamese."

Ambassador Bui Diem

"The paradox is that the Vietnam War, so often condemned by its opponents as hideously immoral, may well have been the most moral or at least the most selfless war in all of American history. For the impulse guiding it was not to defeat an enemy or even to serve a national interest; it was simply not to abandon friends."

Ernest May

I THE U.S. CONDUCT OF THE VIETNAM WAR, 1964–73

PAPERS AND DISCUSSIONS

MISADVENTURE REVISITED

by Richard K. Betts

Each November 22nd there is a memorial ceremony at President John Kennedy's grave in Arlington Cemetery. Prominent in attendance along with members of the Kennedy family are representatives of the U.S. Army Special Forces — the Green Berets. In a small way this combination inadvertently symbolizes the tragedy of the U.S. venture in Vietnam and its legacy for American politics. John Kennedy "made" the Green Berets, elevating them from a minor military component to a heroic vanguard of U.S. commitment to combating Communist revolution. Within several years after the President's death, however, his brothers Robert and Edward had moved into the vanguard of opposition to this commitment as it had unfolded.

In the 1982 ceremony there was an added undercurrent of irony because the Reagan administration had recently moved, as Kennedy did two decades earlier, to expand and reinvigorate the Special Forces. After a dozen years of reaction against ambitious forward strategies of anticommunism, the U.S. government was once again acting as if it would "pay any price, bear any burden" to oppose challenges to the "free world." Yet despite administration rhetoric and reports of deepening U.S. involvement in counter-revolutionary efforts in Central America, history is unlikely to repeat itself; the 1980s will not be the 1960s. Though enervated, the residual effects of anti-Vietnam sentiments of the 1970s remain far more potent than was the comparable opposition (which was far more restricted to the left-wing political fringe) 20 years ago.

To the extent that Reagan's assertive foreign policy is reminiscent of the period in which the U.S. commitment to South Vietnam burgeoned (and as with any analogy, too much should not be read into superficial similarities), two questions seem paramount:

First, why is the interventionist impulse resurgent after the traumatic experience in Southeast Asia? Have the "lessons" of Vietnam been cast aside?

Second, what do we know about the assumptions, deliberations, and expectations in the earlier period that might cast light on current dangers? That is, what *are* the lessons?

The answers are unlikely to offer a reliable guide to the future, but they are related. The U.S. descent into Vietnam was impelled by the overarching postwar goal of containment of communist power.[1] At the time, a few quarreled with the application of the containment principle to a theater so low in priority and interest to the West. Indeed, George Kennan, who coined the term (and subsequently spent much of his career explaining that he didn't mean what those who became custodians of the concept assumed) was an early opponent of military involvement. But not until after the massive escalation of 1965 did many in the foreign-policy establishment or the mass public doubt that Vietnam was a testing ground and the front line in the global battle to keep the world safe for democracy.

By the time the Nixon administration came into office the war had become a fiasco;

the whole notion of containment was on the defensive. Support for the war was not the only casualty; in the early 1970s disillusionment, coupled with Sino-American rapprochement and hopes for United States-Soviet détente and arms control, crippled the constituency for maintaining a high U.S. military profile even in areas outside the Third World. But the reaction proved as excessive as the consensus that had led to Vietnam. As détente deteriorated, Soviet clients scored advances in Angola, Ethiopia, and Yemen, and revolutionary Iran humiliated the United States; assertiveness and containment became popular again.

Contradictions

Is U.S. policy caught on a pendulum, bound to follow some ineluctable rhythmic alternation between introversion and extroversion?[2] Was the Vietnam experience not a unique or epochal turning point after all? In a limited sense this is true, but the real answer cannot be so starkly fatalistic, or else analysis has little to offer to policy, since policy becomes the prisoner of a Tolstoyan view of history that denigrates the ability of leaders to control it. Within certain bounds, such as a general aim to prevent expansion of Soviet influence, there is, and was even during the first two decades of the Cold War, ample room for choice about priorities, costs, and risks. What is critical is the collection of circumstances, beliefs, and judgments that make leaders decide in certain cases that there is only one choice, that taking high risks and bearing high costs are less unacceptable than backing away from engagement.

The United States became gradually but progressively more involved in Indochina after President Truman boosted military assistance to the French in the early 1950s. Vietnam did not become a high priority issue, however, until the Kennedy administration, and it did not become the highest priority until Lyndon Johnson's Presidency. The 1960s were the crucial period for U.S. policy-makers, but this was not because goals changed. Indeed, there was remarkable continuity and simplicity of aims. The problem was that there were two grand but contradictory goals — prevent communist conquest of South Vietnam, and avoid a major war in Asia[3] — and the contradiction was not fully sharpened until the mid-'60s.

Kennedy and Johnson were quite obviously not clones, and the commitments they made were markedly different in scale — the late 1961 decision to increase the number of U.S. advisors and the amount of military aid pale beside the 1965 decisions to bomb North Vietnam and dispatch conventional ground forces to the South. But the similarities of the Kennedy and Johnson approaches outweigh the differences, which were more a function of circumstances than of objectives.

In 1961 and 1965 both Presidents increased U.S. involvement dramatically in order to arrest the danger of imminent South Vietnamese collapse and shift military momentum to the anti-Communist side. The difference was that what was required to do this in 1961 was (though much more than had gone before) far less than what was required four years later.

As George Ball has written, "Johnson. . .was as anxious as Kennedy to avoid an irreversible embroilment. At every stage he moved reluctantly — pushed by events and the well-meant prodding of the same men who counseled President Kennedy."[4]

Kennedy was less willing to consider disengagement than later apologists suggested, and Johnson was less anxious to escalate than later detractors believed. Kenneth O'Donnell has maintained that Kennedy intended to extricate the U.S.

after the 1964 election, but there is little corroborating testimony to that effect, and the notion is belied by the course of policy right up to Kennedy's death: a continuing U.S. advisory build-up, presidential reaffirmations of commitment that would have been gratuitous or self-damaging if Kennedy was looking forward to withdrawal, and support for the coup against Diem. Johnson's rhetoric against Goldwater in 1964 exploited public fears of war, but he never suggested that defeat would be an acceptable alternative to a wider war. Although contingency planning for direct U.S. combat commitment was well under way before November 1964, Johnson continued to hope and search desperately for alternative solutions well *after* the election. When he finally decided to dispatch forces, it was in the context of gloom such as that suggested by McGeorge Bundy in a memorandum on February 7, 1965: "Without a new U.S. action defeat appears inevitable."[5]

Nibbling the Bullet

Johnson's decisions were larger than Kennedy's, but like his predecessor he refused to accept any of the extreme options provided by his subordinates that promised *victory*. Early in 1965 he authorized sustained bombing of North Vietnam, but only in limited and gradually increasing dosages — not the quick and over-whelming program recommended by the Air Force. In mid-1965 he agonized over the decision to send large numbers of ground forces, and eventually did so, despite the lack of ringing promises of early success from Army leaders. In the fall of 1965 Secretary of Defense McNamara estimated that 600,000 U.S. troops (about 20 percent more than the maximum level ever reached during the war) might be needed by 1967 and admitted that even that number "will not guarantee success."[6]

For the next two years Johnson slowly and abstemiously expanded the scope of the bombing program, against persistent military assessments that gradualism vitiated its efficacy, in consonance with civilian advisors' hopes that mounting pressure (which, by sparing targets, still left the enemy with assets to lose) might induce Hanoi to negotiate on American terms.

During that time the ground operations expanded too. And ultimately, after the 1968 Tet Offensive, the cumulative effectiveness of the operations — blunt, wasteful, and strategically uninspired as they may have been, according to critics — had forced the Communists back onto the defensive and rolled back many of their gains, though without eradicating them. But in an unconventional revolutionary war, as the bitter axiom goes, the guerrillas win as long as they do not lose and the government forces lose as long as they do not win. Colonel Harry Summers has ruefully described his postwar encounter with a North Vietnamese officer who, when confronted with the fact that the Communists had never beaten U.S. troops in a battle, replied, "That is correct. It is also irrelevant."

At the March 1967 Guam Conference, General William Westmoreland told LBJ and other civilian leaders that, unless North Vietnamese infiltration could be stopped, the war could continue indefinitely. Later in the year, in Washington, Westmoreland and Chairman of the Joint Chiefs of Staff Earle Wheeler told the President that with then-present U.S. troop levels the war would continue as an indecisive "meat-grinder"; with an increase of 95,000 men it could drag on for three years; and given an increase of 195,000 (to a total of 665,000) it could last two more years. Yet Johnson authorized an increase of only 55,000.[7]

Like Kennedy, though at a higher level, LBJ chose a *limited* strategy — or limited means, if history now makes clear that the approach was too ambivalent and flawed to be dignified by the term "strategy." There were three basic reasons that Johnson chose to nibble the bullet rather than bite it, which would have entailed either withdrawal or escalation to a point that decisive victory would have seemed probable. One reason was the fear of provoking Chinese intervention, as the U.S. advance into North Korea had done in 1950. A second was the desire to avoid having a full-scale war wreck Johnson's primary policy ambition: construction of the Great Society, with all its costly domestic programs. Crude Keynesian instincts allowed him to believe he might manage the trade-off between guns and butter.

But most salient was the third reason — unwillngness to confront a full-scale domestic political assault from either the right (for "selling out" Vietnam to Communism) *or* the left (for going too far militarily). He preferred to compromise and suffer limited attacks from both ends rather than face the full fury of either, although until the Communists' 1968 Tet Offensive he feared the hawks more than the doves. Such a centrist domestic strategy drove the military strategy.

And in this, too, Johnson's approach seems drastically different from that of his predecessors only because the price he had to pay for it was higher than the price they faced. But why did such a course, for any of the Presidents, seem the least damaging instead of the worst of both worlds?

No Optimism

For a quarter century no U.S. President was willing to let Vietnamese Communists conquer South Vietnam — not even Gerald Ford at the end (Congress forced him to accede to the fall of Saigon). Truman and Eisenhower avoided paying a high price for this policy, but only because they — unlike Kennedy and Johnson — never faced a crunch in which major involvement appeared the only alternative to defeat. Although this was the critical factor, there was more behind the decisions of the 1960s to intervene in force. Policy-makers were rarely deluded that the odds for success were high — indeed, escalation decisions were invariably prompted by pessimism rather than expectations that the corner was about to be turned toward victory — but what made them believe that they were running *risks* which might produce failure but with luck might pan out, rather than marching *inevitably* toward defeat?

The principal answer lies somewhere between hubris and hope.

Particularly influential in setting the intellectual scene in which Washington officials operated in the early 1960s were theorists of limited war and counter-insurgency. At their worst these theorists promoted the illusion that American tutelage and economic aid could remold the feeble South Vietnamese polity, creating nationalism, anti-Communist solidarity, and organizational élan that could confront powerful Marxist revolutionary idealism with some sort of vigorous Asian Jeffersonianism.[8] At their best, counter-insurgency theories were borne out, eventually proving reasonably successful in implementation — though with much stumbling and backsliding. For all their deficiencies and failures, pacification efforts — from "Revolutionary Development" to the "Phoenix" program — eventually produced a major increase in population control and road security during the years between the 1968 Tet Offensive and the 1972 Easter Offensive. The southern Communists' National Liberation Front was ground down by attrition and North Vietnamese forces took over most of the burden of combat. The later collapse was brought on by large-scale *conventional* North Vietnamese attacks.

Sending Messages

In the early 1960s previous counter-insurgency successes in the Philippines and Malaya provided grist for those who saw chances of success in Vietnam (though the French experience in Algeria might have been more instructive). Literature on the subject flourished.[9] The works of Mao as well as those of Western analysts like Galula, Trinquier, Clutterbuck, and Thompson were translated and read in government circles. Fascination with counter-insurgency did not flow from ignorance of the French experience in Indochina, but just as much from attention to it and the hope that those mistakes could be avoided.

The mistakes in applying limited war theory in South Vietnam came less in the tactical realm of counter-insurgency than in the strategic area of conventional operations. Limited war theory had developed in opposition to the Eisenhower "massive retaliation" policy and the recognition that in the nuclear era more measured uses of force were the only sort that could be used for political purposes. This led to a focus on using force to convey *messages* of resolve to induce an adversary to negotiate and compromise. The problem with this rationalistic approach was that "revolutionary war could not be encompassed by a doctrine of limited war." The theorists' "recipes of 'graduated response' might be self-defeating in a war between a very great power and a very small one."[10]

This problem was evident in conceptualization of the air war against North Vietnam, as was the difference between devising a theory and implementing a strategy. Designed by civilians (especially Robert McNamara's staff) against the advice of the military, the air war was originally meant to calibrate response to provocation and use incremental increases in pressure to convince Hanoi to desist. The aim of precise calibration and communication was subverted by practical operational difficulties and hesitancy within the government that derailed the "orchestration" of words and deeds.[11]

Most of all, the theory of using force to induce accommodation foundered because it overestimated the basis for compromise.

Vietnam was a civil war involving incompatible ideologies and visions of society, not just a conflict between great powers over influence in a third area. The difficulty policy-makers had in appreciating this carried over into the negotiating phase late in the war. As Henry Kissinger reflected with benefit of hindsight:

> Because the United States had become great by assimilating men and women of different beliefs, we had developed an ethic of tolerance; having had little experience with unbridgeable schisms, our mode of settling conflicts was to seek a solution somewhere between the contending positions. But to the Vietnamese this meant that we were not serious about what we put forward and that we treated them as frivolous. They had not fought for forty years to achieve a compromise.[12]

Dynamics of Decision

Limited war notions and elegant game-theoretic strategies for application of pressure were prime ingredients in the civilian approach to saving South Vietnam. The professional military were never impressed by much of this logic,[13] and it was they who actually fought the war. This split encouraged some critics to cite bureaucratic fragmentation and lack of coordination between planning and implementation as prime sources of our policy failure.

These factors were really secondary in consequence. With scarce exceptions until 1968, all the participants shared the assumption that South Vietnam had to be saved; disputes were over means, not ends.

Only if civilian managers had known for *sure* that graduated pressure would fail (that is, that it was not even a gamble, but hopeless) and that the bleakest military estimates of what would be required to win were correct, would there have been a chance for a White House decision against committing large U.S. forces.

Both Kennedy and Johnson distrusted the objectivity of the Joint Chiefs of Staff, and some of their civilian lieutenants viewed pessimistic military estimates or pleas for "decisive" strategies as untrustworthy worst-case inflation of Vietnam's real requirements, used as a ploy to maximize their options and to cover their reputations in "posterity papers."

This tragic misjudgment aside, the fact remains that the Presidents and their aides knew, at critical junctures, that expanding commitment offered no assurance of success. Yet at each juncture they saw no acceptable alternative to pressing on.

There are two other related points to remember about how much weight should be placed on the intellectually flawed "slow squeeze" air war strategy as a source of miscalculation.

First, even the civilian proponents did not assume that the strategy would be decisive; they knew the ground war in the South was more critical. Only the Air Force and to a lesser extent the Navy believed that bombing (if properly quick, stunning, and massive) might be enough to cripple the Communists. And the ground war in the South was not conceptualized in the "signaling" terms of the civilian-designed air war, nor were its tactics so closely managed by civilian leaders. (The critical restraints on the ground war were White House prohibitions against expanding U.S. operations into Laos and Cambodia, and calling up the reserves at home.)

A Tragic Combination

Second, there is scant evidence that President Johnson, who made the critical decisions and bears responsibility for the Vietnam strategy, was captivated by the game-theoretic logic of the graduated bombing program. He went along with it because it was limited, not necessarily because he had faith in the details of the "signaling" rationale.

The air war strategy was erroneous, but the details of its rationale pale in significance beside Johnson's overarching decision to keep the war effort, as a whole, limited.

Except for the military (whose loyal acquiescence now appears to have had baleful rather than benign effects in terms of the outcomes that those liberals most devoted to "civilian control" would have preferred), there were virtually no officials in the executive branch — and few newspaper editors or legislators — who questioned the premise of limitation.

The tragedy was the iron combination of this premise with the assumption that the war still had to be fought. Tactical confusion or diplomatic discoordination were secondary sources of failure — the strategic dilemma was primary.

In the White House the crucial figures were the President's Special Assistants for National Security — especially McGeorge Bundy, Walt Rostow, and Henry Kissinger. These men were more important than sources such as the *Pentagon Papers* suggest because, first, they had most frequent direct access to Presidents; second, more of their counsel (compared to that of executive departments) was oral and thus lost to the historical record; and third, because they provided cover letters for papers coming from the bureaucracy, they could condition the President's reception of formal assessments and recommendations.

The record is incomplete. But there is virtually no evidence that any of these men, while in office, seriously questioned the imperative of carrying on the struggle. Bundy later had a change of heart — as did several of the architects of Vietnam policy — but during all the time that he was in office in the 1960s he was among the most steadfast and aggressive of advisors.[14] Rostow clearly took an aggressive stance, promoting the war effort energetically (more so than his boss). Kissinger, coming to the scene in 1969 after U.S. involvement in Vietnam had crested, consistently fought a rear-guard action against the antiwar forces in Congress and the public.

Whiz Kids

The role of the State Department may be most difficult to gauge because the most important figure — Secretary Dean Rusk — was renowned for reserving his most important counsel for the President's ear alone. One of Rusk's principal subordinates admitted to me in conversation that he often had no idea what the secretary's real views were, that he was a "sphinx." And Rusk, following the standard of honor set by his mentor George Marshall, wrote no memoirs, since they would breach the trust of his superiors. As far as documents indicate, however, Rusk was staunch for commitment but without illusions about easy success. If anything, he was more attuned to the thinking of military leaders than were top civilians in the Defense Department.

The one legendary figure who opposed escalation was Under Secretary of State George Ball. Much of his argument rested on the priority of our commitment in Europe and the damage that could be done to it by diversion in Vietnam. The negative reception his reasoning received was somewhat ironic, since the original U.S. involvement in Indochina was spurred by the priority of Europe — it was considered necessary to support France in the early 1950s even though Washington had no love for colonialism, because of the need to buttress NATO. But not until 1965 did Ball come close to baldly recommending withdrawal.

The civilian bureaucrats most often tagged with responsibility for flawed strategy were those in the Defense Department, particularly in the offices of International Security Affairs and Systems Analysis. McNamara's "Whiz Kids" (with some support from State Department bureaus trying to scale down the options favored by the military) were instrumental in putting over the "slow squeeze" graduated pressure approach in 1964–65. Systems analysts, however, did not run the war—they wound up, at best, as peripheral kibitzers.

Congress was quite complicit in supporting direct involvement. Only mavericks such as Wayne Morse and Ernest Gruening were opposed to the crucial decisions of the mid-1960s. When J.W. Fulbright turned against the war late in 1965, he was still countered by colleagues of equal position, such as Armed Services Committee Chairman John Stennis, though Fulbright received more attention from the media (as opposition figures always do, on virtually any policy issue).

Though opposition mounted with time it was not until *after* U.S. troops had been withdrawn and POWs returned in 1973 that the raft of legislation was passed constraining U.S. operations in Indochina and presidential war powers.[15] Although there was very little active *support* for the war on the Hill, even until well after the 1968 Tet Offensive nearly all congressional opposition took the form of pressure for quicker de-escalation and more willingness to offer concessions for negotiations — *not* recommendations for unconditional withdrawal.

There is no reason to believe, however, that earlier or quicker moves to accommodate Hanoi would have yielded any better result. Because the Communists' stakes in the conflict were much higher than Washington's, they were more willing to suffer excruciating pain for a long time than Americans were to bear moderate pain for a shorter time.[16] And if the goal of congressional opponents was simply to save U.S. lives and dollars, immediate withdrawal (rather than the compromise alternatives they emphasized until after the 1973 peace accord) would have been the clearest way to do so.

The remarkable consensus behind massive U.S. intervention in Vietnam in l965, unenthusiastic as it may have been, was obscured by the force of later disillusionment. Only *after* it became clear that the price of decisive success was prohibitive — near the end of the Johnson administration — did it begin to seem clear to the emerging majority that the alternative of Communist victory was not such an unimaginable disaster. When that recognition dawned, it understandably fostered a bitter wonderment among those outside government that leaders could have been so stupid. But by that time, compromises that seemed radical during the Johnson administration seemed insufficient.

"By August of 1969," Kissinger recounts, "we had offered or undertaken unilaterally all of the terms of the 1968 *dove* plank of the Democrats (which had been defeated in Chicago). We had exceeded the promises of the Republican platform, expecting by our demonstration of flexibility to foster moderation in Hanoi and unity at home. We were naively wrong in both expectations."[17]

What Do We Know Better Now?

Hindsight highlights three basic misjudgments about objectives and alternatives that pervaded decision-making. One was that Communist victory in Vietnam would be so damaging to United States' interests that preventing it warranted a major effort despite high risk of failure. A second was that a major effort could be undertaken without predetermining its limits or military objectives, and without providing an acceptable escape hatch in advance. Third was that the U.S. polity could sustain an effort that was large but still so limited that it did not yield clear success within a few years. I will discuss these in reverse order.

The last is easiest to grapple with. It is clear that the war effort was not subverted by moral objections or distaste for the use of force (groups with these views remained a minority even to the end), but by a gradually building public perception (dominant by the early 1970s) that all the blood and treasure was simply being *wasted* to no visible end. The United States might be able to fight a limited war again, but only if it is not long and inconclusive: "The most crucial limitation. . . is not the limitation on weapons or geographical scope or goals, but rather the limitation on *time*."[18]

This political recognition reinforces the military inclination against "slow squeeze" signaling rationales for the application of conventional forces overseas. This recognition, though, does not provide a clear guarantee against future mistakes, because the necessary scale and duration of successful military operations can never be known for sure in advance. What the record does show, however, is that top decision-makers in the 1960s knew that, given the limits imposed on U.S. strategy, victory would not come quickly. A similar White House estimate in a future case could thus be grounds for either choosing to make a decisive hard-hitting commitment or no commitment at all.

The second mistake implies that future ventures be undertaken only if a cut-off point, where the game will not be worth the candle, is decided in advance. Richard Neustadt criticizes the government for not seriously addressing "the option of getting out of Vietnam. . . .It was always taken to be unacceptable on the face of it. And it is one of the most distressing aspects of the NSC staff's role in Vietnam."[19] Doing this, however, is politically dangerous; any leak about such a study would necessarily subvert the commitment domestically as well as on the scene.[20]

The Early Days of Commitment

The first misjudgment was the most important and the hardest to deal with. Deciding what is vital is inevitably affected by perceptions of conditions that may not be known to be — or may not be — incorrect until later. For example, much of the motive to fight in Vietnam was to prevent further Communist Chinese advances. The problem was not, as some critics assert, a simple obtuse failure to recognize the Sino-Soviet split. Despite their dispute they were seen to have parallel interests in promoting Third World revolution. And because Sino-American rapprochement happened later does not mean that it could have happened in the mid-1960s — before the Ussuri River clashes and Soviet hints of interest in a preventive attack on Chinese nuclear facilities pushed Beijing to accommodation with Washington.

There is another problem that limits the use of hindsight for lessons about the future. Estimation of how high a priority a commitment should have, or how many risks should be run to prevent a reverse at any particular point, cannot be made in a vacuum; they are inseparable from what else is happening at the time.

Had North Korea not attacked South Korea in 1950, shaking Washington into a fundamental revision of judgments about whether Communist leaders would resort to armed conquest as a strategy, there might have been scant inclination to become more deeply involved, as we did that year, in support of the French in Indochina.

Had Eisenhower not just concluded the Korean War and scored anticommunist successes in Iran and Guatemala, he might not have felt secure enough in 1954 to accede to partition of Vietnam after Dien Bien Phu (though that acceptance encouraged stronger U.S. commitment to the new Diem regime in the South).

Had John Kennedy not experienced the unsettling Vienna summit, the Bay of Pigs disaster, a new Berlin crisis, and setbacks in Laos — all in the first half of 1961 — he might have felt more leeway to avoid the major increase in commitment to Vietnam later that year.

The dilemma is that the crucial phase of a commitment is the early part, the formative period, when presidential rhetoric becomes mortgaged and initial costs are sunk. Yet it is in this phase that consequences are least certain and the commitment is a secondary or dependent variable in the superpower competition, rather than the centerpiece it may become later as involvement grows and costs accumulate.

When costs are still limited, the alternative to commitment seems bleaker than it does when the commitment burgeons into a full-blown national sacrifice.

Policy-makers in the 1960s faced these pressures and ambiguities and decided that a risky gamble on backing up an open-ended commitment with large but limited forces was preferable to the alternative; uncertain prospects of success were better than certain prospects of defeat. The results make clear the folly of this judgment.

No More Vietnams?

After 1973, the immediate, dominant, operative lesson in Washington was that risks should not be taken, that messy military involvements should not be begun if there is any danger that they cannot be concluded without huge sacrifice. Despite the fact that taking this lesson too seriously in the 1970s allowed uncontested advances by Soviet clients in the Third World to accumulate and to poison the public mood in the other direction again, the lesson still has a powerful hold — Congress is unlikely under any circumstances to allow even modest increases in direct U.S. military involvement in Central America. (Covert operations are another matter.)

Yet containment of communist advances, the goal that drove the United States into Vietnam, remains a goal. Few of the major bureaucratic actors in Washington now perceive the challenges in a markedly different light than did those of two decades ago.

If anything, the assertive tenor of the rhetoric of the Reagan administration, its contrary domestic policies notwithstanding, recalls the international staunchness of the New Frontier. What has not rebounded to the same degree is the bipartisan consensus. If anything, there seems to be an implicit yearning for the situation in the Eisenhower years (and it is notable that political scientists have been vigorously rehabilitating Ike's presidential reputation) — that is, the ability to have our cake and eat it too, to bestride the globe and confront Soviet power without spilling blood, to be strong but at peace, to support anticommunist clients but with levels of involvement so modest that they do not raise the spectre of war.

Eisenhower could do that because the crunch in Vietnam that his successors feared — the imminent collapse of the whole row of Southeast Asian dominoes — did not develop while he was in office. If such a prospect looms somewhere in the world later in the 1980s, there is little that the lessons of Vietnam can offer to suggest how instrumental aspects of U.S. foreign policy decision-making and implementation can better avert disaster. We know more now, but we do not know how a disastrous war could have been avoided except at the possible price that was foreseen at the time — acceptance of disastrous defeat. Kennedy and Johnson were wrong in stepping irrevocably into the inferno, but they were not necessarily wrong in estimating that failing to do so could produce a bitter reaction. Now, as then, major communist advances cannot be contained or ignored without running risks, and what we know about the follies of Vietnam cannot tell today's leaders how to make painless choices.

NOTES

¹ See Leslie H. Gelb with Richard K. Betts, *The Irony of Vietnam: The System Worked* (Washington, D.C.: Brookings Institution, 1979). Some of the points in this paper draw on that book.
² The most prominent example of the pendulum thesis is the "Klingberg cycle," resurrected in recent years by Samuel Huntington.
³ Daniel Ellsberg develops this theme in "The Quagmire Myth and the Stalemate Machine" in his *Papers on the War* (New York: Simon and Schuster, 1972), p. 102 and *passim*.
⁴ George Ball, *The Past Has Another Pattern: Memoirs* (New York: Norton, 1982), pp. 374–375.
⁵ Quoted in Larry Berman, *Planning a Tragedy: The Americanization of the War in Vietnam* (New York: Norton, 1982), p. 43.
⁶ Department of Defense, *The Pentagon Papers: The Senator Gravel Edition* (Boston: Beacon Press, 1971), Vol. 4, p. 623.
⁷ *Ibid.*, Vol. 4, pp. 442–443.
⁸ Graham Greene's novel *The Quiet American* (New York: Viking, 1956) takes off from this motif. The central characters are metaphors: the prostitute Phuong (helpless, ignorant, trusting, sullied by foreigners, but outlasting them all) represents Vietnam; the journalist Fowler (decadent, disillusioned, failed) stands for Europe; and the covert operator Pyle (young, virile, naive, altruistic, but a friend more dangerous than enemies) represents the United States. Speaking of Pyle after his death, Fowler says, "The trouble was. . .he mixed up. . . ." [The Frenchman] Vigot said, "I am not altogether sorry. He was doing a lot of harm."
"God save us always," I [Fowler] said, "from the innocent and the good," p. 15.
⁹ See D. M. Condit, *et al.*, *A Counterinsurgency Bibliography* (Washington, D.C.: U.S. Department of the Army, 1963).
¹⁰ Theodore Draper, in Richard Pfeffer, ed., *No More Vietnams?* (New York: Harper & Row, 1968), pp. 39, 27. See also Stephen Peter Rosen, "Vietnam and the American Theory of Limited War," *International Security* 7, no. 2 (Fall 1982).
¹¹ Wallace Thies, *When Governments Collide* (Berkeley: University of California Press, 1980), pp. 81, 56–57, 64–69, 7–90, 262–271.
¹² Henry Kissinger, *White House Years* (Boston: Little, Brown, 1979), p. 259.
¹³ Richard K. Betts, *Soldiers, Statesmen, and Cold War Crises* (Cambridge: Harvard University Press, 1977), chapters 1–3.
¹⁴ Some observers have cited a recently declassified Bundy memorandum of June 30, 1965, as indicating much greater reluctance than he evinced on other occasions. (See the memo, quoted in Berman, *Planning a Tragedy*, pp. 82–83.) While noting many dangers in a large-scale U.S. commitment of forces, however, the memo does not even hint grudgingly at the acceptability of what ultimately would have been the only alternative — withdrawal and defeat. Subsequent contributions by Bundy favored use of forces, but just on a smaller initial scale than McNamara had recommended.
¹⁵ Alton Frye and Jack Sullivan, "Congress and Vietnam: The Fruits of Anguish," in Anthony Lake, ed., *The Legacy of Vietnam* (New York: New York University Press for the Council on Foreign Relations, 1976), pp. 200–202.
¹⁶ Richard K. Betts, "Interests, Burdens and Persistence: Asymmetries Between Washington and Hanoi," *International Studies Quarterly* 24, no. 4 (December 1980), pp. 520–524.
¹⁷ Kissinger, *White House Years*, p. 256.

[18] Samuel Huntington, in "Vietnam Reappraised," *International Security* 6, no. 1 (Summer 1981), p. 7.

[19] Neustadt in *ibid.*, p. 18.

[20] In late 1964, Assistant Secretary of Defense John McNaughton reportedly commissioned Daniel Ellsberg to devise a contingency rationale for U.S. withdrawal. Ellsberg was told not to tell anyone about the assignment, even to type his own drafts. "'You should be clear,' [McNaughton] repeatedly warned Ellsberg, 'that you could be signing the death warrant to your career by having anything to do with calculations and decisions like these.'" David Halberstam, *The Best and the Brightest* (New York: Random House, 1972), p. 366.

WAITING FOR SMOKING GUNS:
Presidential Decision-making and the Vietnam War, 1965–67

by Larry Berman

I have been asked to begin by identifying the types of information we still do not have about the presidential decision-making and advisory process with regard to troop deployments and strategy in Vietnam, 1965–67. To a great extent the situation is unchanged since George Herring's 1981 observation that "historical writing on Johnson's management of the Vietnam war is obviously still in an embryonic stage. Little material is open in the Johnson file for the period after 1965."[1]

Moreover, for those of us interested in serious historical inquiry into the dynamics of the Vietnam decision-making process, the bulk of primary source materials are still under restriction. In some respects we cannot really know what we don't know until these materials are declassified. We know, for example, the kinds of questions which researchers will want answered, but we may have too great expectations of either the historical record or of Lyndon Johnson.

What don't we know that is worth knowing?

What were the specific interactions between and substantive contributions of Rostow, McNamara, Wheeler, and Bunker? Did Johnson ever receive a decisive strategy for winning the war? Did Johnson encourage the military to develop such a strategy? Did the Joint Chiefs of Staff ever challenge the President on the grounds that he was not taking their advice, especially as things got worse? Was there ever legitimate debate in the President's presence for mining Haiphong or cutting the Ho Chi Minh trail? Or, were domestic political considerations so great that Johnson discouraged any critical analysis of basic assumptions or military strategy?

Two years from today we will know a great deal more. The Johnson Library has now declassified the bulk of materials from the Honolulu conference of February 1966, Guam (November 1967), and the March 31, 1968, decision to seek a negotiated settlement. All of these materials are included in the National Security Council History file. In addition, the personal papers of Clark Clifford have been made available for researchers. General Westmoreland's personal papers are currently being declassified by the U.S. Army. Tom Johnson's notes of Tuesday Cabinet meetings as well as the State Department administrative history will be declassified within eighteen months. And the Center for Military History's multi-volume study of Vietnam (in which researchers were given access to all classified materials) should be of great substantive value for us all.

Part of the problem in analyzing presidential decision-making during the Johnson years is that, in retrospect, Johnson's actions seem so poorly conceived. A modern day Rip Van Winkle would be hard pressed to believe that Johnson actually had professional advice. How could the President have made such errors in tactics and overall strategy? Why didn't he ever attempt to bring major U.S. forces to bear in a decisive way? Why didn't he encourage his staff to at least plan the politics of getting out? Because the reality of the situation for Lyndon Johnson was to figure out a way to save his domestic program, not to pick the best alternative in Vietnam.

In *Planning a Tragedy*[2] I utilized hitherto unavailable documents from the Lyndon Baines Johnson Library as well as interviews with most of the principals to recreate the dynamics of President Johnson's July 28, 1965, decision which fully committed the United States not to lose the war in Vietnam. On July 28, 1965, President Johnson announced a 50,000-man increase in U.S. fighting strength in Vietnam, and that additional forces would be sent as they were requested by the U.S. field commander, General William Westmoreland. But, contrary to all previous indications from the White House, no Reserve or National Guard units would be called into service. I depicted Lyndon Johnson not as the infamous Caligula, but rather as a soft-selling *homo politicus* who believed that losing Vietnam in the summer of 1965 would wreck his plans for a truly Great Society. For while the fundamental fact of international politics in July 1965 was South Vietnam's impending fall to communist control, the overriding concern of domestic politics in July 1965 was Lyndon Johnson's intent that the Great Society reach legislative fulfillment.

Drawing the Line

The primary source documents show that Lyndon Johnson was *not* misled by advisors, nor did he cow them into submission. Instead, he created conditions under which all options could be presented (but not analyzed) and then used his great talents to forge a marginal political and military consensus. He utilized the advisory process to legitimize what he knew would later be characterized as a "butter and guns" decision. He did *not* act indecisively. He *chose* between short- and long-term risks; his fatal mistake occurred in that choice. July 1965 shows how a President approached the advisory process not for advice but for political reasons — for building consensus and legitimacy *outside* government by seeking what looked like advice from all with competence in the given policy area. In July, Lyndon Johnson went through an elaborate series of meetings with his formal advisors in order to legitimize the option selection process to political elites.

On the broad question of commitment, President Johnson had clearly made up his mind in early July, but he created the impression that he had not yet done so and encouraged his advisors to debate the question of getting in versus cutting our losses and getting out. Johnson's intent was to foster a public perception that advisors were carefully deliberating *all* policy options, as well as to build legitimacy for a President who hoped to secure domestic political advantage from the decision *not* to mobilize the reserves. An example illustrates the point. As early as June 26, 1965, Secretary of Defense Robert McNamara had developed the basic blueprint for the July 28 decision — except that McNamara *favored mobilizing the country by calling up the reserves* (as did all of Johnson's military advisors).

Opposing this view was Under Secretary of State George Ball, with a plan for cutting U.S. losses and withdrawing under whatever conditions could be arranged. On July 1, 1965, Special Assistant for National Security McGeorge Bundy wrote to

Johnson, "My hunch is that you will want to listen hard to George Ball and then reject his proposal."[3] Johnson did *privately* reject the proposal, but decided that it was in his interest to let everyone hear George Ball.

Between July 4 and July 28 Johnson orchestrated a remarkable set of events. First he sent McNamara to Saigon under the guise of seeking additional information, but immediately recalled the Secretary with instructions to develop a plan for taking over the war. But, on July 20 and 21, Johnson allowed Ball to argue the big question of cutting losses versus getting in — and to try to prove his case — that humiliation would be less costly than commitment and eventual defeat. The burden of proof that a military operation could secure the goal of getting Hanoi to the conference table was placed *only* on Ball, never on McNamara.

Not Too Much

In a recent interview, McGeorge Bundy explained that LBJ "had known when he sent McNamara to Saigon that the purpose was to build a consensus on what needed to be done to turn the tide — not to cover a retreat. Within that purpose he was glad to have all sorts of options . . . [discussed] but his own priority was to get agreement, at the lowest level of intensity he could, on a course that would meet the present need in Vietnam and not derail his legislative calendar." Moreover, the only real decision made in July 1965 was to not call up the reserves — a decision made by Johnson alone against the almost unanimous advice of his advisors.

Worrying About China

There was, however, a peculiar logic to Johnson's actions, and in retrospect it all seems so self-destructive. During a July 26, 1965, meeting between the Joint Chiefs of Staff and President Johnson, General Wallace Greene, the Marine Corps Commandant, told Johnson that if the President agreed that the *stakes* in Vietnam were (1) national security, (2) our pledge, and (3) our prestige — then there were really only two choices facing the President in July 1965: "Get out or stay in and win." But, for Johnson, the goal in Vietnam was always to do "what will be enough and not too much." The difference in perspective between General Greene and President Johnson reflected, at bottom, a fundamental conflict in *ends*. Thus, Johnson the politician developed a third option — stay in and not lose right away, hope for a big break.

"What will be enough and not too much," is an accurate description of what Johnson hoped his policies would achieve: "enough" to bring Hanoi to the conference table, but "not too much" to bring the Soviets or Chinese directly into the conflict. On the basis of this definition of the situation Johnson discouraged any analysis of basic assumptions or rationale for U.S. involvement. The burden of proof rested *only* on those who favored getting out, not getting in.

George Ball always had to prove his case that the dominoes would not fall, that humiliation would not be worse than staying in. Secretary McNamara was never required to prove that a negotiated settlement could be achieved within a reasonable period, or that U.S. infantry would be confronting main force and not guerrilla units. This double standard of proof is best viewed within the context of several tactical issues involving the introduction of U.S. ground troops to Vietnam by July 1965.

A primary constraint on U.S. policy in July 1965 was Johnson's belief that provocative military measures in the North would bring Chinese troops into the war. But under what conditions would such an intervention occur?

The documents show that Johnson *never* encouraged hard analysis of the question *"under what conditions"* would the Chinese or Soviets intervene with substantial military forces of their own in a way which would *change the character of the war*? This is particularly relevant because Johnson made constant public reference to the possibility of Chinese intervention whenever he was challenged for not accepting the military recommendations of his Joint Chiefs of Staff.

Recently declassified CIA documents show that a great deal of institutional intelligence work went into these questions. One CIA document (June—July 1965) concluded that the Chinese would intervene *only* "if U.S. ground forces invaded North Vietnam in such strength as to control the country," and "almost certainly if U.S. forces approached the Chinese frontier." It is significant that the CIA *did not* believe the Chinese would intervene militarily with ground forces "if the U.S./GVN were winning the war in South Vietnam," or "if U.S. air attacks began to damage the industrial and military sector of North Vietnam."

As for Soviet military intervention, it was judged "extremely unlikely." A July 15, 1965, report from the Office of National Estimates on "Soviet Tactics Concerning Vietnam" concluded that:

> We continue to think that the Soviets want to avoid sharp crises on two fronts simultaneously. The new leaders have shown themselves willing, however, to put some pressure on West Berlin while the war continues in Vietnam. We believe that they will further develop the line that the U.S. faces trouble in Berlin if it remains unyielding in Vietnam, perhaps underscoring it from time to time with controlled harassments falling short of a major challenge to the Allied position there.
>
> All these recent moves, in our view, illustrate and are explained by the major dilemmas of Soviet policy. The USSR naturally desires the victory of communism in Vietnam, yet it does not want to see such a victory as would magnify the prestige and power of Communist China. At the same time, in the circumstances of the Sino-Soviet controversy Moscow cannot afford to appear laggard in supporting the DRV and the Viet Cong. Yet it is highly apprehensive of the consequences of expanded war in the Far East, a major military confrontation between the U.S. and Communist China, and the extremely dangerous world crisis that would result therefrom. Finally, the situation is one over which Moscow has little control; it cannot manage the DRV, or the Chinese Communists, or the U.S.
>
> The feasible options open to Moscow are thus limited and unsatisfactory. It is giving more aid to North Vietnam because practically speaking, it cannot avoid giving such aid and because it wishes to strengthen its presence and influence in Hanoi. It is putting some pressure on the U.S. through low-keyed threats about Berlin. Yet it is also keeping open its lines of communication with the U.S. endeavoring somewhat to soften the crisis, to keep alive the possibilities of negotiation at some future time, and to persuade the U.S. not to carry military operation to a degree of extreme severity. *We continue to believe that the Soviets desire a negotiated settlement, because such a settlement would bring least profit to the Chinese, would dampen the dangers of*

extended war, and yet would not necessarily surrender Communist objectives in Vietnam. At the moment there is little the Soviets can do to bring about negotiation. They can only temporize, and lay what foundations they may for the time when negotiations become feasible and they can hope to influence them.

Expanding Containment

Another example of the double standard of evidence can be seen in the question of a third phase. Secretary McNamara's request for 44 battalions in July 1965 was based on the assumption that U.S. troops would be engaging *main force* and not guerrilla units. According to McNamara, "The enemy clearly was moving into the third phase of revolutionary warfare, committing regiments and subsequently divisions to seize and retain territory and to destroy the government's troops and eliminate all vestiges of government control."[4] The case provides an excellent example of how a determined President might have shifted the burden of proof to Westmoreland or McNamara and received answers which were not compatible with the selected option.

After reading McNamara's report, William Bundy instructed the State Department Office of Intelligence and Research to examine whether or not the Communists were moving into the third stage of warfare as predicted by General Giap. A July 23, 1965, "Secret — Limited Distribution" report concluded "that their pattern of behavior in Vietnam to date and their probable expectations as to the future argue against the hypothesis that the Communists are preparing to enter the third stage. . . . We do not believe that the criteria established by Giap for the third stage — size of unit, scale of operation, and nature of attack — have been or are about to be met in South Vietnam. Our examination of Viet Cong capabilities, the campaign against GVN lines of communication, the Communist attack pattern, and the content of Communist propaganda, persuades us rather that the VC will continue to employ guerrilla tactics with only intermittent recourse to spectacular, multi-battalion attacks against major ARVN reinforcements, and are not now capable of initiating a drastically different phase of warfare."

Not Losing

George Ball also rejected McNamara's "unproven" assumption of a third phase. Writing to the President, Ball noted that "implicit in arguments for greatly augmented United States combat forces in South Vietnam is the assumption that the Viet Cong have entered — or are about to enter — their so-called 'third phase' of warfare, having progressed from relatively small-scale hit and run operations to large unit, fixed position conventional warfare. Yet we have no basis for assuming that the Viet Cong will fight a war on our terms when they can continue to fight the kind of war they fought so well against both the French and the GVN." Ball noted that "We can scarcely expect [General Giap] to accommodate us by adopting our preferred method of combat, regardless of how many troops we send. There is every reason to suppose that the Viet Cong will avoid providing good targets for our massive bombing and superior firepower."[5]

In a July 1 memo to the President, William Bundy agreed with Ball's rejection of

McNamara's thesis: "As for major additional ground deployments, the first argument is simply whether they would be militarily effective. As the Ball paper points out, Hanoi is by no means committed to a really conventional type of war and they could easily go on making significant gains while giving us precious few opportunities to hit them." President Johnson never encouraged his staff to investigate these discrepancies in estimates of enemy tactics. To do so would have opened the possibility of admitting that the U.S could never achieve its goal in Vietnam — unless a drastic military plan was implemented.

The documents also show that the principals accepted containment of communism and the domino theory as basic premises for formulating policy and not as hypotheses for analysis. Moreover, the principals approached the problem definition stage with 20 years of intellectual baggage shaped by visions of Soviet-inspired and aggressive communism. There was an almost Talmudic adherence to the containment strategy outlined by George Kennan which called for an "unalterable counterforce at every point where they [communists] show signs of encroachment." But in 1965 the principals expanded significantly on the definition of containment and, for that matter, of world communism. Containment of Soviet aggression was originally conceived as limited in both geographical scope and objective. As Vietnam became an increasingly important component in U.S. global interests, not losing Vietnam assumed an equally high stature.

The logical companion to containment was the domino theory. As a result, even support for the repressive and authoritarian Diem was justified as a regrettable means to a nobler end — saving the world from Soviet-inspired communist aggression. Decision-makers eventually abandoned all of the original preconditions for policy — particularly a stable and meritorious GVN — to pursue the ultimate goal of halting communism in Southeast Asia. Acceptance of the containment legacy led decision-makers to become preoccupied with the question of "how" the government of South Vietnam could be saved, and never with "why" the government was worth saving.

Moreover, the stakes were simply too great — freedom stood in the balance. Dean Rusk placed the stakes within the parameter of another world war: "My generation of students was led down the trail into the catastrophe of a World War II which could have been prevented. We came out of that war with a strong feeling that collective security treaties [were needed] in this hemisphere, across the Atlantic, and across the Pacific. Vietnam [meant] to some of us the integrity of the system of collective security whose main purpose was to prevent World War III."[6]

Perhaps the most perplexing non-discussion within the advisory process involved the question "How do we achieve success and what will it cost us to do so?" When Senator Mike Mansfield wrote to Secretary McNamara, "The main perplexity in the Vietnam situation is that even if you win, totally, you still do not come out well,"[7] McNamara responded not with his plan for success (which did not exist), but instead with the cloak of labels and terms which came to characterize an administration which could not critically examine its own means or ends. McNamara's response reflected just how committed he was to a definition which greatly raised the stakes of losing: "South Vietnam is vital to the United States in the significance that a demonstrable defeat would have on the future effectiveness of the United States on the world scene — especially in areas where people are depending upon our guarantee of their independence. It is a vital U.S. concern to maintain our honor as an ally and our formidability as an opponent. As for how the situation in Vietnam

will ultimately come out, we cannot now know. But there is a range of outcomes —
many less than perfect ones — that would satisfy American vital interests."[8]

Why did it happen? Because Lyndon Johnson dreamed of a Great Society and not
of Asian real estate. "Everyone knew what we didn't want in July 1965," a principal
told me, "and that's essentially what we got — loss of integrity to the United States
and a totalitarian regime in South Vietnam." On the eve of American military
involvement, for example, Johnson described his options to Henry Graff, "There is,
he said, the right-wing solution, which would be a nuclear solution. And, of course,
we could pull out — which is really what Senator Morse and Walter Lippman want.
Neither of the alternatives being satisfactory, what are we to do? Should our forces
just 'hunker up and take it'?" Clearly, no. But what is to be done? "What will be
enough and not too much?"[9]

It was never enough. On October 19, 1967, Robert Manning of *The Atlantic* asked
Johnson, "Do you ever find youself regretting not taking [George Ball's] argument
on Vietnam?" Johnson's answer: *"I don't recall many decisions where there was not full
agreement.* I have never thought there shouldn't have been intervention or bombing.
If history indicts us for Vietnam, I think it will be for fighting a war without trying to
stir up patriotism" — the very warning given from all quarters during the decision
process of July 1965. In the end, the advisory process mattered only incidentally.
Lyndon Johnson mattered a great deal.

NOTES

[1] George Herring, "The War in Vietnam," in Robert Divine, ed., *Exploring the Johnson Years*
(Austin: University of Texas Press, 1981), p. 54.

[2] Larry Berman, *Planning a Tragedy: The Americanization of the War in Vietnam* (New York:
W.W. Norton, 1982).

[3] Bundy to Johnson, July 1, 1965. NSC History. "Deployment of Major U.S. Forces to
Vietnam, July 1965." Hereafter cited as *NSC History.*

[4] McNamara to Johnson, June 20, 1965. *NSC History.*

[5] Ball to Johnson, July 1, 1965. *NSC History.*

[6] Personal letter to the author.

[7] Mike Mansfield to the President, July 27, 1965. *NSC History.*

[8] McNamara to Mansfield, July 28, 1965.

[9] Henry Graff, "Decision in Vietnam: How Johnson Weighs Foreign Policy." *New York
Times,* July 4, 1965.

COMMENTARY: The War in Laos

by Douglas Blaufarb

This is an augmentation rather than a criticism of Mr. Betts's work.

The question put to me was: Did Lyndon Johnson's administration tend to see Laos as a separate war? And the answer is emphatically yes. However, this was not their idea. They took it over from Kennedy. The Kennedy decisions were not challenged by LBJ. These decisions (in 1962–63) were to treat Laos as a separate problem which had been provisionally solved by the Soviet-American Geneva Accords ("neutralizing" Laos) in 1962, and to maintain the stalemate which resulted from the Geneva Accords with minimal and carefully controlled violations required to balance Communist violations and maintain the military stalemate and the political balance achieved by the Accords.

To this end the Muong irregulars (and I call them "Meo" because that's what we called them, but when I say "Meo" I mean "Muong" because that's what they're called now), who were Laotian hill tribesmen supported by the CIA, were the equalizer because they were prepared to fight and willing to fight, and the Royal Laotian Army was not. This made the military stalemate possible.

As time went on, various additional kinds of support were given the Muong, notably vastly increased U.S. air support and Thai irregulars. By these means a rough balance was maintained until the early 1970s when it began to come apart. This completely *ad hoc* formula, developed one day at a time, one step at a time, worked for a period because the North Vietnamese apparently did not wish to escalate to the extent necessary to wipe out this irregular force. Washington's purposes were to avoid the necessity of U.S. intervention with ground forces in a forbidding area very close to North Vietnam and China, in an area where the Russians had directly intervened and might end up doing so again if challenged. This was Kennedy's motivation and continued to be the principal motivation under LBJ and Nixon; also, Laos was to be used as an example of the type of settlement which might eventually emerge in Vietnam.

I would say the first purpose was accomplished more or less, up until the early '70s at least, and the second, of course, was not. So the policy might be called a limited success in that Laos was shunted into a secondary position and the United States was able to avoid the risks which seemed imminent in 1961 when the decision was taken.

However, the policy could not cope with one major aspect of the Laos puzzle, which directly impinged on the Vietnam War, namely the Ho Chi Minh Trail supply corridor. Here the Geneva Accords were simply ignored and intensive U.S. bombing was conducted from 1965 on. But North Vietnamese personnel continued to move south through Laos in ever-increasing numbers in spite of the bombing. The whole arrangement was entirely provisional and collapsed when the United States withdrew from Vietnam.

AMERICA AND VIETNAM: THE FAILURE OF STRATEGY, 1964–67

by Herbert Y. Schandler

Vietnam was a political disaster for the United States. Although our military forces won every battle, the nation was unable to pursue the war to a satisfactory conclusion. This produced a rather short-lived national trauma in the United States, but the effects have conditioned American policy in many other areas of the world. Some have concluded that the whole effort was for naught. Indeed, based upon the Vietnam experience, some have questioned the utility of military forces as a viable instrument of American foreign policy in the future. "No more Vietnams" has become a foreign policy imperative for many of the nation's political leaders.

The causes of this failure, however, have never been carefully examined.

American failure in Vietnam was both strategic and tactical. In both cases, political and military objectives were not clear and the strategy and concept of operations adopted did not accord with the realities of the situation. American introspection and lack of knowledge, indeed unwillingness to understand the motivations of a dedicated enemy, led to policies which did not address the actual problem, but addressed only the problems that we chose to see.

In response to a new challenge, to an unconventional threat, the initial U.S. response was almost entirely conventional. We fought the war American-style rather than adopting our responses to the nature of the conflict. In 1964–65, Lyndon Johnson saw the effort in Vietnam as an integral part of the Cold War.

The successful defense of South Vietnam was also seen by President Johnson as essential to the domestic political well-being of the United States. Vietnam itself was not seen as of great strategic importance to the United States. Rather it was seen as a test of the United States' military commitments to its allies around the world, as a vital clash of wills between communism and the system of alliances established by the United States after World War II. It was the testing ground where the challenge of communist wars of national liberation would be met by counter-insurgency warfare.

Not to intervene and assist a beleaguered ally, the President felt, meant that communism would spread throughout Southeast Asia, other United States commitments would be called into question, and the nation would be split by a vicious internal debate as to the wisdom of the policy adopted. President Johnson has been quoted as saying as early as 1962: "I am not going to be the President who saw Southeast Asia go the way China went."[1]

The long-term goal was a political settlement that would "allow the South Vietnamese to determine their own future without outside interference." In a speech at Johns Hopkins University in April 1965, the President laid out for the American people what would be done in Vietnam: "We will do everything necessary to reach that objective (that the people of South Vietnam be allowed to guide their own country in their own way). And we will do only what is absolutely necessary."[2]

Thus, the President's policy objectives translated into doing the *minimum* amount militarily to prevent a South Vietnamese defeat while convincing Hanoi that it would not succeed in its aggression.

To the President and his Secretary of Defense, then, this policy meant a war for limited purposes using limited resources in a geographically constricted area. The allocation of American manpower, resources and materiel would not be allowed to reach the point where the war would unduly affect the civilian economy or interfere with the burgeoning programs of the Great Society. Operations would be restricted geographically so as not to incite Soviet or Chinese intervention.

To repeat, the objective would not be to "win," either in North or South Vietnam, but rather to convince the North Vietnamese (and their Soviet and Chinese sponsors) that the cost of continuing the war in South Vietnam would be, over time, prohibitive to them and that they could not succeed.

In actuality, however, there was no clear conception in Washington as to when this elusive psychological goal would be achieved.

The President's strategy, then, was defensive in nature and, in effect, left the decision as to when to end the war in the hands of the North Vietnamese.

Underestimating Hanoi

And, most important, the proponents of this strategy greatly underestimated the willingness of the old revolutionaries in Hanoi to take terrible punishment in the pursuit of their objective: taking over the South.

This rather naive U.S. strategy saw the conflict in South Vietnam simply as a communist aggression on the Cold War model — a challenge to a free nation by expansionist international communism. The questionable legitimacy and in-efficiency of the fledgling South Vietnamese government, and the anti-colonial tradition and nationalist credentials of North Vietnam were overlooked. Thus, the enemy was much too simply described and the Saigon government had ascribed to it by Washington capabilities and qualities which it never possessed.

But the Joint Chiefs of Staff — the President's principal military advisors — saw the White House's limited political objective as essentially negative and ineffective. The White House "no-win" approach yielded the initiative to the enemy and ultimately placed primary reliance upon the fragile South Vietnamese armed forces. If the U.S. was to go to war, the Joint Chiefs felt that a more ambitious objective was necessary, that of defeating the enemy both in North and South Vietnam. They advocated the classic doctrine that victory depended upon the rapid application of overwhelming military power through offensive action to defeat the enemy's main forces.

Thus, in the air war against the North, the military chiefs advocated a forceful, massive, and concentrated bombing campaign. In the South, the military chiefs advocated a strategy of taking the war to the enemy wherever he might appear, attacking his main force elements in South Vietnam and his sanctuaries and support installations in Laos and Cambodia. This strategy, of course, would require a virtually open-ended U.S. military commitment to Vietnam.

A debate behind closed doors concerning the limited strategy advocated by the President and his civilian advisors and the more forceful strategy advocated by the military chiefs continued intermittently throughout Lyndon Johnson's Presidency.

The Joint Chiefs of Staff continued to request additional American troops for South

Vietnam, increased bombing of North Vietnam, and expanded authority to strike in Laos, Cambodia, and North Vietnam. They felt that any U.S. effort to win the war in the South was thwarted by the availability to enemy troops of crucial sanctuaries and supply routes in Laos and Cambodia where they would refit, re-equip and escape destruction by American ground and air power.

Further, the constraints on the use of air power in North Vietnam, they felt, allowed the enemy to adjust to the bombing campaign so that its pressure did not become unacceptable. Of equal consequence and concern to the military chiefs in 1965–67 was the fact that the White House decision not to call up U.S. reserve units depleted American active forces outside of Vietnam to the point where the nation might not be able to respond to overseas military contingencies elsewhere.

President Johnson and his Secretary of Defense, Robert S. McNamara, continued to disapprove any major increase in operational leeway in Indochina and approved only that gradual force build-up in Vietnam which could be supported without the necessity for a reserve mobilization.

The Bottom Line

As the war developed, the debate within the administration concerning the level of American effort in South Vietnam, in fact, came to revolve around this one crucial issue of mobilization. When the President searched for the elusive point at which the political costs of the effort in Vietnam would become unacceptable to the American people, he always settled upon mobilization — that point at which reservists would have to be called up to provide enough manpower to support the war.

This domestic constraint, with all its political and social implications, *not any argument concerning long-range military strategy*, appears to have dictated American war policy. Lyndon Johnson saw reserve mobilization as the threshold at which the nation would see itself as being on a war footing. His top priority continued to be the passage by Congress of the social programs of the Great Society. He would not be a wartime President.

Denied a clear presidential strategy and the freedom they felt was necessary to win the war, the military chiefs were mollified by the President by being granted, over time, gradual increases in Vietnam force levels and, to some extent, in bombing targets; and, eventually, by the replacement in 1968 of Robert McNamara, who had become anathema to them. But these increases in military authority and resources were always within the President's guidelines.

Thus, fundamental differences between military and civilians at the national level concerning the war in Indochina were never resolved.

There was no agreed coherent strategy to achieve American objectives and, indeed, no agreement as to those objectives. Decisions concerning the allocation of American resources to Vietnam were made on the basis of what was the minimum additional effort that could be made while maintaining congressional support for (or acquiescence in) the administration war policy and for the programs of the Great Society. There was to be minimum disruption of American life.

The President made at least eight separate decisions concerning United States manpower levels in Vietnam in 1964–68. The issues addressed and the decisions that were made were always tactical and short-term in nature. The only alternative policies examined involved different force levels or alternative bombing campaigns.

On the other hand, the Joint Chiefs made no independent analyses of what manpower levels would be needed to achieve White House objectives (denial of Communist victory), *within* the restraints placed upon the military operations in Vietnam by the President, or of what military gains actually could be achieved within those constraints. Their advice on how to "win" was always predictable: "Do what General Westmoreland asks, lift the political and geographic restraints under which our forces operate, and increase the size of the strategic reserve."[3] But this was advice which the President was never willing to accept.

So the U.S. policy at the national level was piecemeal and contradictory throughout. Each decision in Washington represented a compromise between a President determined to preserve his domestic programs while warding off communist victory in Southeast Asia, and the Joint Chiefs of Staff who saw no alternative to defeat in Vietnam but an American takeover of the war and an all-out effort against a dangerous and tenacious enemy, while mobilizing to maintain American military capabilities to deal with contingencies in other parts of the world.

The Johnsonian Compromise

Surprisingly enough, however, it does not appear from the available documents that any of the senior military leaders threatened or even contemplated resigning in 1965 to dramatize his opposition to the limitations on the conduct of the war insisted upon by the President and his civilian advisors. President Johnson was aware of the possible political repercussions of such a military defection, and he temporized over the years in order not to push his loyal military leaders to such a point.

Although he never approved the decisive strategy that the Joint Chiefs continued to recommend, he never explicitly ruled it out either in 1965–67. He allowed the military chiefs gradual increases in their combat forces in Vietnam and held out the possibility of greater operational leeway in the future. He pointed out the political and fiscal realities that, he felt prevented his meeting all of their requests while never rejecting completely all of those requests. He slowly increased the resources and authority of General Westmoreland in a process of gradual and reluctant escalation.

But this Johnsonian compromise did not produce a coherent concept of what increased American forces were to achieve on the battlefield.

Far from seeking to present their views in public, each member of the Joint Chiefs, who (with the exception of the Chairman) was also chief of his respective service, sought to protect the position of his service and his own status "inside" the administration while striving to change White House policy from within. The ventilation of disagreements with presidential policies did not become a high priority for the senior members of the military establishment during the entire period of U.S. involvement in Vietnam.

The consequences of this failure to develop a precise, clear military strategy were certainly unintended by President Johnson. They included a costly bombing campaign against North Vietnam and the commitment of half a million American troops to a ground war in Asia without any fundamental agreement within our government as to how success was to be achieved.

This disagreement at the national level over military strategy was reflected on the ground in South Vietnam on the tactical level. By White House orders, the mission assigning the first American Marines to land in Vietnam in March 1965, was simply to protect the airbase at Da Nang and the facilities then being used to aid the new "Rolling Thunder" air campaign against North Vietnam. The orders clearly stated, "The U.S. Marine Force will not, repeat will not, engage in day to day actions against the Viet Cong."[4]

Enclave Theories

The policy of using these forces only for base security was short-lived, however. The Marines hardly had their feet dry when several proposals were brought forward to get U.S. troops actively engaged in the ground war.

That issue initially took the form of a debate between advocates of an "enclave" strategy and those who advocated an all-out military struggle of attrition, but this debate was also short-lived. The enclave strategy, first proposed by General Harold K. Johnson, Army Chief of Staff, in 1965, was tenaciously advocated by Ambassador Maxwell Taylor in Saigon. Taylor, a former Army general, saw many advantages to it:

> The. . .role which has been suggested by U.S. ground forces is the occupation and defense of key enclaves along the coast such as Quang Ngai, Qui Nhon, Tuy Hoa and Nha Trang. Such a disposition would have the advantage of placing our forces in areas of easy access and egress with minimum logistic problems associated with supply and maintenance. The presence of our troops would assure the defense of these important key areas and would relieve some GVN forces for employment elsewhere. The troops would not be called upon to engage in counter-insurgency operations except in their own local defense and hence would be exposed to minimum losses. . . .[5]

Thus, the proponents of an enclave strategy envisaged denying the enemy victory because he would be unable to seize crucial coastal areas held by U.S. forces, despite whatever successes he might enjoy throughout the rest of the country. Realizing his inability to gain a final victory, the enemy would be moved to a negotiated settlement of the conflict. Moreover, U.S. forces would be limited in number, could be brought in and supplied with ease over sea lines of communications controlled entirely by the U.S. Navy, and could be withdrawn with equal ease should the situation so dictate. Beyond the enclaves, the South Vietnamese army would be expected to continue to prosecute the war against the enemy's main forces. This enclave strategy, then, would have faithfully reflected the President's goal of denying Hanoi victory at the "lowest possible cost" and would have limited the commitment and objectives of U.S. military forces.

But as Ambassador Taylor also pointed out, the enclave strategy was "a rather inglorious static defensive mission unappealing to them (U.S. forces) and unimpressive in the eyes of the Vietnamese."[6] It also was perceived by General Westmoreland as a negative strategy, yielding the tactical initiative to the enemy and designed to frustrate rather than to defeat him, with no firm prospect of success. As Westmoreland saw it: "I am convinced that U.S. troops with their energy, mobility, and firepower can successfully take the fight to the VC."[7]

In requesting a build-up to a total of thirty-five maneuver battalions (infantry or armor units, roughly 900 men each) with a further nine battalions to be prepared for deployment if needed at a later date, Westmoreland spelled out his concept for employing these mobile forces. Sweeping away the last vestiges of the enclave strategy with which he had never agreed, Westmoreland described his plans for assuming the offensive and defeating the enemy. He saw the war developing in three distinct phases as follows: *Phase I.* Commitment of U.S. and other Free World forces necessary to halt the losing trend by the end of 1965. *Phase II.* U.S. and Allied forces mount major offensive actions to seize the initiative to destroy guerrilla and organized enemy forces. This phase would be concluded when the enemy had been worn down, thrown on the defensive, and driven back from the major populated areas. *Phase III.* If the enemy persisted, a period of a year to a year and a half following Phase II would be required for the final destruction of enemy forces remaining in remote base areas.[8]

No Enclaves

The concept, of course, was a traditional military one, that of defeating the enemy's military forces. Aware of LBJ's sensitivities, Westmoreland did not mention enemy "base areas" in Laos or Cambodia.

President Johnson, on July 28, 1965, approved the deployment to South Vietnam of General Westmoreland's thirty-five battalion force (with ancillary units) totaling 175,000 troops (later raised to 219,000).[9]

Whatever they may have thought personally of the wisdom of this momentous decision of July 1965, all the participants realized that a major threshold had been crossed. A new course had been taken, the end of which was not in sight. As General Westmoreland understood: "Explicit in my forty-four battalion proposal and President Johnson's approval of it was a proviso for free maneuver of American and allied units throughout South Vietnam. Thus, the restrictive enclave strategy with which I had disagreed from the first was finally rejected."[10] And as President Johnson later stated, "Now we were committed to major combat in Vietnam."[11]

Under Westmoreland's plan of action, U.S. forces could gain and maintain the tactical initiative in South Vietnam through their great mobility and firepower, but the enemy always maintained the strategic initiative by his ability and willingness to increase his commitment of forces, via the Ho Chi Minh Trail, to the struggle. Thus, the pace and level of the fighting would be dictated by Hanoi, using the Laos and Cambodia sanctuaries, and not by the United States and the Republic of Vietnam. The size of U.S. forces required to defeat the enemy depended entirely on the enemy's response to the U.S. build-up and his willingness to increase his own commitment to the struggle.

From that point on, the American effort in Vietnam was for the large part a conventional military one. The military defeat of the enemy seemed an achievable goal, and thus became an end in itself, as it has been in more conventional American wars.

Westmoreland's Hopes

Paradoxically, General Westmoreland had adopted a basic concept of operations for which his civilian superiors in Washington would not provide the necessary operational leeway or, finally, the necessary level of forces. Westmoreland always hoped, as he stated in his memoirs, that the President would eventually allow him the authority to pursue the strategy — notably cutting the Ho Chi Minh Trail — that he and the Joint Chiefs saw as essential to a decisive outcome.

The Viet Cong and the regular North Vietnamese units were not vulnerable to U.S. ground forces until they crossed the borders into South Vietnam. Likewise, enemy units in South Vietnam could escape pursuit and engagement by U.S. units by crossing over the borders into Cambodia, Laos, or beyond the Demilitarized Zone (DMZ). Thus, the enemy could enter the battle when he wished and could withdraw from the battlefield when he chose.

Success in this kind of war did not depend on General Westmoreland's ability to defeat the enemy in South Vietnam; it depended instead on how long the North Vietnamese were willing to feed the pipeline with men and materiel. For the United States, it was necessary to kill the enemy even faster than he could supply replacements via the sanctuaries. The White House constraints on Westmoreland granted crucial advantages to the enemy that could not be overcome by U.S. actions in the field. The war became a protracted war of attrition. If he were willing to pay the price, the enemy could keep American forces tied up indefinitely. As it turned out, Hanoi was able and willing to pay a very high price.

In addition, the build-up of U.S. forces and their use in an offensive role throughout Vietnam was an explicit expression of U.S. loss of confidence in the South Vietnamese Armed Forces (RVNAF) and a corresponding willingness on the part of U.S. commanders to take over the major part of the war effort in 1965–67.

The paradox arose of the Americans fighting on behalf of an army (and a government) that they treated with disdain, even contempt. The South Vietnamese were dealt with as if they really were irrelevant. Thus, there grew a naked contradiction between the political objectives of the war — an independent self-sufficient South Vietnam — and the U.S. neglect of the South Vietnamese government and army in the formulation of American war strategy during the 1965–67 build-up phases. There was little realization among American unit leaders that crucial to South Vietnam's security was the development of an honest and efficient South Vietnamese government able and willing to improve the welfare of its people.

Until 1968, after the failed Communist Tet Offensive, U.S. military operations were seldom coordinated with or directed toward progress in the pacification program. U.S. military leaders on the ground failed to grasp the causes or the significance of the steady attrition of GVN authority in the countryside, a loss of political authority that was directly linked to the way the war was conducted. Indeed, the effects of U.S. military operations — the uprooting of the rural populace, its concentration in refugee camps or in the large cities of South Vietnam, the creation of "free fire zones," the breakdown of government in the rural areas, the demoralization of many aspects of traditional Vietnamese life — worked against the objective of gaining the support of the populace for their government. As one observer noted: "Instead of the weaknesses within South Vietnam being eliminated they were being aggravated. . . . It was never understood that nation-building was the offensive construction program designed to strengthen the government's assets and eliminate its weaknesses, while the military operations were defensive and destructive, designed to hold the ring for the constructive program and in so doing, to weaken the enemy's military assets."[12]

As Colonel Harry Summers has pointed out, the military's efforts in Vietnam could be seen, from one point of view, as an enormous success. He states that "as far as logistics and tactics were concerned we succeeded in everything we set out to do. At the height of the war the Army was able to move almost a million soldiers a year in and out of Vietnam, feed them, clothe them, house them, supply them with arms and ammunition, and generally sustain them better than any Army had ever been sustained in the field. To project an Army of that size half-way around the world was a logistics and management task of enormous magnitude, and we had been more than equal to the task. On the battlefield itself, the Army was unbeatable. In engagement after engagement the forces of the Viet Cong and of the North Vietnamese Army were thrown back with terrible losses. Yet, in the end, it was North Vietnam, not the United States, that emerged victorious. How could we have succeeded so well, yet failed so miserably?"[13]

An Enormous Success

The point was, of course, that the many and spectacular American military victories in 1965–67 over VC/NVA forces were not translated into lasting gains for the South Vietnamese government or, no less important, into a decisive military success for the allies. When American forces withdrew from an area, the enemy continued to find shelter, or at least passive acquiescence to his presence, from the rural population of South Vietnam. At least until mid-1967, the two wars — political and military — were pursued as two relatively unrelated activities. But success in the military war could make no lasting difference without corresponding success in the political war.

There was some recognition that more was needed in Vietnam. Lip service was given to a "positive program," to "pacification," or to "Revolutionary Development" programs designed to bring social justice to the countryside in order to win the "hearts and minds" of the people and gain their active support for a government interested in their welfare and responsive to their needs. Often, such programs as were developed were largely planned, financed, and implemented by Americans with little GVN involvement. And certainly there was no agency within the United States government solely responsible for such programs.

The administration of American civil programs in Vietnam was long marked by fragmented and inefficient planning and execution. CORDS, an innovative and unique organization which integrated all U.S. civil and military pacification support and provided a single channel of advice and assistance to the Vietnamese at all levels, was finally instituted in South Vietnam, under Robert Komer and the overall direction of General Westmoreland, in May 1967. Unfortunately, unification in the field was not paralleled by similar unification among the many interested agencies in Washington.

Indeed, there was a general shallowness of knowledge of and indifference to South Vietnam as a society with its own structures and history. Even though a constitution was written in 1960 and generally fair democratic elections were held at the national level in 1967, the basic structure of South Vietnamese governmental and power relationships was not disturbed. And so the existence of South Vietnam as a nation continued to be sustained, as it had been at the outset of the American involvement, only by the commitment of American military power.

Tet 1968 and the Effect on Strategy

The shock of the Communist Tet Offensive in January 1968 finally shattered the facade of national policy. After Tet, despite the severe military setback to the National Liberation Front in South Vietnam, the decisions in Washington that had been avoided in past years could no longer be avoided. The senior military made it clear to President Johnson that the price in American manpower to sustain the war and provide for contingencies elsewhere had now reached the point where it could no longer be met without a large reserve call-up.

The political reality that faced President Johnson in February—March 1968 was that more of the same in South Vietnam, with an increased commitment of American lives and money and its consequent impact on the country, accompanied by no guarantee of victory in the near future, had become unacceptable to political Washington and to major opinion leaders in the country at large.

The Tet Offensive seemed to show that the attainment of LBJ's goals in Vietnam, if possible at all, was to be far in the future. To produce quicker or more decisive results, the U.S. commitment of manpower and money would have to be vastly increased, and the whole nature of the war, its strategy, and its relationship to the United States would have to be changed. There were strong indications that much of the American political elite had begun to believe that the cost in lives and money had already reached unacceptably high levels and that the objective — a noncommunist South Vietnam — was no longer worth the price.

The road to ending the U.S. war in Vietnam, it finally became clear to American leaders, depended at least as much on South Vietnamese political and military development as it did on American arms. This realization made it possible, in a sense, to return to the original purpose for which American forces were sent to South Vietnam by Lyndon Johnson, that of preventing the defeat of the South Vietnamese government.

March 1968, then, represented *de facto* a turning point in American policy toward Vietnam. The President's objectives in Vietnam remained the same. But after years of military effort and political anguish, the administration finally began to develop a strategy for attaining those objectives that it hoped would not place an unlimited burden upon national economic and military resources, and that could, over time, hold public acceptance.

American forces, in the number then deployed (close to 540,000), would continue to provide a shield behind which the South Vietnamese forces could rally, become effective, and win the support of the people. More weapons and equipment would be made available to the South Vietnamese, and pressure would be applied on the Pentagon to allow, indeed to require, progress in this long-neglected area. Thus, the eventual outcome of March 1968, that of limiting the further increases in American manpower in Vietnam and improving Vietnamese forces to the point where they could take over more of the effort, were opposite sides of the same coin. They represented an attempt at rationalization of the American effort in Vietnam and a return to the basic "minimum-cost" goals that had been used initially to justify American intervention in Vietnam.

The Failure of Strategy

The American failure in Vietnam up to the time of Tet 1968 was not a failure caused by the limitations placed upon military action, as some military and other commentators continue to charge. It was not caused by the press or dissent on the homefront. Indeed, overwhelming American military power had finally been brought to bear. The United States enjoyed complete control of the sea and air and had a striking superiority in mobility and materiel on land.

The American failure was caused by the lack of realization in Washington that military power alone could not solve a long-range political problem, that of the competence and political stability of the South Vietnamese government. Despite much hand-wringing in Washington, American strength and energy were never directed toward solving that political problem.

More fundamentally, the American effort fell short because of a failure at the national level to develop an agreed-upon strategy for success. Fundamental differences within the administration were never resolved. There was no agreed, coherent strategy to achieve American military and political objectives and, indeed, no agreement as to those objectives.

Wary of domestic reaction, careful not to take any actions that might possibly lead to Chinese or Russian intervention, President Johnson sought to achieve his objectives — saving South Vietnam — through gradual escalation of the military effort. The major cost that he felt had to be considered was continued public support for the war effort. This domestic consideration dictated to him the minimum necessary disruption in American life. Lyndon Johnson shied away from decisive action, failed to examine ultimate costs, and attempted to appease both the pressures for winning and for disengaging. He undertook a gradual military escalation to satisfy the "hawks" while trying to placate the "doves" by restricting air and ground operations and calling for peace negotiations.

The United States did not stumble into Vietnam. Each step was a deliberate choice by a careful President who weighed the alternatives as he saw them, limited each response, and took into account the opinion of the public. Some analysts have concluded that this indicates that the American decision-making process "worked," that all points of view were heard and accommodated, and that the war was conducted in a series of limited responses as desired by the President.

The Debate That Wasn't

But this is hardly a decision-making process that should be praised or emulated, nor did it yield a satisfactory result. The effort in Vietnam was piecemeal, indecisive, and misdirected. Each decision in 1965–67 represented a compromise between a President determined to preserve his domestic programs while defending freedom in Southeast Asia and the Joint Chiefs of Staff who saw no alternative but an American takeover of the war and an all-out military effort against a dangerous and tenacious enemy.

By presenting a facade of unanimity in 1964–65 concerning the conduct of the war and of the objectives being pursued, the President and the Joint Chiefs of Staff, in effect, inhibited rational national debate within the American body politic concerning United States objectives in Southeast Asia and the forces and resources to be devoted to the attainment of those objectives. When this debate did come, it was initiated by scattered groups of antiwar protesters and their congresssional allies who offered no workable policy alternatives.

Had the Joint Chiefs of Staff, who felt strongly about their own position, made public in 1965 their dissent from White House policy even at the risk of their jobs, or had the President at some point explicitly and publicly rejected the views and advice of his military leaders, Congress and the American people early on might have had a timely opportunity to debate and evaluate the basic issues facing the United States in Southeast Asia.

Indeed, such a debate might conceivably have resulted in wide support for President Johnson's approach. Our Vietnam involvement might then have focused on limited goals and our military effort would have been limited in keeping with those goals. The nation might then have addressed later the results of that limited effort without bitterness, recriminations, and accusations.

But no such debate took place.

NOTES

[1] Tom Wicker, *JFK and LBJ: The Influence of Personalities on Politics* (Murrow, New York, 1968), p. 208.

[2] *Public Papers of the Presidents: Lyndon B. Johnson 1965*, Vol. 1 (U.S. Government Printing Office, Washington, 1966), p. 395.

[3] Alain C. Enthoven and Wayne K. Smith, *How Much is Enough? Shaping the Defense Programme, 1961–1969* (Harper and Row, New York, 1971), pp. 299–300.

[4] *U.S.-Vietnam Relations, 1945–1967*, IV C (4) (a), p. 1.

[5] *U.S.-Vietnam Relations, 1945–1967*, IV C (3), p. 57.

[6] *Ibid.*, p. 58; General William C. Westmoreland, *A Soldier Reports* (Doubleday and Co., Garden City, 1976), pp. 129–30.

[7] Military Assistance Command Vietnam, 19118, 070335Z, June 1965, MACV to Commander in Chief United States Forces Pacific.

[8] General William C. Westmoreland, *Report on the War in Vietnam: Section II, Report on Operations in South Vietnam*, January 1964–June 1968 (U.S. Government Printing Office, Washington, 1969), p. 100; *U.S.-Vietnam Relations, 1945–1967*, IV C (5), pp. 118–19.

[9] *Public Papers of the President: Lyndon B. Johnson, 1965*, Vol. II, pp. 794–9.

[10] Westmoreland, *A Soldier Reports*, pp. 144, 146–52.

[11] Lyndon B. Johnson, *The Vantage Point: Perspectives of the Presidency, 1963–1969*, p. 153.

[12] Sir Robert G. K. Thompson, *No Exit From Vietnam* (Chatto and Windus, London, 1969), pp. 146–149.

[13] Col. Harry G. Summers, Jr., *On Strategy: A Critical Analysis of The Vietnam War* (Presidio Press, Novanta, Ca., 1982), p. 1.

COMMENTARY: On Betts and Schandler

by Larry Berman

First of all, it strikes me that throughout this whole 1960s period we really are dealing with the case of a powerful political personality, Lyndon Johnson, and the way it inhibits to a great degree any rational discussion of strategy and choice because so much in hindsight looks irrational as to how Johnson chose the course that he did for what, I have argued, were pure political reasons.

My first point is that as early as July 28, 1965 — or really the week before the July 28 announcement — McNamara had brought to the President the figure of 600,000 troops as a likely requirement for Vietnam, and that Johnson knew full well that down the road he was looking at a major commitment.

On the question of the reserves, a very important one that didn't manifest itself in either of the papers, McNamara initially favored the mobilization of the reserves in 1965. Indeed, his first recommendations to the President as early as July 1 called for the mobilization of at least 44 battalions. He wanted the mobilization of the reserves and he knew full well the impact on American public opinion, and the danger of fighting the war without the reserves, but Johnson turned it around. There was no way that Johnson would allow that. Documents for that are now available and are really quite interesting.

Betts does a good job of outlining the three reasons Johnson didn't bite the bullet. I would certainly like to do research in this area. What about these assumptions? The first one, the fear of provoking Chinese intervention: How much staff work was really done on that? To what extent did he ask either his military or intelligence staffs to give him a scenario about what level of escalation would actually send these hordes of Chinese along this Korean model. I've produced in my paper just one of the early CIA documents, but I wonder how much of it ever reached the President if it was done; and secondly, if the President had any interest in having it done.

On the Soviets and the Soviet response: The general assumption is that the limited policy was pursued because of fear of agitating the Soviets. I'd like to know if Johnson actually ever commissioned [staff] work on this and just what exactly was done, because the reason Johnson later gave for not mobilizing the reserves and the one he gave publicly, was his fear of provoking Chinese and Soviet reaction, and I would hope that serious staff work went into that. I haven't seen evidence of any in my work although I did for this conference publish what I did find.

On the assumption of "limited response": There's something that I want to go back to Texas to find out if it's available in the Johnson Library, or perhaps some of the military historians here can tell us: Was there any dissent among the military itself, or were some of the members of the military actually unanimous in their disagreement? It is said that all civilian advisers favored limited response and all the military advisers didn't. I for one am skeptical if unanimity existed to that degree. Again it's something that the record will have to show us.

In the various disagreements within each sector, civilian or military, how were people allowed to debate this within themselves, or within the group? I think that is an interesting question to pursue. Generally, I think the historical record provides a little more data than Betts would lead us to believe, and that's only because we do now have a wealth of material on McGeorge Bundy's role, particularly his role initially.

It's quite interesting to see in the early Bundy memos how he was able to criticize McNamara and McNamara's plan, but not to go to the President with that. Those people who have read my book find it a tragedy to see McGeorge Bundy's response to that in the interviews he gave to me. But basically it was clear that McNamara, among all civilian advisors, was *primus inter pares* at the time, and that nothing was going to derail his program. Powerful civilian advisors knew that you could try to argue with McNamara privately, but you couldn't argue directly with Johnson.

I think a wealth of material is coming out on that. All of Bundy's memos to the President are now available, and certainly Bundy's memos to McNamara are available, where you see Bundy very critical of McNamara's program for escalation in July 1965 (that eventually became operationalized), but backing off on that when he wrote to the President. He actually went so far as to tell the President that he should let Under Secretary of State George Ball become a kind of domesticated devil's advocate: "Let's all listen to him but eventually the decision should be a narrow one between my brother, Bill Bundy [Assistant Secretary of State], and McNamara."

The politics of getting out: Betts cites historian Richard Neustadt's point that he believes one of the failures of the National Security Council staff during the time was their failure to investigate the politics of getting out. It's interesting that more and more, as documents are becoming available, we see that Johnson was advised at various times by his press secretary Bill Moyers in early 1965 to work on this. A new memo that just became available is one that Moyers sent to Johnson in June '65 in which he says, "You should take George Ball and myself [Moyers] and one other person and let them just work alone, get them out of the institutional network for a while and let them work on the politics of getting out." Nothing apparently ever came of that, but it was clear that it did reach Johnson's desk.

The overriding concern of Lyndon Johnson in 1965 was, as Betts accurately points out, that he feared a right wing or a left wing backlash. We must realize that this was a President who wanted to be a great legislative president and whose Great Society took precedence over everything.

If you look back over the documents now available, you see a man who really destroyed himself and his strategy. Particularly in the failure, if he was going to fight the war, not to mobilize the reserves and not to play it straight with the American public. His decision of July 28, 1965, to go ahead with a major build-up in Vietnam, has all the seeds of his own destruction.

Something that doesn't appear in the Betts paper, but does appear in Colonel Schandler's paper, and which is a most essential point, is the way that Lyndon Johnson very craftily and cagily — and this is well documented — used the advisory process in July of 1965 really to legitimize a decision that had already been made, calling in the Joint Chiefs for a series of meetings and letting everyone have their two cents worth when he already knew very well what the course was going to be.

McNamara had already devised it, giving Ball his day in court simply to allow everyone to feel that they had considered the option of getting out and that they had given it their due. Johnson was a President who manipulated the advisory process in a way that most of us never thought presidents used advisory processes for. If you're going to lead a country into war, you have to let Americans think that you're deliberating and advising. What better way to do that than to let the *New York Times* and the *Washington Post*, as I've shown and others have shown, report about the "war climate" permeating Washington: What will happen? Will the reserves be mobilized? Will 600,000 men go or not go?

By July 28 Lyndon Johnson seemed like a moderate President, in a way, not mobilizing the reserves, only sending 50,000 men to Vietnam when he had all the documents in front of him.

One of the lessons of the whole thing is the need for an honest President, and no advisory process at all can guarantee that. In this case I think the advisory process did "work" in the context employed by Gelb and Betts. But it mattered only incidentally; it was used to legitimize a decision for which advice was not necessary at the time.

COMMENTARY: The President and the Generals

by Paul Miles

First, with regard to the role of the President as Commander-in-Chief, Larry Berman has expressed some doubt about whether Johnson continued to hope and search desperately for alternative solutions well after the elections of 1964, although I think that he would agree with the other point that was made by Richard Betts that, in mid-1965, he did agonize over the decision to send large numbers of ground forces, and that he eventually did so despite the lack of promises of early success from Army leaders.

The pattern I see emerging from the documents, beginning immediately after the election of 1964 and extending at least until mid-June of 1965, is that of a President who is asking questions of the chairman of the Joint Chiefs of Staff, questions which are being communicated to General Westmoreland and Ambassador Taylor in Saigon — not just questions, but indeed comments — comments in the form of the criticism of the military program in Vietnam during that period, which in turn produced recommendations and unleashed a chain of events that the President desperately then attempts to reassert some control over.

In illustrating that pattern, I would give more attention to the message that President Johnson sent to Taylor and Westmoreland on December 30, 1964. This is the one that is referred to by Taylor in his *Memoirs* where he said he was surprised that the President once again declined to initiate so-called reprisal bombing of North Vietnam, but yet seemed to have an open mind about a far more hazardous course of action, a land war in Asia.

This is the message in which Johnson says, "What I want to do in this message is to share my own thinking with you and ask for your full comment so that we can lay a basis of understanding that will give us a base line not only for prompt reprisal, but for other actions, mainly within South Vietnam, which can help to turn the tide."

LBJ mentions his concern about the failure to provide security for American bases in Vietnam; he has not yet been told, in any convincing way, why aircraft cannot be protected from mortar attacks and officers' quarters from large Viet Cong bombs. He then goes ahead to make the statement that has been paraphrased and quoted in part elsewhere, "Every time I get a military recommendation, it seems to me that it calls for large-scale bombing. I've never felt that this war will be won from the air. It seems to me that what is much more needed and would be more effective is a larger and stronger force of rangers, special forces, Marines, other appropriate military strength on the ground and on the scene. I am ready to look with great favor on that kind of increased American effort directed at the guerrillas and aimed to stiffen the aggressiveness of the South Vietnamese military units up and down the line. Any recommendation that you or General Westmoreland make in this sense will have immediate attention from me, although I know that it may involve the acceptance of larger American sacrifices."

Now the significance of that message was, I'm reasonably certain, from the point of view of the military command in Saigon, that this was LBJ's invitation to Taylor and Westmoreland to start thinking seriously about providing security for the U.S. air bases within South Vietnam. This, along with an intensified concern which came from the February 1965 decision to bomb North Vietnam, later prompted a recommendation for the deployment of the very limited Marine forces in March 1965 which, some analysts have said, represented some kind of a crossing of the Rubicon.

But beyond that, LBJ's invitation was the catalyst for what admittedly was still a kind of an embryonic plan for the commitment and eventual utilization of division-sized U.S. elements within South Vietnam, a catalyst not only for the Joint Chiefs in Washington, even though they may have for their own reasons favored such a commitment earlier, but more importantly, for Westmoreland.

Let me just mention two or three other documents from that period to reinforce that. I think more attention needs to be given to the visit to Saigon of General Harold K. Johnson, Army Chief of Staff, in March 1965, and the instructions that the Secretary of Defense gave once again to both Taylor and Westmoreland. "We're sending General Johnson to South Vietnam and developing a list of requirements and assume no limitations on funds, equipment or personnel. We will be prepared to act immediately and favorably on any recommendation you and General Johnson may make." The President is asking, "What more can be done?"

Similarly, the message of 16 April 1965: "Highest authorities concluded the situation is deteriorating. We're ready to send brigades. . . .Westmoreland to submit proposals."

And a very interesting bit of guidance from Admiral U.S.G. Sharp, Commander-in-Chief in the Pacific, to Westmoreland on 11 June 1965. He has been in Washington, he has conferred with the Secretary of Defense. According to Sharp, McNamara does not want to depend on ARVN. He wants to know if U.S. troops could do the job in Vietnam and he assumes future mobilization at home of the reserves. This, of course, sheds additional light on the background of the so-called Americanization of the war.

I mention these documents, and there are others that we will find in the Westmoreland papers, now deposited at the LBJ Library, which, when processed and declassified, will illumine this period. We need to know more about the interaction between the President and Wheeler and Westmoreland and Taylor during that 1964–65 period, and how that interaction, on an incremental basis, added up to some kind of White House strategic concept for Vietnam.

With regard to strategic concept, Schandler has mentioned that the Joint Chiefs of Staff made no independent analyses. I think that is true. But I think it's also useful to recall a vignette that General Wheeler mentioned once in an interview back in 1971: When the Joint Chiefs of Staff sent their strategic concept for Vietnam on 27 August 1965 to the Secretary of Defense, McNamara mentioned that he found it very interesting, the sort of thing that we should consider again in the future. But it was not formally approved by the White House and therefore did not really become, even with all of its shortcomings or inadequacies, any kind of catalyst for more intensive debate or discussion of a strategic concept which would have included not only the Joint Chiefs but others with the Department of Defense, at the White House, and at other governmental agencies.

I might add that General Wheeler said that among the sins of omission he regretted committing during the course of the war, the one he would emphasize was his failure to insist that McNamara take some formal action on that concept of the Joint Chiefs and forward it to the President.

Schandler notes that there was a reluctance on the part of the military to expose controversial military disagreements to the President. Here again the role of the President casts some light on that reluctance. On one occasion in March 1965 when the President had apparently said to all of the Joint Chiefs, "We need to kill more VC" (quoted in the *Pentagon Papers* and elsewhere), it did lead to a debate between General Wallace Greene, Commandant of the Marine Corps, General Johnson, and others about the employment of American forces in Vietnam, specifically over how they should be based and used. The President was visibly uncomfortable and told McNamara he never again wanted to be exposed to that kind of awkward discussion.

Apparently there was then some kind of gentlemen's agreement between Wheeler and McNamara that they would adhere to the President's wishes in that regard.

With regard to the role of Westmoreland in promoting some kind of a more coherent, strategic concept in Vietnam: One point that needs to be mentioned is that he was, of course, only the field commander in Vietnam, and probably did not see himself as an especially influential, independent, autonomous advisor in 1965. He does not become one until his rather mysterious meeting with the President in August 1966 at the LBJ Ranch, where no one else of senior rank was present. After that he became considerably more assertive and began to see himself as a military advisor to the President, and even more so to the Secretary of Defense.

Nevertheless, I do think that Westmoreland was asking questions in the spring of 1965 which he assumed were also being asked at the Washington level. In some cases they were being asked by people he did not anticipate, like George Ball. For example, on the 14th of February 1965, before the Marines landed at Da Nang, Westmoreland raises the question of the relationship between performance of U.S. ground forces in South Vietnam and the philosophy of the "graduated reprisal bombing" program. To him this connection between the conduct of the air war and the ground war at that time was not clear, and there are similar expressions of concern along those lines that we find in his papers.

It is especially unfortunate, given many of the comments that have been made about the inadequacy of the strategic concept, that one particular Westmoreland message of the 24th of June 1965 which McNamara quoted from just briefly in his recommendations to LBJ of the 26th of June, was not quoted by McNamara in greater detail.

This is the one when, in response to Wheeler's remark, "We need to start thinking about forces in 1966," Westmoreland replies that he is uncomfortable with the arithmetical approach to the war that the Secretary is taking, and he thinks there needs to be more attention given to the employment of the U.S. forces; that the premise behind whatever further actions we might take either in South Vietnam or against the North must be that we are in for the long haul. "The struggle has become a war of attrition. I see no likelihood of achieving a quick, favorable end to the war." He then proceeds to outline his views on some of the questions which, as we have suggested here, were not being considered in detail at the Washington level.

Finally, with regard to the "enclave" strategy: There's been a lot of confusion, a kind of intellectual confusion, over the distinction between so-called "logistic islands" of 1965, which were nothing more than a rather practical and realistic concept for deploying American forces incrementally, particularly at a time when most of them were going by ship to bases in South Vietnam where they could be supplied by sea, coupled with the interest of the President, as explained to Ambassador Taylor on the 3rd of April 1965 by Dean Rusk, citing the emphasis of the President on avoiding language suggesting an offensive mission, specifically saying, "We must emphasize logistics."

With regard to the initiative of Ambassador Taylor and what seem to be confused motives on his part, I think if we, for example, read in its entirety the message that Schandler quoted in his paper, we will find that there is the suggestion that Taylor is still primarily concerned in postponing any kind of deployment and, along with giving the advantages of an enclave strategy, he outlines the disadvantages. But he also outlines the advantages and disadvantages of deploying forces to the logistic islands. The bottom line of that message is, "Let's consider this situation more carefully."

Finally, what I want to emphasize is that I don't think a coastal "enclave" policy was a practical alternative because of the reality of politics, both domestic and international; and that our allies, the South Vietnamese, did not want American forces in the populated enclaves, an opinion expressed not only by them directly to McNamara in July 1965, but also expressed by the CIA station chief through Chester Cooper to McGeorge Bundy.

And second, it was Westmoreland's impression, based on his reading of Rusk's comments on a *Today* television program, that American forces were not expected to act like scared jack rabbits in coastal enclaves. This impression was strengthened by the rhetoric of LBJ, who began to anticipate his statements of the Honolulu conference and at Cam Ranh Bay in 1966 about "bringing home the bacon." A proposal to employ American forces in a "constabulary" role in Vietnam was not acceptable either to the President or the Congressional leadership at that time.

COMMENTARY: The Role of the Military

by Edwin Simmons

I agree with Schandler that Johnson and McNamara are the main villains in the Vietnam drama, but the civilian strategists come a close second.

Schandler is correct in criticizing Johnson's reactive, defensive strategy that left the initiative in the hands of the enemy, and his failure to call up the reserves. He is incorrect in claiming that the Joint Chiefs of Staff made no independent analysis of the force needed to achieve U.S. aims within the restraints imposed by the President. I know of numbers of studies, some originated by the Joint Chiefs, some by the Service planning staffs, on what needed to be done and the forces that would be required. I remember a 1964 study that put the force needed in South Vietnam at 700,000, a remarkably accurate prediction.

When one asks military leaders why they did not resign in protest against the President's unworkable policy, they invariably say they felt they could be most effective working within the system. Actually, the military chiefs were sheltered from exposure to hard, ethical choices by the umbrella of civilian control. It was one of the distortions of the Vietnam War that civilian control of the military became civilian direction and management, and that military leadership at all levels of command used "civilian control" as an exoneration from moral responsibility. Pushed to the extreme, this thought comes out that without mobilization, as signaled by a call-up of the reserves, the war — or the non-war — was fought by the regulars, the "professionals," and these "professionals" were more than willing to accept the role of automatons controlled by their civilian masters.

No one openly favored a war of attrition, but then that is what we were engaged in. I recall a Marine Corps study that showed, mathematically, that the North Vietnamese could keep up the struggle forever, rather like the mythical march of Chinese, four abreast, past a given point, for all eternity.

COMMENTARY: The Pacification Effort

by Richard Hunt

Herb Schandler contends that there was a serious imbalance between the U.S. military and non-military pacification programs in Vietnam. That contention is true for the period 1965–67, but I think you have to keep in mind that the Johnson administration was aware of this imbalance as early as the end of 1964. In the Johnson Library I have read several memos written by McGeorge Bundy and his assistant Chester Cooper addressing specific questions of how to redress this imbalance. The memos serve to keep the President aware of the serious organizational problems and the failings of settling the pacification problem in Vietnam. They are a kind of a bridge leading to the Honolulu conference of February 1966 and the appointment of Robert Komer in March 1966 to oversee from Washington the American support of pacification.

With this support of Secretary of Defense Robert McNamara, Bundy's successor Walt Rostow, and above all the President himself, Komer became the catalyst for a more cohesive and better managed program of support for pacification. Komer's efforts culminated in the establishment of an organization named CORDS that placed both the military and civilian support components for pacification under a single manager. Starting in May 1967, Komer directed CORDS and worked, in turn, for General Westmoreland. Komer is quite appreciative of Westmoreland's full support of CORDS and his willingness to accept innovations that Komer proposed.

One key innovation was Westmoreland's support of the "Phoenix" program. This was a program which sought to target and apprehend members of the Viet Cong infrastructure, and he let Komer run this in spite of the objections of his J-2 who wanted to retain that particular function himself. This is a clear example of U.S. adaptation to circumstances of war that should be brought out.

Komer's arrival in South Vietnam in 1967 marked the beginning of a coherent pacification program. Pacification only became an effective program after the Tet Offensive of '68. The effect of the Tet Offensive on pacification is an important subject needing further treatment. The initial reaction in Washington to the offensive was that pacification had suffered a serious blow. Herb Schandler's book on Tet makes clear that the press and many in the government shared that perception. What has not been appreciated is that by March 1968, while LBJ was reassessing his Vietnam policy, MACV and CORDS were concluding that the enemy's military failure at Tet gave them an opportunity.

Komer and his staff began to plan for a special pacification counter-offensive to make visible gains in Saigon's control of the countryside. They wanted to do this in order to convince the American people that the war could be won and to strengthen Saigon's territorial claims in case of a cease-fire in place. Komer and his deputy, William Colby, drafted a broad plan whose most prominent goal was to add to

Saigon's control an additional 1,000 contested hamlets in the brief span of three months. Ambassador Ellsworth Bunker, General Creighton Abrams, and Komer persuaded President Thieu to embark on this plan. It initially was called the Accelerated Pacification Effort, but the acronym APE was not very congenial, so it was changed to Accelerated Pacification Campaign, APC.

The campaign brought good news and bad news. The good news was that the APC met its statistical goals; the bad news was that it made no difference on policy in Washington. By January 1969 when the campaign ended, there were sharp disagreements in Washington, as recorded in NSSM-1, about what the pacification statistics meant. State and CIA remained skeptical that any permanent progress had been made. MACV, the Joint Chiefs, and of course CORDS, on the other hand, believed the gains were real and would last. The only unanswered question was whether the Viet Cong would be able to disrupt the pacification program. They had not done so during the Accelerated Pacification Campaign and that was the key reason for the campaign's statistical success.

According to statistics compiled by Thomas Fair, now published in unclassified form, the war changed in character after the Tet Offensive in 1968. (Fair worked in Systems Analysis in the Pentagon during the war and worked on something called the *Southeast Asia Analysis*, which was a periodical in-house journal.) Combat deaths, both enemy and friendly, peaked in 1968, but afterward allied fatalities dropped by a greater percentage than did enemy deaths.

Between 1968 and 1972, the aggregate strength of Viet Cong and NVA forces in South Vietnam dropped, although the number of Viet Cong and NVA battalions remained fairly constant. If these figures are correct, there were fewer soldiers per battalion. The number of Viet Cong and NVA battalion-size attacks dropped from 126 in 1968 to 34 in 1969 to 13 in 1970 to 2 in 1971. The number of small assaults, raids on villages or outposts, was slightly higher in those years compared to 1968. There was a change in the enemy style of fighting because the Communist battalions were weakened during 1968 and also because you had the impact of the pacification program.

During 1967–71, say from the year of Tet, 1968, the combat death rate was higher for the RF-PF, the Regional and Popular Forces. These were the South Vietnamese local militia forces providing population security. The combat death rates were higher for the RF-PF than they were for the ARVN. This is another possible indication that the Communists were concentrating against pacification after Tet 1968.

During the period 1969–71, the pacification program continued to make headway. There are numerous statistical measures that were used and abused during the war, and those indices still have to be used cautiously. Still they show that gains were made, but these numbers cannot and did not assess the permanence of any gains that were made.

The percentage of population living inside secure settlements rose from 47 percent in 1968 to 84 percent in 1971. The South's RF-PF nearly doubled in size between 1967 and 1971, from 300,000 to 532,000. Police forces also increased substantially over the same period. The strength of the Viet Cong infrastructure (agents, tax-collectors, etc.) was estimated to drop by nearly one fourth between August 1967 and October 1971, with the heaviest losses among low-level Viet Cong cadre assigned to villages and hamlets. The Viet Cong was thus a weaker organization after Tet.

I conclude with the thought that what happened during the period 1969–72 has not really had the serious scholarly scrutiny that such an important period deserves.

DISCUSSION

MUELLER: It would be useful if Betts and Schandler could offer a definition of strategy.

KARNOW: Can one refer to a planned strategy of attrition, or is it a war of attrition without a strategy?

LOMPARIS: Given LBJ's political objectives, was not a limited enclave strategy as proposed by Gavin the best option?

KOHN: What evidence does Betts have that LBJ knew before July 1965 that huge numbers of American troops were necessary in Vietnam? And how do we know if this information stood out in all the "noise"?

WEBB: In the late JFK and early LBJ years, Communist activity was on a less than overt military level. How did American planners expect to deal with it?

AVERY: What was the role of intelligence — faulty, non-existent, or what? For instance, did American officials really consider North Vietnam to be a stand-in for Red China? Also, was there any real contingency planning for a U.S. combat commitment before November 1964?

GOODMAN: Did LBJ ever look at statistics on the Viet Cong and other matters?

SCHANDLER: Let me talk about strategy for a minute. I haven't necessarily given this a great deal of thought, but General Simmons mentioned the divergences between strategies — the blending, the lack of precise detail. The way I looked at it was on various levels. There is a national strategy which is the strategy for using national power to achieve national objectives. Then it would seem to me that within that strategy, you have various elements of national power. You have the strategy for employing your political power, you have the strategy for employing your military power.

So there was a national strategy which was never really enunciated by the President. What was in his mind was having a limited war for limited purposes, with geographic constraints, not to win but to convince the North Vietnamese that they could not win.

It would seem that from that national strategy, there would then evolve a strategy for employing military forces, political forces, other elements of national power to achieve that end. And this is where the breakdown came.

First of all, the White House strategy was not clearly enunciated, the objectives that the strategy were designed to achieve were not clearly enunciated on a national level, and were not accepted by the other leaders who were in charge of applying their part of the forces to the achievement of that national strategy. So indeed the military strategy on the ground and in the air in North Vietnam was undertaken by the military in such a way that it could not possibly succeed within the limits and the objectives of the national strategy which again was not accepted or enunciated.

So this failure was all the way down the line: to agree on the objectives of the strategy on a national level and to enunciate it clearly so the military knew what they were supposed to be doing; and then in the field the military developing their own concept of operations from the Joint Chiefs of Staff on down to the field, which did not accord with and could not succeed within that national strategy.

My discussion on the enclave theory (keeping U.S. forces in coastal bases), whether or not this was really very important in the Washington deliberations in 1965, is an attempt to show that there were options in this military strategy which perhaps could have been followed and which would have been in accord with the President's strategy to deny victory to Hanoi. If we had done this, perhaps this could have been more successful, but it would have been more rational, in any case. And I think this leads to a larger lesson on the concept of civil/military relations wherein if you are going to have a national strategy and then implement it with military force, the military better know what that strategy is and be informed as to the manpower and materiel constraints under which they must implement it.

This has not been the American tradition since World War II. The military is independent, the war is on, you guys go out and win it, and don't bother with the politics of it. And consequently this may be the lesson that we must learn from Vietnam: that, as Harry Summers has pointed out so well, the military is one instrument which must be directed toward the achievement of the national strategy, and in Vietnam, this did not happen.

SUMMERS: Strategy is the application of means to achieve an end. Enclave "strategy" is really only a tactic.

SCHANDLER: We get down to the question of the strategy of attrition. Was this a strategy? Well, it was a means to an end, I guess, under this definition, but it was not deliberately chosen. General Westmoreland's objectives in Vietnam, and he stated these in his request for the 44 battalions, he saw in three phases: the commitment of U.S. forces to stop the losing trend, whatever that meant; the mounting of a major offensive to seize the initiative and destroy the guerrilla and organized enemy forces; and then the final destruction of remaining enemy forces.

He never really got past the second stage, and it evolved into a war of attrition because it was an attempt to destroy the enemy forces and these enemy forces were never destroyed. The enemy always had the option of reinforcing from their sanctuaries in Laos and Cambodia, of retreating to the sanctuaries, of determining tactically the level of combat.

BRAESTRUP: It seems to me that what you are saying in part is that there was no military strategy either on Lyndon Johnson's part or on anybody else's part that accorded with the objective, however vaguely defined, that was sought, namely, to persuade Hanoi to call off its efforts to take over the South.

SCHANDLER: And the realities of the situation: the geography, the dedication of the enemy. . . .

BRAESTRUP: It's instructive to keep in mind the geography. So much of the discussion, now as during the 1960s, of Vietnam seems based on the assumption that Vietnam was an island. Lyndon Johnson's greatest achievement with the press and with Congress was that he succeeded in getting us all to think about the war in terms of South Vietnam primarily, and of North Vietnam solely in terms of bombing. Somehow he succeeded in getting everybody to think that the whole argument was kind of based on that — all about pacification and revolutionary warfare, search and destroy, etc. — and we always forgot that the other side had two other countries, Laos and Cambodia, to which they could repair and from which they came.

KOHN: How does Schandler differentiate between strategy and policy?

SCHANDLER: The policy of LBJ was not winning the war. He was, as Larry Berman pointed out, the principal actor. He had an idea of how the war should be conducted in Vietnam — limited war with limited resources over a period of time, not interfering with the civilian economy. That was his policy and that was his objective, but this was never enunciated. He never sat the Joint Chiefs down and said, "This is what we're going to do. Don't tell me about mining Haiphong, bombing Hanoi, invading Laos, invading Cambodia, and mobilizing the reserves. We're not going to do that. Now, within those constraints of our national policy, how are we going to implement this strategy?"

It got to be funny in the Pentagon because every time, every six months, the President would come back to the Joint Chiefs and say, "How can we make greater progress in Vietnam?" and they would say, "Mine Haiphong, bomb Hanoi, invade Laos, invade Cambodia, and mobilize the reserves." And the President would laugh and say, "We're not going to do that, but within these constraints, how can we achieve greater success?" And they'd say, "Give the Air Force more targets, and give the Army some more men, and the Marines some more, and the Navy a little bit more, and everything will be all right." After four or five reiterations of this, if I were President, I'd say, "Listen, guys, you don't get the message." Or if I were on the Joint Chiefs, I'd come to the President and say, "We can't do it. You're asking us to do an impossible thing." So the policy was never translated [into strategy]. They didn't agree.

BETTS: I think it is true certainly that Johnson was clearly the activist and dominating figure by '65 as he usually was in most of his political roles. But I don't think that negates his anxiety and ambivalence a lot of the time. And I think part of the problem with the decision-making records is trying to deal with the problem of ambivalence and how that shows up in historical evidence, because it was there in most of these people (Washington civilians), even if there was a dominant strand of thinking that drove their decisions.

The evidence on whether Johnson really sought desperately for alternative solutions after the 1964 elections — maybe "desperate" was an infelicitous choice of words. But I think that the fact that he did direct another strategy review in November 1964 to go over other options indicates that he either was the cynical manipulator of the advisory process that Berman suggested, or was maybe hoping that something would turn up, even though by that time the accumulation of events made him see that probably we were going to have to do more. But I think that he was hoping that maybe something might turn up. I associate myself with Paul Miles's comments about the dynamic of interchange between Johnson and some of his subordinates during this period between the 1964 election and the critical decisions in mid-'65.

And I think you're right that the Great Society and domestic concerns were his dominant preoccupation. That's one of the reasons that he was interested in alternatives. It's one of the reasons that, whether or not he was thinking earlier that we definitely were going to have to do something [in Vietnam], he didn't really decisively act until people were telling him, or at least some people were telling him, that there was a crunch. And certainly by July '65, as you [Berman] point out in your book, a lot of people were telling him, "If we don't act now, South Vietnam's going to go down the tubes." Now maybe he would have done it anyway, but that suggests to me, at least circumstantially, that he was hoping to avoid major troop commitment as long as there was some other possibility. And he came up against the fact that there didn't seem to be another possibility.

Also a distinction that Les Gelb made in our book, [*The Irony of Vietnam*], was between the pre-'65 period of doing the minimum necessary to avoid defeat and the post-'65 period of doing more, in a sense, of the maximum feasible to have a chance of winning, even though it was not the amount that most advisors said would be necessary to have much assurance of winning.

The question of how much investigation there was in Washington on the danger of Chinese intervention: I think you point to some of it in your paper and raise the question of whether Johnson really considered it. I imagine he probably didn't, but it's true that most Presidents, and Johnson maybe more than most, was known for not being a great reader of NIEs and things of that sort. But also I don't think you can blame any President for not directing that process himself. That's the job of the director of Central Intelligence and his assistant for National Security, at that time, McGeorge Bundy. So maybe a more interesting question is how well they did that and brought it to his attention.

Whether there was really a unanimous military against unanimous civilians, no. The center of gravity clearly was different, and there was also a difference on the alignment on the air war and the ground war. Certainly the Army was more flexible and less strident on most of these matters than the Air Force, with the Navy in-between but generally more favorable towards the Air Force point of view; and certainly there was much more military vehemence about the air war because that was much more closely managed [by the White House] in its details. The standard cliché is the portrait of Johnson picking individual bombing targets at the Tuesday luncheon. Certainly there were differences between, say, Rostow and McNamara and other civilians, especially over time, with McNamara clearly shifting by the end of his tenure in 1967 to being close to an in-house dove.

The role of McGeorge Bundy — there's another instance of what gives me a problem of dealing with ambivalence. Professor May [in his commentary paper] looks at some of the documents of Bundy's and indicates that this raises some doubt about a categorical assertion [that Bundy was] not questioning the imperative of carrying on the struggle. In an economy of words, I made things too stark, but I think even in those documents and in other things I've seen, Bundy, as a number of other actors, did manifest ambivalence at some time and did raise questions about what the hell we might be getting into, but never seriously even in those documents, as I saw it, suggested the acceptability of the alternative and that alternative was pulling the plug.

George Ball and those others up until '65, in Ball's case, always thought there was maybe some third course — do less, emphasize negotiation, do other things, but these ultimately would have led to the same crunch anyway. So to me it was the basic commitment not to question whether or not we could allow South Vietnam to fall. That was what I was emphasizing.

There's a question of the managerial relations between civilians and the Pentagon and the professional military. I have in the past argued and still do believe that there was in some rough sense equal measure of irresponsibility on both sides. I'm a little bit troubled by almost too much agreement of some of what I've said. I think it would be wrong to say that there were some civilian Whiz Kids who really screwed everything up and were sort of the criminal actors in this fiasco. They made a lot of mistakes. I think the military were complicit, though, in not being adamant about their estimates of what would be necessary for conventional victory.

Part of the reason that their advice was downplayed in the earlier period was that Vietnam was not viewed by the White House as a conventional war; it was viewed as a highly political war, a revolutionary situation, in which military judgment was not sufficient, and in which military actions could not be disentangled from political strategy, and therefore the Joint Chiefs' views were not regarded as being professionally sufficient under those circumstances. When the war did shift to a conventional war, after 1965, it is more arguable that civilian restraints were less justifiable, but those restraints had been made clear long in advance.

That's why I argued in my first book that probably, at least with hindsight, which is always easier to employ, the Joint Chiefs would have performed a greater service in the summer of 1965 if they had resigned, or at least confronted the President with the choice: Either give us what we say we need or we'll resign. As it was, they were good soldiers, they saluted.

Their anxieties were sort of known in the defense community, but they didn't make great headlines and the President didn't have to face that choice. If that choice had been posed in '65, I suspect he might have had more of a motive and also an excuse to disengage, had it been clear [to the public] that there were military professionals saying that winning in Indochina was going to take a million men.

The questions of whether civilian control was excessive, though, is still a secondary question. The basic problem was the larger policy and strategic problem of simultaneously defining avoidance of defeat in Vietnam as vital and the cost of victory as unacceptable. I think civilian and military were equally irresponsible and muddled in their approach to the issue in not forcing the resolution of the contradiction between those goals.

How ample was the military warning? Again that's hard to say. Who knows with what vehemence a position that you see on paper was articulated? Who knows really about what Wheeler told Johnson about needing between 700,000 and a million men, whether he sort of mentioned that and then sort of winked? I don't know. There are indications, though, that these figures were mentioned more than once. I think there are also indications that the President and some of his other supporters probably believed that the military [was] inflating the problem and that maybe we might get by with less, which is at least the only logical excuse for why they tried to get by with less. But I can't answer the question about how much of the military advice was lost in the noise.

The requirements for victory in the classical sense were overlooked for a number of reasons, one of which was the hope that we might get lucky with other options, too. We needed a big injection of force to beat the North Vietnamese over the head, show them that they couldn't win, make them hurt, and that combined with a gradual build-up of the South Vietnamese, which later was called Vietnamization, the hope of some kind of negotiation, other things, altogether might raise the odds of some kind of compromise success.

In early 1965 there was an exercise undertaken at McNamara's direction asking the Joint Chiefs and the services to estimate what it would take to win if we did everything we could. I don't know anything more about that exercise than what was in the *Pentagon Papers*, which isn't much. But there, too, there was sort of a kicker: They were saying, "if we do everything we could," when it was clear from the beginning, or at least was clear to the civilians, that we were not going to do everything we could.

This relates to one question about why I say the Vietnam commitment was a misjudgment. I think it's important to add a qualifier that I had on the end of the sentence; that is, the misjudgment that communist victory was so damaging, that preventing it warranted major effort despite high risk of failure.

It's one thing if we knew that with a major effort we had great odds for success; that would have been a different calculation. Or if we had said saving Vietnam is so important that we'll do anything necessary. But neither of those was the case.

What we wound up with was a high-risk strategy, and the reason I would still say it's a misjudgment, the results clearly show that it wasn't worth it — 50,000 dead Americans and God knows how many thousands of dead Vietnamese, and communist control over all of Indochina.

The alternative of invading North Vietnam, sending over a million U.S. troops, and probably leaving them there for a long time, I would say, and this is just a policy judgment, was not worth it and most of the participants would have said it was not worth it. But they weren't faced with the absolute inevitability of that alternative; they still hoped that things might work out otherwise. We lost and it was tragic, but Southeast Asia today [as a result] is probably not a more dangerous place for the United States than a lot of other places around the world. And the rapprochement with China makes the war look even less necessary.

On Goodman's question on whether the President looked at the numbers generated on Vietnam, I frankly don't know. I think it's clear that McNamara and Rostow were fascinated with them, and Rostow particularly was reported to have waved numbers around at various points to buck up morale; but the details on that I just don't know, maybe someone else does.

About negotiation, I won't say much. Allan Goodman can say more about that since he's written a book about it. My basic feeling from looking at the record was that the essential problem was that, until 1968, neither side wanted unconditional negotiations. Both sides wanted negotiations on conditions that would reduce the military activities of the other side during the negotiation period and that's why nothing ever happened until after Tet on negotiations.

Why were the Joint Chiefs of Staff mistrusted? There are a lot of reasons for that, most of them probably not very good. There's a lot of second-hand testimony from people in the Kennedy and Johnson administrations that the Bay of Pigs, the fights during the 1961 Laos crisis, and the Cuban missile crisis soured a lot of civilians on the Joint Chiefs as being either reckless or manipulative or dense. Whether those were reasonable judgments or not is another subject. But I think that accounts for some of the instinctive distrust among the people in those administrations.

My model of civil/military relations? I'd associate myself generally with Harvard scholar Samuel Huntington's notion of objective control, which means that the military should sort of give advice untarnished by political considerations. But that's entirely dependent on the character of the administration. You can't have model civil/military relations divorced from the operational modes and norms of conduct and expectations of particular administrations because the latter will determine whether military advices are listened to or valued in any sense, regardless of any norms which can be articulated about how the Joint Chiefs should act in general.

THE NIXON STRATEGY IN VIETNAM

by George C. Herring

Ten years after the attainment of "peace with honor," it remains extremely difficult to assess the Nixon-Kissinger policies in Vietnam. The source materials are very limited and selective. We have no equivalent of the *Pentagon Papers* for these years, and only a handful of scattered documents have been declassified. All we know is what Nixon and Kissinger want us to know and have told us, or what their disgruntled associates (the Haldemans, Ehrlichmans, and Roger Morrises) have themselves divulged or told researchers like William (*Sideshow*) Shawcross and Tad Szulc.

In short, we now have a very limited fund of information, much of it revealed to settle old scores or score debating points.

It should be unnecessary to add that Nixon's Vietnam policies have been the subject of bitter controversy.

Whatever their differences, Nixon and Kissinger agree that they pursued the only responsible course open to them and insist that, despite North Vietnamese intransigence and irresponsible opposition at home, they succeeded in constructing a workable peace, only to be undercut after 1973 by the liberal press and Congress.[1]

Liberal critics, on the other hand, paint a devastating picture of an administration literally at war with itself, for whose intrigues the word "Byzantine" is far too tame, presided over by an insecure and vindictive chief executive who, among other faults, could not hold his liquor.[2]

The liberals charge that instead of cutting their losses and getting out of Vietnam, the only sensible and ultimately moral course, Nixon and Kissinger were tempted by visions of victory and pursued a futile quest which eventually produced what Roger Morris called one of the "most savage retreats in history," wreaking vast destruction in Indochina and in Washington as well.[3] Limited evidence and heated controversy thus create serious problems for those who seek to make sense of an extraordinarily tumultuous era.

It should be apparent by now to all but the most inveterate Nixon-haters that his administration inherited an enormously complex, perhaps intractable problem in Vietnam. Elected on a deliberately vague foreign policy platform by a margin of less than one percent of the voters in an extraordinarily low turnout election, the new President had no clear mandate to do anything in Vietnam. The Democrats retained control of both houses of Congress.

The polls make abundantly clear, moreover, that the nation was deeply divided on the war. Vocal minorities at either extreme advocated getting out or escalating to "win," but the majority remained ambivalent. Increasingly frustrated by a war the government would not or could not win, most Americans wanted to get out but hoped to accomplish this in a way that did not smack of surrender or defeat.[4]

Whether these conflicting impulses could have been reconciled now seems quite unclear.

In the aftermath of the 1968 Tet Offensive, the United States and North Vietnam had committed themselves to negotiations, but neither side was yet willing to make the concessions required to bring about a settlement. Hanoi's determination to drive the United States from Vietnam and to eliminate the Saigon regime had not slackened, but its military power had been appreciably weakened by the losses suffered during Tet. The United States remained committed to the Saigon government, but Johnson's decisions to stop the bombing of North Vietnam and put a ceiling on American ground forces, along with the growing war-weariness at home, limited America's ability to protect South Vietnam and exert pressure on Hanoi. Rather than breaking the long-standing stalemate, the bloodshed of Tet may merely have reinforced it.

By 1969, extreme measures of one kind or another may have been required for America to end the war.

Going for Vietnamization

The available evidence suggests that the new administration rejected the extreme options out of hand. During the transition, Henry Kissinger's staff prepared a list of options ranging from A to Z, from unilateral withdrawal to massive escalation, and the same range was reflected in the questions posed for the NSSM-1 study ordered by Kissinger. Nixon and Kissinger make clear, however, that they never seriously considered withdrawal, which they viewed as a callous abandonment of South Vietnam and as potentially destructive of America's credibility abroad and their own standing at home. By the same token and apparently to their later regret, they also rejected escalation, which, they feared, might revive the moribund antiwar movement and put the administration on the defensive at the very outset.[5] Nixon and Kissinger appear also to have rejected the extreme steps because they thought such measures unnecessary. Following a pattern that is repeated time and again in U.S. policy-making with respect to Vietnam, they came to office certain that *they* could solve difficulties that had baffled their predecessors.

Beyond a general agreement that the extreme options should be rejected, the Nixon administration was deeply divided in its assessment of the situation in Vietnam and a proper American response. NSSM-1 was designed to dredge information from the bureaucracy and produce a wide range of policy choices, but, according to Kissinger, it did neither. The departments and agencies differed sharply in their appraisals of conditions in Vietnam. The military and the U.S. Embassy in Saigon were relatively optimistic about the position of the United States and South Vietnam and the chances of a favorable settlement. The Office of the Secretary of Defense, the Central Intelligence Agency, and the State Department were much more skeptical. According to Kissinger, none of the participants came up with imaginative new policy proposals. Thus, he complains, "Our desire to develop a coherent strategy immediately ran up against the paucity of facts, our attempt to modify established practices against the inertia of conventional wisdom."[6]

Nixon's top advisers pushed widely divergent policy recommendations. The military fell back on long-standing proposals to resume and expand the air war against North Vietnam and to invade North Vietnamese sanctuaries in Laos, Cambodia, and across the demilitarized zone — policies proposed and routinely rejected since 1965.

Secretary of Defense Melvin Laird, on the other hand, was skeptical of the possiblity of a military victory and of the value of negotiations. A politician through and through, the former Wisconsin Congressman wanted to get the United States out of Vietnam before the war cost the administration its domestic support. Most likely permitting the wish to father the thought, he persuaded himself that turning over the war to the South Vietnamese — what would be called "Vietnamization" — was a viable solution. From the day he took office he pressed relentlessly for a hard line in negotiations, for Vietnamization, and for withdrawing American troops as quickly as possible.

Secretary of State William Rogers shared Laird's concern about domestic pressures and also favored troop withdrawals. Reflecting the State Department's pre-eminent interest in negotiations, however, he put primary reliance on a negotiated settlement, and he regularly put forward proposals emanating from the State Department, most of which, Kissinger claims, were based on items the North Vietnamese had hinted they might accept.

Faith in Negotiations

Kissinger concedes that at this stage he, too, was optimistic about negotiations. He doubted that Vietnamization would work or that any sort of military victory could be attained. He favored the two-track negotiating strategy originally developed by Averell Harriman and Cyrus Vance, by which the United States and North Vietnam would work for military disengagement and withdrawal, while the South Vietnamese (GVN and Viet Cong) arranged a political settlement among themselves.

Nixon's views are the least clear. During the campaign he claimed to have a secret plan to end the war, but this now seems to have consisted of nothing more than some vague notions about using diplomatic leverage with the Soviets and military threats against Hanoi to force a favorable settlement. According to Kissinger, the President did not believe that negotiations would amount to anything until the military situation had improved significantly. Accordingly, he sought to exert maximum military pressure against the enemy in South Vietnam without stirring domestic protest, a challenging task to say the least.[7]

It seems clear that a Vietnam policy of sorts had taken shape by the summer of 1969. This consisted of public and private appeals for substantive negotiations (not accompanied by major political or military concessions), combined with quiet and limited military escalation in the form of the secret bombing of North Vietnamese sanctuaries in Cambodia and stepped up pressure against enemy units on the ground in South Vietnam. Massive materiel aid was provided to the South Vietnamese army (ARVN). The final element of the policy was a series of phased withdrawals of American troops, beginning in June with the announcement that 25,000 would be pulled out immediately.

The way in which this policy evolved and the assumptions and expectations it was based on remain quite unclear, however. Nixon appears never to have conducted a full-fledged in-house debate on Vietnam policy, even to the extent that LBJ submitted the 1965 troop decision to such debate. Policy appears rather to have emerged on an improvised *ad hoc* basis in response to developments in Southeast Asia and at home. At a time when Nixon had not apparently established firm control over his own administration, moreover, Vietnam policy also appears to represent a classic case of the President appeasing various bureaucratic constituencies by giving them a bit of what they wanted. The military got the bombing of Cambodia, Laird his troop withdrawals and Vietnamization, and the State Department its negotiations. Incredibly, from the perspective of ten years, both Nixon and Kissinger concede that they harbored what can only appear now as a naive faith that this makeshift strategy would produce an acceptable settlement within no more than a year.

No Stick, No Carrot

It now seems quite clear that the Vietnam decisions did not add up to an integrated strategy. The bombing of Cambodia hampered but did not cripple North Vietnam's capacity to support the war in the South, and whatever signal it may have conveyed to Hanoi must have been more than offset by the conflicting signal sent by the U.S. troop withdrawals, which suggested that there would be a payoff for patience and persistence. From the enemy standpoint, the new negotiating position announced by the administration in May probably represented an improvement over that offered by Johnson; but it was not sufficiently attractive to produce a settlement. Stripped to its essentials, the Nixon strategy (tailored to a considerable degree to American public opinion) did not provide sufficient force to compel North Vietnam to negotiate on American terms, or sufficient concessions to entice Hanoi to make a deal. Like the earlier and equally improvised strategies of the Johnson era, it offered only extended stalemate.

Nixon's apparent efforts to break the stalemate in the summer of 1969, by what he referred to as a "go for broke" initiative, raise some of the most intriguing questions about this stage of the war. The strategy seems to have been modeled on Nixon's belief that Eisenhower had ended the Korean War by threatening to use nuclear weapons if a settlement were not forthcoming; and it reflected his persistent — and, as it turns out, unwarranted — faith that the United States could use its leverage with the Soviets to secure a settlement in Vietnam. In his memoirs, Nixon indicates that in the summer of 1969 he passed to Hanoi, through Soviet and French intermediaries, an ultimatum that unless progress toward a settlement were made by November 1 he would have no choice but to resort to "measures of great consequence."[8] Kissinger adds that in the early fall of 1969 his staff began to develop detailed plans for an operation code-named Duck Hoop, which provided for a drastic escalation of the war up to and perhaps including the use of tactical nuclear weapons.[9]

Whether Nixon took this initiative seriously is a matter of debate. In his memoirs, he gives detailed coverage to the ultimatum and implies that he was quite serious, but he does not indicate that plans were developed to implement the threat. Much of the evidence for the "Duck Hoop" planning comes from several members of Kissinger's staff who later resigned in protest against the invasion of Cambodia. They suggest that the President and Kissinger were deadly serious and were eager to unleash the full scale of American military power against North Vietnam, but their bias is obvious and they were not really privy to the thoughts of their bosses.[10] By contrast, Kissinger dismisses the entire episode as nothing more than an academic exercise. He insists that planning for a drastic escalation of the war was never more than "desultory" and that he, at least, never examined the military option more than "half-heartedly." He even minimizes the significance of Nixon's deadlines, suggest-ing that the President himself did not take the ultimatum seriously and never pursued the threat actively. It was, Kissinger concludes, "a way to convince himself — and perhaps the historical record — that he was the tough leader thwarted by weaker colleagues."[11]

No Massive Escalation

Whatever the case, the go-for-broke initiative produced nothing. The North Vietnamese ignored Nixon's ultimatum, if indeed it was an ultimatum and if the message got through to them. In the meantime, the Kissinger study group recom-mended against massive escalation, on the ground that such action would not compel Hanoi to stop the war and would cause an outburst of domestic protest. Nixon acquiesced in the recommendation, perhaps reluctantly, later calmly ration-alizing his decision to do nothing on the grounds that Ho Chi Minh's recent death might create new opportunities for negotiations (a conclusion that Kissinger admits flew in the face of most intelligence reports).[12]

His early efforts having failed to bring about the settlement he had anticipated, Nixon in late 1969 appears to have settled on Vietnamization as *his* policy and as the solution to what increasingly appeared to be a long-term problem. As well as can be determined, his hope was to mobilize American public opinion behind him, inten-sify the build-up of South Vietnamese military strength, and in time persuade Hanoi that it would be better to negotiate with the United States in the immediate future than with a vastly strengthened South Vietnamese government later — thus per-mitting him to extract from the North Vietnamese concesssions necessary to secure an acceptable settlement.

Again, however, it is not at all clear how, or precisely why, Nixon settled on this policy. As before, the decisions appear to have been made on an *ad hoc* basis without a full-scale debate or even wide consultation. Nor is it clear whether Nixon embraced the policy optimistically or out of desperation. He concedes that he moved toward it after his ultimatum had failed. He goes on to note, however, that he acted on the basis of an optimistic public report from the British counter-insurgency expert Sir Robert Thompson on the prospects for Vietnamization.[13]

Raising questions about this explanation, Tad Szulc claims that in a simultaneous secret briefing at the Pentagon, Thompson was in fact quite pessimistic.[14] Although he admits that he did not press his case, Kissinger claims to have expressed to Nixon grave doubts about the viability of the policy.[15] In light of this, it seems entirely possible that Nixon fell back on Vietnamization because he felt he had no other real choice, and that he acted with no expectation that it would work, or indulged in a good bit of wishful thinking to convince himself it would work.

The decisions of 1969 set the administration on a course from which it would not, perhaps could not, deviate, and which appears to have heightened rather than eased its dilemma. Vietnamization required above all else time, a luxury the administration did not have. Once initiated, the U.S. troop withdrawals had to continue — to pacify an increasingly restless public and insatiable critics — regardless of the impact on Vietnamization. Problems with the Vietnamization program appear to have made the incursions into Cambodia (1970) and Laos (1971) seem necessary if not absolutely essential, and the incursions in turn weakened the administration's already shaky domestic base.

What Were the Assumptions?

There is, of course, much that we still do not know about the implementation of Vietnamization and the expansion of the U.S. war in Indochina. Internal assessments of the progress of pacification and Vietnamization are generally unavailable to scholars. Because of the work of William Shawcross and because Kissinger felt compelled to respond to Shawcross at some length, we have more information on Cambodia than perhaps on any other topic related to the 1969–73 war years.[16] As with other key issues, however, we lack reliable evidence on the assumptions and expectations behind key decisions. Did the administration have reason to anticipate the Lon Nol coup, or was it taken by surprise?

Kissinger portrays Nixon as eager to get involved in Cambodia from the outset. Was this in fact the case, and if so, what did he expect to gain that would compensate for the domestic uproar he appears to have anticipated? Did the administration feel that it had no choice but to expand the war, as Kissinger suggests, or did it eagerly and with some enthusiasm seize the opportunity created by the fall of Sihanouk?

In contrast to Cambodia, almost nothing has been written about the Laotian incursion of 1971. Kissinger devotes a mere several pages to it — virtually nothing by his standards — and Nixon shrugs it off in passing as a military success but a "public relations disaster."[17] The Laotian operation raises, however, many of the same questions which seem to pop up in the case of other major decisions. Why did the U.S. Joint Chiefs of Staff and General Creighton Abrams, then the U.S. Commander in Vietnam, conclude at this point that ARVN was capable of accomplishing what Westmoreland had earlier indicated would require *larger* numbers of U.S. troops?

CIA Director Richard Helms apparently raised serious warnings about possible North Vietnamese responses to the operation. Why were his warnings ignored? Kissinger claims to have had serious doubts but concedes that he did not push them. He concludes merely that "We allowed ourselves to be carried away by the daring conception, by the unanimity of the responsible planners in both Saigon and Washington, by the memory of the success in Cambodia, and by the prospect of a decisive turn." He admits also that much of the administration's energy was consumed in getting key officials to support the operation rather than analyzing its potential.[18]

To a considerable extent, of course, judgments on the Nixon-Kissinger strategy rest on the events of 1972–1973 and after. Nixon, Kissinger, and their defenders argue that whatever the flaws of their earlier policies, their timely and forceful military response to the enemy's 1972 Easter invasion and skillful diplomacy (combined with the 1972 Christmas bombing) extracted a settlement that was far from perfect but was certainly workable. It would have ensured an honorable peace, they go on, had not it been undercut by Watergate and the callous betrayal of South Vietnam that stemmed indirectly from it.[19]

The argument contains a large element of truth. Because of the Air Force's use of the so-called "smart" bomb and because the North Vietnamese conventional offensive was dependent on spare parts and petroleum, the bombing and the mining of Haiphong harbor were more decisive than many previous U.S. military moves. Perhaps to the surprise of Nixon himself, they also won widespread popular support in America. For the short term, at least, the administration emerged from the crisis of the summer of 1972 with its position significantly strengthened. Nixon's politically daring actions spared South Vietnam the fate that would befall it in 1975. Along with important political concessions, they led directly to the peace settlement of October 1972.

Could Saigon Have Survived?

The Nixon-Kissinger argument omits a great deal, however, and assumes a great deal more. It assumes first that preserving South Vietnam intact, rather than Kissinger's famous "decent interval," was in fact the administration's intent, something that cannot be established definitively from existing evidence. If the former was indeed the aim, then the peace settlement, which left North Vietnamese troops in South Vietnam and in sanctuaries in Laos and Cambodia, severely compromised its attainment. It assumes that without Watergate Nixon would have been able to make a credible threat of reintervention if the peace were threatened, or would actually have been able to use force if required. It assumes that the Thieu government would have been strong enough to survive with limited American support in the face of direct or indirect challenges from North Vietnam.

Before this argument can be accepted, we need to know a great deal more about the actual progress of pacification, the strength of the ARVN, and the solidity of Thieu's government. The Nixon-Kissinger argument also ignores the fact that Watergate itself was to a considerable degree a product of the administration's ill-conceived response to its domestic foes. The ultimate irony may be that the U.S. position in South Vietnam was stronger at the end of 1972 than at any previous point in the war, but that domestic impatience and eventually Watergate prevented the considerable American commitment that would have been required to attain an honorable and workable peace.

This brief overview of the Nixon policies suggests several general conclusions. At this point, nearly ten years after the withdrawal of American military power from Vietnam, we still know very little about the formulation and implementation of policy, and what we know is obscured by the controversy that has raged since the events themselves. The outlines of the Nixon strategy are clear enough, but we have only a dim picture of why and how it took form. We lack detailed, first-hand information on assessments of the situation in Vietnam, on policy recommendations, and on the debates that preceded choices.

The evidence we do have, combined with a large dose of hindsight, suggests that the Vietnam problem may have been even more intractable than it was perceived at the time; that by 1969 it may have reached the point where extreme solutions were required.[20] This "extreme" type of choice may be the most difficult to make within the American political system. In any event, there is nothing to suggest that in 1969 it was seriously considered.

The actual choices made at that time, and after, consistently suggest a certain wishful thinking about the determination of the adversary and the strength of the ally. In the early stages, a seemingly casual optimism may have been the function of newness to power. Later on, it may have reflected the bind in which top officials found themselves — a faith born of necessity that partial measures would somehow bring results. In this regard, the Nixon administration, despite what had occurred in the preceding decade, fell victim to many of the same delusions that had vexed its predecessors.

NOTES

[1] See Richard M. Nixon,*The Real War* (New York, 1981), pp. 127–133, and Henry M. Kissinger,*White House Years* (New York, 1979), p. 1470.

[2] See especially Seymour M. Hersh, "Kissinger-Nixon in the White House," *The Atlantic,* 249 (May 1982), 41ff.

[3] Roger Morris,*Uncertain Greatness* (New York, 1977), p. 154.

[4] See, for example, "Americans on the War: Divided, Glum, Unwilling to Quit," *Time* (October 31, 1969), p. 13.

[5] Kissinger,*White House Years,* pp. 227–228; Richard M. Nixon, *RN: The Memoirs of Richard M. Nixon* (New York, 1978), p. 347.

[6] Kissinger, *White House Years,* p. 236. NSSM-1 is discussed at some length in Henry M. Brandon, *The Retreat of American Power* (New York, 1972), pp. 52–59. It is printed in the *Congressional Record,* 92nd Cong., 2nd Sess., 1972.

[7] Kissinger, *White House Years,* pp. 226–265.

[8] Nixon, *RN,* pp. 393–394.

[9] "Duck Hoop" planning is discussed at some length in Morris, *Uncertain Greatness,* pp. 163–166; Tad Szulc,*The Illusion of Peace: Foreign Policy in the Nixon Years* (New York, 1978), pp. 150–156; and Kissinger, *White House Years,* pp. 284–286.

[10] Morris, *Uncertain Greatness,* pp. 163–166.

[11] Kissinger, *White House Years,* p. 304.

[12] Nixon, *RN,* p. 405. Robert Haldeman claims, on the other hand, that Nixon was enraged when the North Vietnamese ignored his threat. See *The Ends of Power* (New York, 1978), p. 98.

[13] Nixon,*RN,* p. 405.

[14] Szulc, *Illusion of Peace,* pp. 162–163.

[15] Kissinger, *White House Years,* pp. 285–288.

[16] William Shawcross, *Sideshow: Kissinger, Nixon, and the Destruction of Cambodia* (New York, 1979), and Kissinger, *White House Years,* pp. 433–521.

[17] Kissinger, *White House Years,* pp. 987–1002, and Nixon,*RN.*

[18] Kissinger, *White House Years,* p. 994. William Safire, on the other hand, quotes Kissinger in the early days of the Laotian operation as taking credit for its approval, boldly claiming that "we have a chance of winning this thing." See Safire, *Before the Fall* (New York, 1975), 390–391.

[19] Nixon, *Real War,* pp. 127–133.

[20] Raymond Aron, "Kissinger, Vietnam, and Cambodia," *Policy Review* (Summer 1980), pp. 163–165.

COMMENTARY: Nixon's Policy

by Peter Rodman

I would like to make a couple of points which are partly methodological and partly factual. There isn't all that much dispute over the facts, but I think there are a lot of problems about one's perspective on the facts.

First of all, I think Mr. Herring overstates somewhat his point about the inadequacy of the source materials. I think we do have quite a bit of material, and I think perhaps the best proof of it is the fact that his paper is able to make a number of very good analytical points. He is able to focus on what the key questions were in fact in 1969 and to comment on them very intelligently on the basis of what record we have. Now, perhaps you are all spoiled by the *Pentagon Papers*, and perhaps it is unfortunate that a sufficient amount of material hasn't yet been stolen from the Nixon administration. But I think also I have a personal interest. I happen to be personally associated with a couple of huge volumes (Kissinger's memoirs) on precisely these issues and with I think a lot of documentation, and this is the first time I have heard anyone imply that the Kissinger books were too short.

But I would just point out to get this out of the way that in these books, in both the Nixon and Kissinger memoirs, there are documents, there are quotations from documents, there are quotations from meetings, from conversations, from messages, and I think it is accurate, I think it is relevant to these issues, and I can assure you that when the mass of documents does become available that you are not going to be able to make much sense out of them unless you do go back to these memoirs to get a sense of what the principals had in their minds and what they thought they were doing, particularly since so much does depend on what was in the minds of these two men. In general I would say as an epistemological point that if one suspends all belief in the evidence one has, one isn't going to get very far, and it is a sort of self-defeating procedure for historians to take.

My second point is partly a factual one. Professor Herring does focus on the strategy in 1969, the strategy or absence of strategy, and he asks what the alternatives were. He raises the question whether perhaps extreme solutions were necessary. Now, these are the key questions to ask. I think he has a point about at least in the first several months Nixon and Kissinger may not have had a clear idea of what they were going to do. But I think by the time 1969 was over, they did have an idea of what strategy they were pursuing. Now, perhaps it was the wrong strategy; perhaps it wasn't going to work. These are all valid questions to discuss. But I think it is a little bit overstated, again, to say that there was no coherent idea.

For example, he makes the point somewhere that it was all appeasement of bureaucratic constituencies. I think this is one thing that it was clearly not. He says the military got the Cambodian bombing, Defense Secretary Laird got his troop withdrawals, State got its negotiations. I think this is factually incorrect. I mean, the military were not really pushing for a Cambodian bombing at the beginning of 1969. It was really the President who seized on this as a way of retaliating for the wave of attacks by the North Vietnamese in February 1969 which was in violation of the bombing halt understanding and we were looking for something to do other than resuming the bombing of the North.

The State Department didn't get its negotiations. The State Department wasn't even informed of the secret negotiations until the beginning of 1972, and it was Kissinger who believed all along that there was some hope for a negotiated settlement, and Nixon allowed him to proceed somewhat skeptically but at least allowed this route to proceed.

And Laird in a sense did get his troop withdrawals, but the White House spent an awful lot of time struggling to rein him in to try to keep control over the increments of troop withdrawals, over the timing of troop withdrawals, precisely in order to relate it to some kind of coherent strategy.

Now, as I said, what all this suggests to me is that the White House did try very hard to keep control over all of these elements, to relate these various instruments to each other and to relate them together to some sort of coherent policy. The President's speech of November 3, 1969, which is not mentioned in the paper but I am sure you are aware of, stated what the concept was: It was the two-track approach of Vietnamization plus negotiation.

We in fact stuck to this policy for four years. I am fully aware of all the weaknesses of it and the flaws in it, and as I said it is perfectly valid to debate whether this was a totally wrong approach. But I think it is wrong to claim that everything was *ad hoc* and all was confusion and all was incoherent.

I think the centralized presidential decision-making under Nixon and Kissinger was probably the most coherent policy-making we are ever going to get, whether you like the content of it or not.

There was an interesting sentence in the paper about decisions being made without a full-scale debate or even wide consultation. Now, this to me reflects a kind of nostalgia for the Johnson administration, with all these memoranda going back and forth and this infinite kibitzing and participation and consensus-building, as the phrase is in Mr. Berman's paper. The system under Nixon was obviously different. There was a major effort to collect all the options, all the information, all the different points of view. I mean, the White House sought these, drew them in, and listened to them. Then the President went off and made his decision, usually in collaboration with his security adviser. It was obviously more hierarchical, less collegial, but given the kind of lowest-common-denominator decisions we saw in the Johnson period, it is not self-evidently bad to have had a sort of more focused centralized decision-making.

So the problem obviously was not procedural at all. Mr. Herring is right to focus on the choices that were faced at the time and to raise the question whether extreme solutions one way or another were what should have been addressed in 1969. Raymond Aron makes this point. Even Kissinger in his book wonders whether perhaps something more drastic should have been attempted. This is a valid subject for discussion.

I also believe that of all the administrations that wrestled with this [Vietnam] problem, Nixon had the least freedom of maneuver. The fact that he ended up in 1972 in not such a bad position (as Mr. Herring seems to admit) is also relevant to this discussion.

But that brings me to the Paris agreement and all of those problems, which I take it you would rather defer to another time.

COMMENTARY: Nixon, Laos, Cambodia

by Stanley Falk

Herring has done a good job summarizing what we know about the Nixon strategy in Vietnam. But as he points out, the available sources are limited, and there is still a great deal of ignorance about the dynamics of decision-making within the Nixon administration — not only on the part of researchers in the public area, but also among the official army historians. We lack a Nixon presidential library where the papers of key individuals like Nixon, Kissinger, and Laird could be found. The NSC, JCS, and high-level MACV are still highly classified. Even official historians face great challenges reporting their findings because of declassification problems.

Regarding the paper, the decision on Vietnamization was not as new as Herring suggests. Westmoreland himself "had pressed for building up self-reliant South Vietnamese forces, the difference being that the pace of his efforts had been slower, and without the pressure of withdrawing American forces that Nixon faced. Nixon himself, two months after he took office, directed that major preparations be made to enable the ARVN to stand on its own" (NSDM 9, 4/1/69). The emphasis on the term "Vietnamization" was just part of the Nixon administration's public relations campaign to win support for the withdrawal.

The apparent early success of Vietnamization, as well as real progress in the Pacification program was part of the reason behind the Cambodian incursion. This operation was attractive because 1) the American military, for sound tactical reasons, had long sought it; 2) it promised more time for Vietnamization to take effect; 3) the ARVN appeared more ready to participate; 4) a spoiling attack is always a good maneuver during a major withdrawal; 5) the North Vietnamese build-up in the Cambodian sanctuaries and the western movement of NVA forces within Cambodia greatly concerned General Abrams and the Joint Chiefs.

About the same motives explain ARVN's push into Laos the following year. American officials had long wanted to cut North Vietnamese supply lines through the Laotian panhandle, and the closing of Sihanoukville in 1970 made the Ho Chi Minh Trail more important than ever.

Herring suggests that the Joint Chiefs and Abrams now felt that the ARVN alone was capable "of accomplishing what Westmoreland had earlier indicated would require *larger* numbers of *U.S.* troops." Actually, what Westmoreland meant was forces necessary to seize and hold a permanent blocking position across the Laotian trails, which indeed would have required a major American deployment. Operation LAM SON 719 was no more than a heavy raid, not the sort of operation Westmoreland had considered.

COMMENTARY: The South Vietnamese Viewpoint

by Bui Diem

The South Vietnamese have been largely silent about their perspective on the war, and I wish to thank the sponsors for allowing me to speak on this subject. The Nixon policy — Vietnamization and negotiations — was mostly correct, but the faults lay in the implementation. As a concept, Vietnamization began in 1965, not in 1968, but Americans never got around to implementing it because they expected early victory without Vietnamese participation. From the Vietnamese viewpoint, we had serious doubts about American seriousness about Vietnamization: Was it carefully thought out, or was it designed just to pacify American opinion and calibrated to meet the geopolitical aims of Nixon and Kissinger?

Nixon backed negotiations with military pressure. But from Saigon's perspective, Nixon seemingly tried to keep the GVN in the dark about the negotiations until the very end. In October 1971, Kissinger accepted the presence of NVA troops in South Vietnam without consulting us. The Vietnamese often noted how Nixon and Kissinger talked about U.S. credibility in the world, but asked if this concept was incompatible with U.S. interests in South Vietnam. If Nixon had sought to coordinate negotiations with the South Vietnamese, the outcome might have been different.

DISCUSSION

KARNOW: When did the Nixon administration reconcile itself to the "cease-fire in place," that is, allowing North Vietnamese troops in the South under a peace agreement?

POPKIN: When the Cambodian invasion was planned, were many estimates made of how it would affect the viability of the ARVN and the GVN, rather than just the timing of the American pullout? Cambodia may have caused long-range damage to the ARVN, leading to false hopes about ARVN capabilities.

PIKE: When LBJ threw in the towel in March 1968, did that mean that the Nixon administration came in knowing that it had to get out?

CAMERON: One thing which we have not discussed is the role of Congress in restraining the Executive, especially with Nixon's advent.

DESTLER: Herring does not treat the American domestic front very extensively. Nixon and Kissinger did not accept the domestic constraints, and their obstinacy greatly complicated their strategy in Indochina and at home.

LOMPARIS: When Herring speaks of the lack of an integrated strategy, what is he comparing it with?

ISAACS: While Nixon and Kissinger accepted the fact that the U.S. would have to withdraw, they never accepted the logic of it: They tried to negotiate a satisfactory peace even as the United States was pulling out. Also, Nixon and Kissinger thought that the Cambodian invasion would end U.S. interests there soon, but it did not, causing major problems.

KARNOW: Nixon at first expected the withdrawal to be only partial. A few thousand troops would remain, but American air power would still be available on a major scale.

BRAESTRUP: Walt Rostow once said that LBJ expected a 50,000-man U.S. residual force in South Vietnam after a peace agreement.

SHEEHAN: Did Nixon and Kissinger really expect South Vietnam to be viable after the American withdrawal or not, as Herring implies?

CAMERON: Regarding Karnow's point, Nixon did not regard the Paris talks to be the end of U.S. military involvement in Indochina. The Paris agreement had huge holes in it, allowing extensive U.S. intervention if necessary, such as another "Linebacker II" (the 1972 Christmas bombing of Hanoi).

SPECTOR: Is it true, as the New Left says, that the U.S. had to pull out because of declining morale among U.S. troops?

HERRING: On Vietnamization, I agree that Vietnamization as a concept is embraced in 1965. Certainly the Johnson administration's March 1968 deliberations include Vietnamization as a basic concept. The term is even coined, although Nixon's Defense Secretary Melvin Laird is usually given credit for it. It's used freely in the internal documents of February and March 1968. My point is that Nixon finally settled on Vietnamization as the policy, or at least a major element of policy in November 1969. Up to this point, he had been bouncing a lot of balls in the air. It's the failure of his ultimatums that make him fall back on Vietnamization as the route to take from this point on. That's the distinction I would make.

The "decent interval" question? I don't think I can answer that satisfactorily and I don't suppose any amount of documentation will ever permit anyone to answer it definitively because it's the type of thing that simply is not going to be put on paper. My feeling, and it is just a feeling by and large, is that probably both Nixon and Kissinger varied day to day, maybe hour to hour, from the "decent interval" to maintaining an independent South Vietnam. I think they started in 1969 with the feeling that perhaps they could; I'm not sure why. This is one of the things that really perplexes me: Why they felt (and both of them say it in their memoirs) that they thought they could get a settlement within six months to a year without making fundamental concessions and negotiations, and without exerting major military pressure.

I really don't understand this at all. Perhaps by November 1969 both may have been thinking more in terms of the "decent interval" because by then the early strategems had collapsed. They were by this time aware that they were in for a long haul, that these early, naive assumptions had not been borne out. Maybe again after June—July 1972, after Hanoi's stalled Easter Offensive, when things came out perhaps better than they had ever anticipated, maybe they again began to conclude that the situation could be solved. I'm not really clear in my own mind.

I think maybe there's a difference between Nixon and Kissinger. Look at what they say about the U.S. commitment in Vietnam before they come into office — Nixon in a 1967 article, for example, seems to indicate that the commitment was both necessary, wise, and moral. He's probably much more serious about that all the way through than Kissinger.

Kissinger does not say that in his 1969 *Foreign Affairs* article. He says maybe Vietnam was an example of reckless U.S. over-commitment in the early stages, but now we're there and we're saddled with this big commitment. There's no sense of a deep-seated moral obligation going back to the very beginning. I think this is a factor, too — that there may be a degree of difference in their perceptions. It may be the type of question that can never really be satisfactorily answered.

Why didn't Nixon and Kissinger do in 1969 what they finally did in 1973? I can only answer that they didn't do it at the outset because they didn't think they had to. I'm not sure why they didn't think they should do it. It's a pattern that crops up time and time again with respect to Vietnam from 1950 on: a new American administration coming in, inheriting a problem that at each time becomes more complicated, but each time there's this sense of "Somehow we can do what our predecessors did not. They really botched it; we can straighten it out."

Was there an integrated Nixon administration strategy? As I looked at Kissinger's account of it, what struck me, and I know that Peter Rodman disagrees with me on this, was what seemed the same sort of pattern we saw in the Johnson administration. Maybe it's inherent in the American system. But Nixon and Kissinger were always compromising, going down the middle of the road, without moving in any straight direction. More of the same.

What was Nixon's sense of the war when he inherited it? I wish I knew more. The memoirs repeat the same sorts of things he was saying publicly and don't offer much in the way of insights. What you glean out of Kissinger's memoir — whether he regarded this as something that was manageable or a serious commitment that had to be upheld — I'm not clear at all.

RODMAN: I'd like to start by replying to a point raised by Ambassador Bui Diem about the conduct of the negotiations and the South Vietnamese involvement in the secret negotiations. As a matter of fact, President Thieu was kept personally informed of the secret negotiations from even before they started. He was briefed before and after every meeting from the beginning, from 1969. And, in fact, every proposal that was made to the North Vietnamese in the secret talks was a joint proposal until near the very end, until September 15, 1972, when we included one element in a proposal that President Thieu had objected to. Every proposal until that point was a joint U.S.-GVN proposal, including the October 1970 cease-fire proposal, which gets me to Stanley Karnow's point about North Vietnamese forces remaining in the South.

When did we relinquish our insistence that the North Vietnamese leave — or when did we tacitly or explicitly accept the presence of the North Vietnamese in the South? I would have to say the key point was Nixon's October 1970 standstill cease-fire proposal. It had something in it about North Vietnamese forces would be discussed or whatever. Some refined version of this was also handed over in October 1971, in the secret talks. I think Kissinger would say in retrospect that once we got on this course of unilateral U.S. withdrawal in 1969, and once it became clear that politically we couldn't stop this process, then I think we had implicitly unlinked American withdrawal from the mutual withdrawal which had been the concept up to, say, the May 14, 1969, proposal. "Mutual withdrawal" was obviously the Lyndon Johnson formula and I think it carried on into the Nixon period. At some point, when we started talking about standstill cease-fire, by definition we had made a big step with respect to North Vietnamese forces remaining in the South.

I would also say that getting the North Vietnamese out of the South was a pretty good definition of winning the war.

Once it was decided that we were going to try to settle this on some compromise basis, once we had settled on a strategy basically of trying to get out in an honorable way, it was inherent in the situation that we were not going to get the North Vietnamese out.

The 1973 Paris Agreement had its own way of addressing this problem. It didn't say anything about the forces in the South, but it had all sorts of prohibitions against re-supply and it had, implicit or separate from the agreement, the fact that we had the right to re-supply South Vietnam.

The compromise was, in our minds, that the South Vietnamese had a decent chance to survive even with the North Vietnamese troops in the South as long as we continued our support for them, as long as there was a threat of possible American re-intervention, as long as the balance of forces we had achieved in 1972 was maintained.

In a sense this is maybe something that we had conceded a long time before, that we were getting out, American troops would not be there anymore, and that obviously at some point we had unlinked this from North Vietnamese withdrawal.

What we still retained, even after the Paris agreement, was 1) the right of unlimited re-supply of the South Vietnamese—military and economic aid was blessed by the agreement; 2) the possibility of re-intervention; and 3) the balance of forces that had been achieved on the ground during the summer of 1972.

It was not an ideal situation; but it was probably better than a lot of people imagined possible, and given the domestic political context in this country, it was a better deal than the Congress would have allowed us if we had stayed there two more months without an agreement. It was better than George McGovern's position. It was a very fragile situation. There was a balance of forces at that time and the government was intact and could guess about the future. I happen to think that nothing was foreordained. In 1969 there were 500,000 American troops in South Vietnam and again the regime was intact. To say at that point that the regime had no chance of surviving — one can have that view but it was not foreordained.

PIKE: North Vietnam's de-coupling of political and military issues (i.e., not insisting any longer on Thieu's ouster as a condition for a cease-fire agreement) was a major concession, and the North Vietnamese still debate the wisdom of it.

RODMAN: I would add a couple of other things: I think the North Vietnamese were taking a risk in signing the agreement.

They were shifting from a military struggle to a political struggle. They had to prepare all their cadre for cease-fire conditions and for political struggle, and I think the NLF people were unhappy with the agreement because it left them to a great extent at the mercy of the South Vietnamese.

There was a long battle in the negotiations over political detainees. We had made it absolutely firm that our prisoners of war had to be released and they could not be linked with political detainees in the South, which is what the North Vietnamese had insisted on until about mid-October 1972. One of the toughest, one of the last concessions we squeezed out of them was that they basically said, OK, unconditional release of U.S. POWs and the NLF prisoners were going to remain where they were.

They were taking risks in the post-agreement situation; they didn't know how much support they could get from the Russians and the Chinese, given the diplomacy we had started. The Russians were giving out assurances (for whatever Soviet assurances were worth) that they had reduced military aid to Hanoi to almost nothing, which I think was more or less true, at least at the beginning of 1973, until a couple of years passed. So they were taking some risks.

Both sides were gambling on the future and gambling that they would maintain enough control over their own instruments of power to shape it or to prevent it from collapsing. I agree with you, we were taking probably a bigger risk.

This is also the answer to Mr. Sheehan's question about the "decent interval." I have to say that from the beginning the intention was to do the best we possibly could do and assure their survival. We thought it could be done; probably there were moments of pessimism and moments of optimism about whether this would work in the end, but I think there was enough chance that it would work to make it the compelling force; it was the only morally honorable course to take. Nixon and Kissinger ruled out unilateral U.S. withdrawal. If they had been prepared to let the South Vietnamese go down the drain, they could easily have done this in the very beginning of 1969, but they thought it was totally immoral and totally disruptive of America's world position to do this to an ally.

I think it's clear now we were attempting to do too much; we were attempting to withdraw and yet attempting to assure the survival of the government. This was clearly very risky, but after the 1970 Cambodian operation, Nixon and Kissinger were even more optimistic about the chances of pulling it off. The Paris Agreement for all its risks we thought was sustainable.

I want to say one other thing about the Cambodian incursion and whether it was unplanned. I would have to say that everything was triggered by the 1970 overthrow of Norodom Sihanouk and that was totally unplanned and caught us by surprise.

You can believe Mr. William Shawcross [author of *Sideshow*], if you like; there's plenty of evidence that the first week or so Kissinger thought it was all a trick by Sihanouk — a device so he could put some pressure on the North Vietnamese to get out. I think Nixon said in a press conference he was still thinking in terms of when Sihanouk would come back. For a couple of weeks we all just assumed that somehow Sihanouk would wangle his way back into power.

What happened was that by the end of March and the beginning of April, the North Vietnamese started expanding all over eastern Cambodia and we were faced with a decision that could not be avoided. If we did nothing, the change of government in Phnom Penh would have proved to be totally temporary, and we would have been faced by all of eastern Cambodia's being a base area, instead of by a string of small North Vietnamese border bases. It would have changed the military situation disastrously against us unless we did something. The decision was made obviously in late April to do something — to act against the base areas. It was an opportunity in a sense, but more importantly, there was some urgency because if we didn't do something, we would have lost the whole thing and all of our Vietnamization strategy would have been totally unviable at that point.

KARNOW: Why did not the United States accept the French proposal for a Geneva conference to restore Sihanouk to power?

RODMAN: This was proposed by the French to the Chinese and North Vietnamese and they both rejected it. Sihanouk had declared himself on the Communist side within about a week of his overthrow. The idea of a conference was proposed. We were waiting to see what Sihanouk was going to do. If he had gone to Paris and said, "I represent the legitimacy of neutral Cambodia," he certainly would have had American support. But he did some very strange things: He went on to Peking, in fact he was told about his overthrow when he was going to the airport to leave for Moscow.

The first thing he did in Peking was to make statements about the unity of all Indochinese communists against American imperialism. He was making a lot of decisions very rapidly that proved to be very sadly mistaken. He burned a lot of bridges behind him very quickly and closed off all our options before we could even have realized that we had those options.

It's another illustration of how little we were in control of events, which makes it even more absurd to think we had somehow engineered all of this. We were way behind on events and there was no real option then to put it back together. Within a few days, Sihanouk had totally destroyed his own neutrality and left us with very few options at all except to support the new regime in Phnom Penh.

DIEM: Thieu had been fully informed of the results of the [Paris] talks, but he was not consulted, and the final 1972 agreement was simply dropped in the lap of the GVN. The Americans gave the agreement in English, and we had to spend much time translating it before responding.

RODMAN: I agree that we paid a huge price for the way we dealt with the South Vietnamese government at the very end. There's no way to dispute that.

II THE NORTH VIETNAMESE AND THE SOUTH VIETNAMESE

PAPERS AND DISCUSSIONS

THE OTHER SIDE

by Douglas Pike

As the year 1965 began, Ho Chi Minh, his Defense Minister Vo Nguyen Giap, and the other members of the ruling Politburo in Hanoi saw triumph ahead. The long-sought goal of unification of North and South under the Communist banner would be achieved during the next twelve months. Broadcasting the leadership's annual State message, Radio Hanoi did not say that 1965 would be a "year of victories," or of "moving toward victory." It said flatly "the year of victory."

This confident judgment in Hanoi, later confirmed by captured documents and prisoner testimony, was based on the Politburo's survey of the battlefield in South Vietnam and its interpretations of Washington's capabilities. All in all, it was not an unrealistic estimate.

Outside Saigon, Da Nang, and the South's other major cities, the People's Liberation Armed Forces (Viet Cong) regulars were chewing up, one by one, the South Vietnamese government's dozen mobile reserve battalions of paratroopers and marines as they were sent in with American advisors to rescue local garrisons under attack. Soon the Saigon regime, its faction-ridden military and political leadership in chronic disarray since the 1963 overthrow of President Ngo Dinh Diem, would have no reserves to spare.

At that point, the Viet Cong, evolving, under Hanoi's control, into regular regiments and divisions equipped with mortars, rockets, and automatic weapons, could begin a series of set piece assaults, first against one isolated city or base, then another. One by one, the Army of the Republic of Vietnam (ARVN) strongholds would be taken, and the demoralized Saigon regime and its widely dispersed forces would collapse.

That Washington might intervene was a strong possibility. But to the Politburo, it seemed that the rot had already set in in the South. Despite the presence of U.S. helicopters, aircraft, and 23,000 advisors, Communist battlefield gains were now too far advanced to be arrested by necessarily piecemeal injections of U.S. combat units. (Indeed, by mid-1965, Communist agit-prop cadres had a new slogan: "The Greater U.S. Intervention, the Greater U.S. Defeat.") The Viet Cong continued to hit U.S. advisors' barracks, airfields — and the U.S. Embassy in Saigon.

Sporadic American air strikes had already begun (in mid-1964) against the Ho Chi Minh Trail in Laos. Lyndon Johnson ordered retaliatory bombing of the North in August 1964 after the Gulf of Tonkin encounter between North Vietnamese patrol boats and U.S. Navy destroyers. (Yet to come were the regular, but still limited, "Rolling Thunder" bombing raids that began in February.) As the North Vietnamese leaders saw it, provision by the Soviet Union of modern air defense radar and weaponry would blunt the impact of any U.S. air effort, although the North would still have to take heavy punishment.

Had the men in Hanoi adhered to this assessment, rather than losing confidence and switching strategy, the year 1965 might well have been the year of Communist victory.

However, by mid-March 1965, with the landing of 3,500 U.S. Marines to defend Da Nang air base, the ever-cautious Giap began to hedge his bets. He did not press for an all-out effort to win the war before the Americans were in South Vietnam in force, although he had already started moving regiments of the North Vietnamese Army (People's Army of Vietnam or PAVN) south along the Ho Chi Minh Trail in 1964. Instead, he spent the first six months of 1965 in what, in effect, was a holding operation. His calculation was that he faced a new war against a new enemy that required new tactics and a readapted grand strategy. This decision, coupled with the psychological lift given to Saigon by the American intervention, served to pull the South Vietnamese out of the jaws of defeat.

The actual onset of the sustained U.S. bombing of the North, despite confident-sounding Communist public pronouncements, engendered enormous apprehension in Hanoi. The French, during the 1945–54 Indochina War, had been able to employ only a feeble air arm (some 100 combat aircraft); the Americans had more than 1,000 fighter-bombers available, plus the B-52 bomber with its 30-ton bomb-load.

Yet the American bombing efforts during 1965–68 were (by Washington's orders) sharply delimited, confined mostly to roads, bridges, power plants, barracks, supply dumps. The B-52s were not used. Hanoi was off-limits. So were North Vietnam's major Mig fighter bases, such as Phuc Yen (until 1967), and the key port facilities of Haiphong.

Friendly Geography

Among the North Vietnamese leaders the belief grew, and then became entrenched, that, aided by increasingly sophisticated Soviet-provided missiles and other weaponry, the North was absorbing the *worst* punishment that the United States could deliver. This view persisted until the shock of Richard Nixon's all-out "Christmas bombing" campaign of 1972, which was followed by the Paris peace agreement of January 1973.[1]

As 1965 wore on, and American ground strength grew in the South, Giap decided (despite contrary advice from some Politburo colleagues) to meet the United States head-on. No longer applicable, he later wrote, were the techniques which had worked for the Communists against the French (and the ARVN): the regimental ambush, the entrapment of mobile units, the isolation and destruction of enemy garrisons, the slow, steady gain of territory and population. The Americans had enormous firepower (fighter-bombers, artillery, helicopter gunships), superb communications, and the ability, lacked by the road-bound French, to move troops rapidly by helicopter and air transport.

For his part Giap had some long-term advantages. Geography, the implications of which were usually overlooked by American pundits and politicians, was on his side. The Saigon government (and the newly arrived Americans) had more than 600 miles of open border to protect and more than 16 million people to defend in an area the size of Washington state, with 44 provincial capitals, 241 district towns, and upwards of 15,000 hamlets that were all vulnerable to terrorism and guerrilla attack. Jungle and mountains covered more than half the country.

In such terrain, the Viet Cong had long enjoyed secure bases and rest areas; these in turn were linked to "sanctuaries" in southern Laos and eastern Cambodia, tied to the Ho Chi Minh Trail transit routes from the North. According to recent North Vietnamese accounts, it took cadres and military replacements six months to traverse the trail when it was first organized in 1959; its roadnet was steadily improved, despite U.S. bombing, after 1965 and soon accommodated well-organized truck traffic and, by 1972, tanks. The trail was the key to Giap's war.

To support Communist forces in the Mekong Delta and north of Saigon, Hanoi also secured (in 1966) secret permission from Prince Norodom Sihanouk of "neutral" Cambodia to use Sihanoukville (now Kompong Som) as a supply port.

Lastly, the North ("the Great Rear") was bombed but not blockaded or invaded. Soviet freighters unloaded SAM missiles, tanks, Moltava trucks, and artillery at Haiphong. From neighboring China came light weapons, ammunition, and rice. U.S. air strikes could slow but not halt these goods — and North Vietnamese reinforcements — on their way to the battlefield.

The ruling Lao Dong (Workers') Party also had strong human assets. A decade after victory over the French, Ho Chi Minh, Giap, Party Secretary Le Duan, Premier Pham Van Dong, and their colleagues commanded a Spartan, highly organized party, purged of dissenters, led by a generation of cadres tested in war, and convinced that "unification" of North and South under Hanoi's rule was a "golden" objective worthy of any sacrifice.

Just Us Southerners

There were periods in the North of low morale and discontent, of malingering and petty corruption, as party documents made clear. But the iron grip of the party cadres and the society's own strong discipline and ethnocentrism sustained the war effort, allowing General Giap repeatedly to suffer enormous losses (perhaps 900,000 dead by 1973), then to rebuild PAVN units for yet another battle. "The North Vietnamese," observed Laos's French-educated Premier Souvanna Phouma in 1967, "are the Prussians of Southeast Asia."

What drew most attention in Washington during 1961–65 were the guerrillas in the South, whose early local cadres were Viet Minh veterans of the French war. One of the myths fostered by Hanoi and accepted by many Westerners was that the National Liberation Front (NLF), or Viet Cong, was an independent creation set up by Southerners in 1960 to combat the injustices of the Diem regime and allied to, but independent of, Hanoi.

In fact, Hanoi decided in May 1959 at the 15th Party Plenum to reunify the North and the South by force. The 559 Unit was established to develop the Ho Chi Minh Trail from North Vietnam through "neutral" Laos and Cambodia for southbound political and military cadres; by Hanoi's own recent account, some 20,000 men moved South during the first few years to help organize and lead the Viet Cong insurgency.

The NLF changed after Diem's overthrow in 1963. Northerners took over the organization with unification under *Hanoi's* leadership as the main aim. The NLF's public face was Southern; it issued its own communiqués, had its own representatives abroad. Hanoi always refused to admit it had troops in the South. But, remembering the 1954 division of Vietnam, Hanoi kept a tight leash on the NLF. Northerners, or northern-trained Southerners, directed most major military operations and held the key political party posts. (Hanoi kept similar control over the Communist Pathet Lao forces in Laos.)

Reviving the old Viet Minh techniques — propaganda, indoctrination, "selective terrorism," and tight organization — drew rural recruits and cowed local government officials. With its network of agents, tax collectors, and porters, the Viet Cong was stronger in some provinces (usually those where the Viet Minh had been active during 1945–54) than in others. It was unsuccessful in enlisting significant support from dissident Buddhist factions, urban workers, the ethnic Chinese, or the *montagnard* (hill) tribesmen. Even so, thanks to the administrative chaos that followed Diem's ouster, the NLF was able to make steady progress, recruiting and sustaining 85,000 well-armed regulars and 115,000 paramilitary local troops by 1966.

America as Domino

Giap used all these assets as he experimented with PAVN thrusts against U.S. units in the Ia Drang Valley in 1965 and below the Demilitarized Zone (DMZ) against the Marines in 1966–67, with a view toward devising a winning strategy. At the same time, he used Viet Cong battalions to fight allied forays into contested areas and to raid allied outposts and district towns. These tactics variously eased or interrupted the growing allied pressures against the elusive local Viet Cong and inflicted losses, but they did not end the steady attrition of the guerrillas. Nor did Giap, taking heavy casualties, succeed in overrunning a U.S. defensive position or destroying a major U.S. unit.

By mid-1967, Giap had completed his strategic experimentation. He then launched the most important campaign of the war, the winter-spring campaign of 1967–68. Giap combined "coordinated fighting methods" — set-piece battles with his main force regiments, usually on battlefields close to his bases in Cambodia or Laos — with "independent fighting methods" — simultaneous small-scale attacks all over the country — to launch a "continuous comprehensive offensive." After his usual lengthy build-up of men and supplies, he combined these assaults with a major political effort. The chief aim was to collapse the Saigon regime's administrative apparatus and its 650,000-man armed forces, thereby undermining the whole U.S. effort.

The climax neared as two PAVN divisions laid siege to the U.S. Marines' outpost at Khe Sanh, near Laos. Then, in what is now called the 1968 Tet (or lunar new year) Offensive, Saigon, Hue, and 100 other places were hit on January 30–31. Some 84,000 troops, mostly in Viet Cong units, were committed in the first assaults. Agents were sent to urban areas to promote a "general uprising" by the inhabitants against the Thieu regime.

Just as the allies underestimated Giap's boldness, so Giap overestimated the Saigon government's weaknesses and the popularity of the Viet Cong; his intelligence agents may have erroneously equated urban complaints against the Thieu regime and the Americans with pro-Viet Cong "revolutionary" sentiment. In any event, no general uprising occurred. ARVN fought back. Khe Sanh held. Even as Washington was shaken, the Saigon regime, buttressed by U.S. aid and advisors, coped with one million new refugees and muddled through. And in and around the cities, the Viet Cong lost heavily, exposed for the first time to the full weight of Allied firepower. Truong Nhu Tang, one of the NLF's founders now in exile, observed:

"The truth was that Tet cost us half of our forces. Our losses were so immense that we were simply unable to replace them with new recruits."[2]

Giving Ground

This military failure was followed up by a weaker "second wave" attack in May, coinciding with the onset of peace talks in Paris. North Vietnamese regulars and local Viet Cong battalions struck at Saigon and several other points. This effort failed, too, although Saigon was penetrated, with heavy urban damage.

By mid-1968, Giap, a better logistician than tactician, was back on the defensive. Against the strong allied effort to take territory and population away from the now-weakened Viet Cong, he made few countermoves. He did on occasion, during 1969–71, launch what the allies called "high points" — simultaneous attacks by sappers and rocket teams against several dozen bases and towns — but these employed mostly local forces. He launched a few thrusts in border areas. But he usually kept his big units in base camps in, or close to, eastern Laos and Cambodia, as his engineers kept developing the Ho Chi Minh Trail.

He did not abandon the Viet Cong; as they slowly gave ground, he sent in North Vietnamese "fillers" to sustain their local battalions, and tried to keep the supply lines open. Even so, by U.S. estimates, the Viet Cong guerrilla strength dropped by 50 percent between 1968 and 1972.[3] In some districts, the surviving Viet Cong simply stopped fighting.

However, by mid-1969, even as the Communists lost ground in the South, from Hanoi's point of view, the "contradictions" in the enemy camp promised new gains. Thanks to U.S. domestic political pressures, Hanoi had already achieved two major concessions, *gratis*: first, Lyndon Johnson's pre-election day total halt to the bombing of the North in 1968 and a "cap" on U.S. troop strength (549,500) in the South; then, Richard Nixon's mid-1969 decision to start withdrawing U.S. troops unilaterally from Indochina. If American antiwar sentiment had been underestimated before Tet, it became an important part of Hanoi's political *dau tranh*;[4] strategy during 1969–72. At the Paris peace talks initiated by LBJ, Hanoi's Le Duc Tho stalled for time; the North Vietnamese periodically hinted in public of possible "breakthroughs," thus stirring new clamor in Washington, then held firm in secret talks with Henry Kissinger.[5]

By early 1972, after mauling an ill-fated ARVN thrust against the Ho Chi Minh Trail in Laos a year earlier and surviving the allies' 1970 Cambodia incursion, General Giap was ready to return in force to the South. He would launch not a "people's war" but a conventional assault. He sought to re-establish his regular units back inside the South, upset Richard Nixon's "Vietnamization," and lend succor to the remaining Viet Cong guerrillas. Giap and the Politburo felt that Nixon's rapprochement with Beijing and détente with Moscow threatened to isolate the North Vietnamese over the long term. Hanoi's leaders, thinking of Tet 1968, believed that a spectacular success during a U.S. election year amid pervasive antiwar sentiment would force Nixon to agree to the replacement of the Thieu regime by a pro-Communist coalition in Saigon.

A Decent Interval

Giap failed to anticipate the resilience of the South Vietnamese, the vigor of the U.S. response, and the lukewarm backing of Hanoi's allies, China and the Soviet Union. Neither Mao nor Brezhnev canceled his scheduled summit with Nixon.

Seeking once again to shatter the South Vietnamese, Giap massed his new Soviet-supplied tanks and artillery at three points: the DMZ, the Central Highlands near Kontum, and An Loc north of Saigon. For the first time, he committed 14 regular North Vietnamese divisions, virtually his entire army, to battle in the South. The initial gains were considerable: The green Third ARVN Divison broke at Quang Tri, and other ARVN units retreated. But nowhere did Giap deploy enough forces to score a breakthrough. American C-130 transports shifted ARVN's paratroops and marines from crisis to crisis. Although most of the 95,000 U.S. troops still "in-country" eschewed combat, American advisors coordinated firepower, helicopter support, and logistics. And Nixon quickly reinforced U.S. air power and naval gunfire in the South, resumed bombing the North, and mined the supply port of Haiphong. General Creighton Abrams was able to use 129 B-52s to strike hard whenever the North Vietnamese regiments massed to attack. As at Tet 1968, Giap's forces were unable to exploit initial gains; once again the ARVN, despite its heaviest casualties of the war, and the Regional and Popular Forces militia muddled through. This time, the Viet Cong played almost no military role. The Easter Offensive stalled by June, then receded slightly, leaving behind prisoners and scores of wrecked tanks.

At a price of an estimated 100,000 dead, Giap did score some significant gains. His PAVN regulars were back inside the South and, here and there, in good position to threaten ARVN units, or to ease the pressure on surviving local Viet Cong guerrillas. As he began to rebuild his decimated forces, Giap was well positioned for another drive, and his foe, as events would show, was badly overextended.

But to his colleagues in Hanoi, the Easter Offensive did not count as a glittering success. The decision was made to embrace a "talk-fight" strategy, resuming the Paris peace negotiations, putting reliance on war-weariness in the United States and on Nixon's quest for a quick ending.

When Hanoi obstructed the talks in November and took advantage of a U.S. bombing halt to rebuild its defenses (and resupply its troops in the South), Nixon unleashed the Navy and Air Force and for the first time sent B-52s over Hanoi (and Haiphong). During a 12-day campaign (interrupted by a Christmas cease-fire), the U.S. bombers left the North Vietnamese capital largely unscathed but smashed up both air defenses and transport, leaving North Vietnam open to further attack. A peace agreement was signed in Paris on January 27, 1973.

In dealing with Henry Kissinger, Le Duc Tho succeeded in securing an American withdrawal, coupled with a continued North Vietnamese presence in the South and in Laos and Cambodia. Soon, Hanoi realized that Saigon could not count on further American support. PAVN commanders prepared for a final offensive in 1976. Their chief worry, the possible return of American B-52s, eased after Washington failed to react to the PAVN's seizure of Phuoc Long, a border province north of Saigon, in early 1975, in a clear violation of the Paris cease-fire accords. Even more surprising to the Politburo was the failure of ARVN, poorly deployed and badly led, without direct American support, to fight effectively, as they had in 1972.

Hanoi sped up its timetable. General Van Tien Dung's Great Spring Offensive, with Soviet artillery and tanks, began in March with a push through the Central Highlands; the ARVN defense turned into a rout. Saigon was captured on April 30, 1975. Thieu fled into exile, and the war was over. Hanoi quickly abandoned any pretense of autonomy for the Viet Cong. By 1976, the NLF was dissolved, and the South was part of the new Socialist Republic of Vietnam.

Liberation brought tens of thousands of South Vietnamese, including former critics of the Thieu regime, into Communist "re-education camps," and eventually sent hundreds of thousands more escaping by sea — the "boat people." More than 425,000 Vietnamese are now in the United States. Their children speak English and attend local schools. In Washington, D.C., in Los Angeles, in San Francisco, Vietnamese names are cropping up with increasing frequency on lists of National Merit Scholars and high school valedictorians. Meanwhile, back home, General Giap's forces, supplied by the Soviets, are still at war, this time to prop up a friendly regime in Cambodia.

NOTES

[1] In my view, this sequence suggests that a similar "all-out" bombing effort in early 1965 could well have prompted Hanoi's leaders to negotiate an agreement, then sought by Lyndon Johnson, providing for a cease-fire and mutual withdrawal of Northern forces and U.S. troops from South Vietnam. Such an accord, of course, would not have ended Hanoi's quest for unification; it would simply have brought a change in tactics and a new timetable.

[2] *The New York Review of Books*, Oct. 21, 1982.

[3] Source: U.S. Army Center of Military History. Few Viet Cong "hard-core" cadres surrendered or rallied to the Saigon side. However, even before Tet 1968, thousands of Viet Cong wearied of life in the bush, on short rations, far from home. In 1967 alone, there were some 27,000 *chieu hoi* (ralliers), mostly rank-and-file guerrillas, porters, and the like.

[4] *Dau tranh* was a strategic concept meaning "struggle," with both military and political emphases. See Douglas Pike, *War, Peace, and the Viet Cong*, MIT, 1969.

[5] In a February 1969 interview, Italian journalist Oriana Fallaci said to Giap: "General, the Americans also say that you have lost half a million [men]." Giap replied: "The exact number." Fallaci: "Exact?" Giap: "Exact." Assigning responsibility for the failed 1968 Tet Offensive to the NLF, Giap went on to say that the Americans would lose eventually: "The Americans will be defeated in time, by getting tired. And in order to tire them, we have to go on, to last. . .for a long time. That's what we've always done." Fallaci, *Interview with History*, Liveright, 1976, pp. 82–84.

COMMENTARY: The Two Vietnams

by Stanley Karnow

Juxtaposed, the papers by Douglas Pike and Allan Goodman might bear the title: "Know thy enemy, know thy ally." Or to put Sun Tzu's famous dictum into a Vietnamese context: "Ngo your enemy, ngo your ally." But after reading both analyses, I don't feel that I know (or ngo) much more about either.

This is not to suggest that I have the answer. More then 30 years of reporting on Vietnam — from the early period of the French war through the American conflict to a recent trip there — have at last taught me the wisdom of recognizing my ignorance. In response to the two papers, therefore, I would only offer some general ideas that might serve as guidelines to a further study of the contemporary Vietnam experience.

Looking back at the years from 1954 through 1975 — from the Geneva Conference through the fall of Saigon — we are confronted with two questions: Why did our enemy prevail? And why did our ally fail?

Oversimplified, of course, those questions frame the story of the war. For the Communists were pursuing a very long range, protracted struggle of attrition in the expectation that the United States would eventually lose patience and withdraw, thus undermining the South Vietnamese government, which had become almost totally dependent on the American presence.

This was not a straight-line strategy.

Just as General Giap ambitiously tried to defeat the French quickly in his Red River offensive of 1951, so he attempted a fast one in the Tet Offensive of 1968 in order to improve Hanoi's position for negotiations. Similarly, the North Vietnamese preceded their 1972 diplomatic approach with an offensive, and they matched Nixon's concessions in order to get a cease-fire agreement. They reckoned that sooner or later the Saigon regime would collapse. Throughout, however, they were operating on the theory that time was on their side.

Colonel Harry Summers put his finger on this point when he recalled having reminded a North Vietnamese officer that the United States had never lost a battle. "That may be so," replied the Communist, "but it is also irrelevant."

I bow to Douglas Pike's emphasis on the concept of *dau tranh*, or struggle, as the key factor in the Communist approach. As usual, Pike has convincingly described the importance of this concept in the development of Communist policy and practice. But I would like to offer a few thoughts in an effort to explain why and how the North Vietnamese population and its Viet Cong confederates in the South subscribed so ardently to the concept. For, after all, they were not brainwashed. Or as Konrad Kellem observed in his Rand studies of prisoner attitudes, you do not have to indoctrinate people who are already indoctrinated.

In the first place, the Vietnamese are extraordinarily sensitive to their own history — and to the nature of their history. It is a history of almost constant resistance against foreigners, dating back two thousand years to wars against the Chinese. The

Trung Sisters and all that may very well be mythology, and we know for a fact that the Vietnamese rulers, including Ho Chi Minh himself, often behaved as tributaries to the Chinese. The reality, though, is that the Vietnamese forged a sense of nationalism that at times has bordered on xenophobia. They borrowed Chinese culture, just as they borrowed French culture, but they maintained an implacable hostility to alien intrusion onto their soil. They are, perhaps, comparable to the Irish.

The Ferocity of Nationalism

It is difficult for us, I think, to empathize with the ferocity of their nationalism, much less comprehend it. In Hanoi not long ago, I asked a veteran Communist officer to explain it to me, but all he said was: "You may find it hard to understand, but we really do believe fervently in the sanctity of the fatherland." At any rate, the U.S. Marines who landed at Da Nang in March 1965 were not the first invaders in their eyes. They had dealt with the Chinese, the French, and the Japanese, plus occasional skirmishes with Cambodians and Chams — and they are back to fighting the Chinese today.

So those thousands of North Vietnamese and Viet Cong whose corpses we tallied in the "body count" were very largely motivated, as individuals, by the conviction that they were national saviors. It is interesting, traveling in the northern part of Vietnam today, to note that every village has the same cemetery with the same whitewashed memorial and the same whitewashed tombstones, each marked "Liet Si," or "hero." There are no bodies in the graves. They were all bulldozed into the ground in the South.

A point worth underlining in logical sequence is the sacrifice that these people were prepared to make in the pursuit of their cause.

Every American planner from the start of the U.S. commitment to Vietnam should have been compelled to memorize Ho Chi Minh's words to Jean Sainteny on the eve of the French war: "I will lose ten men to every one of yours," Ho said, "but I will win and you will lose."

Ho may have minimized the casualties his people would take — especially if the two wars are combined. The Communists have still not revealed their losses, but the figure of some 600,000 North Vietnamese soldiers killed in the U.S. war alone is in the ballpark. In relative population terms, that is something like six million American lives.

Observing these sacrifices in the form of battlefield cadavers, General Westmoreland and other Americans could only conclude that the Vietnamese put a different premium on human life than did Westerners. But anyone familiar with Vietnamese and other Asians knows this to be nonsense. What the Americans never understood was the enemy's priorities. They believed that the Communists could be bombed into submission, but they were restrained by the limitations imposed by the President. In any case, the North Vietnamese were prepared to take limitless losses. Paul Warnke, who left the Pentagon in 1969, observed that "We guessed wrong with respect to what the North Vietnamese reaction would be" to the bombing, having anticipated that "they would respond like reasonable people." Or as Leslie Gelb and Richard Betts put it:

The [Pentagon civilians'] rationale imputed to the North Vietnamese an economic motivation, a mechanistic calculation of costs and benefits, a logical willingness to lower demand as price rose . . . . It implicitly assumed that Vietnamese reunification was a relative value to Hanoi that could be relinquished as the pain threshold rose, rather than the absolute value it was.

To give this notion a hometown angle, visit a battlefield of the American Civil War, and the Communists become somewhat easier to fathom. The bodies that piled up at Manassas and Gettysburg were of young men who believed themselves to be fighting for an "absolute value."

Another question arises: why the Communists managed to capture the leadership of the nationalist movement, when there were rivals like the VNQQD, Dai Viets, and others. Here, I would suggest, the answer is the revolutionary dimension. Or, as Ev Bumgartner once put it in the most elementary terms, the kid in the Mekong Delta who joined the local Viet Cong guerrilla unit was simply looking for a piece of land he could call his own.

A Pragmatic Appeal

Having spent a good deal of time focusing on the Chinese and other revolutions, I tend to be skeptical about ideological appeals. Peasants are not moved by abstractions. They are conservative, concrete, and pragmatic, and they will side with anyone who can offer them something. During the French war and afterward, the Communists offered them agrarian reform programs and, motivated more by their pocketbooks than by their hearts and minds, they gave their support in exchange.

That, in oversimplistic terms, was what the revolution was all about — and it was doubly fortuitous for the Communists because the French controlled the big estates and plantations, especially in the South, and so the revolutionary and nationalist struggles coincided. A landmark study, incidentally, is Chalmers Johnson's "Revolution and Peasant Nationalism," which describes how Mao Zedong used the Japanese invasion of China to mobilize the Chinese peasantry. Substitute the French for the Japanese in Vietnam and, with some other variations, the phenomenon is similar.

So, by the time the United States became involved, there was already in Vietnam what the academics call a "political culture" largely influenced by the Communists, in which the idea of struggle against capitalist foreigners was considered to be normal. Nothing was more ridiculous than our idea of providing security for the peasants against the Viet Cong. In many parts of the country, they were the same people, viz. Pogo: "We have met the enemy, and he is us."

Against this background, the mechanics of the Communist operation fit easily. Pike and others make much of the organizational structure, the role of cadres and suchlike, all indisputable. But the organizational structure was only able to work effectively because, behind it, there were enough people for whom it meant something very real. You can find in Vietnam today any number of men who have spent their whole lives at war — who joined the Viet Minh as teenagers, fought at Dien Bien Phu, went on to devote years to the conflict in the South, and survived to take over Saigon. Their stories are almost incredible.

In Allan Goodman's paper, the question of what went wrong with "our Vietnamese" answers itself: They were "*our* Vietnamese." Well, not quite, as far as we were concerned, because they didn't always behave as we wished they would. But in the eyes of the Vietnamese, the Saigon leadership in the post-Diem period had very thin nationalist credentials indeed.

No Match for Ho

Here again, it is important to reach back into recent history to understand the fragility of the South Vietnamese government.

Both the communists and their adversaries make much of ideology and organization, the role of the party, and the rest. But communism, perhaps more than any other political system and certainly more than capitalist democracy, is centered on one-man rule: Lenin, Stalin, Mao, Khrushchev, Tito, Brezhnev. So it was Ho. His anticommunist rivals simply had nobody to match him. The French, unbelievably, tried Bao Dai—whom S.J. Perelman, after meeting him in Hong Kong, described as having the "consistency of Crisco." The United States tried Ngo Dinh Diem — a notch better, but no contest.

We could look back to the late 19th century to find the forerunners of the people who staffed the Saigon regime. They were the Vietnamese who collaborated with the French, especially in Cochin China, where they became the local elites. Many emigrated afterward to Paris — which at one stage had more Vietnamese doctors than did Saigon.

I do not intend to demean these Western-oriented Vietnamese, these products of the *mission civilisatrice*. Indeed, they are my kind of people, personally speaking. But they were not the dynamic leaders of a future nationalist movement.

After 1954, Diem may have been the best of a poor lot. But he had very little in the way of an establishment — and he dismissed whatever talent he did have by placing loyalty to himself above competence. His regime was essentially a family oligarchy in which the most influential figures were his older brother, Archbishop Thuc, and his younger brother, Nhu, who was close to madness. His generals — Big Minh, Tran Van Don, Le Van Kim, Nguyen Khanh — were hand-me-downs from the French policy of *jaunissement*. A South Vietnamese army officer had to have a *baccalaureat* — a *lycée* diploma — which meant that he probably came from a middle-class urban family. A village was as alien to him as it was to me. His objective was to survive and make his way back to a job in Saigon, where the promotions, the money, the girls, and the fun were. Ted Serong, a very shrewd Australian in Vietnam, once remarked to me: "One of the advantages for the Viet Cong is that they have no Saigon to go to."

Goodman is correct to point out that the courage and the heroism of the ARVN "grunt" were too often neglected. Ordinary South Vietnamese soldiers fought and died, frequently despite poor leadership. They also panicked on many occasions, because of poor leadership.

Looking back with 20-20 hindsight, it seems to me that the great Vietnam tragedy really began with the overthrow of Ngo Dinh Diem in 1963. I think it was true, as those of us who criticized him at the time said, "We can't win the war with Diem." Having been involved in his ouster, however, the United States assumed a responsibility for Vietnam that was to lead inexorably to the American combat intervention.

The arrival of the American war machine in Vietnam in 1965 was one of the great logistical feats of all time. Ho Chi Minh once described his war against the French as a conflict between a grasshopper and an elephant. Now he was a microbe pitted against a leviathan. The paradox, however, was that the policy designed to strengthen the South Vietnamese actually weakened them.

I will leave to the sociologist the disruption of South Vietnamese society — the corruption, venality, and so forth caused by the inflow of American money. Just a couple of points, which Ambassador Bui Diem cites in the Rand study on why Saigon fell, bear mentioning.

Microbe versus Leviathan

First, the overwhelming American presence created a crippling sense of dependency in the South Vietnamese officialdom, so that the Saigon regime's days were numbered after the United States withdrew in 1973. I had always assumed that the B-52s were crucial (in 1972). Military specialists tell me that the American advisers with ARVN units were even more important. The reliance, incidentally, worked both ways. American pacification advisors counted for promotions on good progress reports by South Vietnamese province chiefs, which made for a good deal of fakery of reports — thereby contributing to illusory optimism.

Second, the huge American investment lulled the South Vietnamese into believing that the United States would never leave. Their thoroughly rational conclusion turned out to be wrong. Nobody in his right mind would spend $11 billion to build the complex at Cam Ranh Bay, and then depart. The Americans must be crazy. They were crazy. The South Vietnamese were left holding the bag.

To Bui Diem's observations I would add another — which also touches on Goodman's reference to Americans' lack of knowledge about Vietnam.

I do not believe that 10,000 Americans with Ph.D.s on Vietnam would have made a difference — except perhaps to have advised us not to get involved. The real problem, as I see it, lay in the way Americans from Lyndon Johnson and McNamara to Westmoreland and Bob Komer perceived the problem of our relationship with the Saigon regime. They saw it more as a management problem than as a political or social problem. Whether they were dealing with military operations or pacification, the approach was always quantitative — or, as McNamara used to say: "By every quantitative measure, we are winning."

The South Vietnamese, who learn quickly, quickly learned to play the quantitative game. Vietnam has been called the first television war — and Larry Lichty calls it the first Xerox war. It was also, I would add, the first computer war. Out poured the statistics until the mind reeled. In Suitland, Maryland, I am informed, a warehouse the size of three football fields is filled with official documents from Vietnam that have yet to be catalogued.

This is not to argue, as some do, that the alternative was counter-insurgency. The late Nguyen Be (a South Vietnamese counter-insurgency specialist) made a lot of sense, but his revolutionary cadres could not, even with the best training, promote a revolution against the Communist revolution for a Saigon government that lacked the foggiest notion of what went on in a hamlet at night. And the United States was not about to support an alternative Saigon government, whose leaders threatened to disrupt the middle-class South Vietnamese establishment that was the pillar of the regime. In short, we Americans do not have a revolutionary vision for agrarian societies — as we are demonstrating in Central America.

Ruthless, Repressive, Dogmatic

Once again, I am not trying to cast the Communists in a romantic glow as a band of Robin Hoods. They could be ruthless, repressive, and dogmatic. As they themselves now admit, their heavy losses in the Tet Offensive and Phoenix program weakened the southern guerrilla and political elements and turned the war by 1970 into a big conventional war. But it had become by then a war between U.S. and North Vietnamese units. The Nixon administration, calculating that the domestic costs had become too great, made the concession of permitting the North Vietnamese to remain in the South in 1972 and, though Hanoi made in exchange the concession of allowing the Thieu regime to remain intact, that augured the darkness at the end of the tunnel.

Speculating in retrospect is always interesting, but I am inclined to doubt that there were "lost opportunities" for the South Vietnamese to have saved themselves — at least not without an interminable American presence. It was essentially the American weight that sustained them. And it was the American weight, when it suited the United States, that crushed them. Nixon was determined to get a cease-fire agreement despite Thieu's objections — and my guess is that he would have staged a Diem-like coup against Thieu had that been necessary. After all, as Henry Kissinger said in reply to John Negreponte's criticism of the agreement: "Do you want us to stay there forever?"

What, then, went wrong in our effort to know our enemy and know our ally? We underestimated our enemy's willingness to take sacrifices. And we overestimated our own ability to wage a fundamentally political war through a surrogate that did not, politically, measure up to its adversary.

What could the alternative have been? Visit Lang Son, on the Chinese border, and the answer is there. The trip is obligatory so that the Vietnamese Communists can show the destruction inflicted on them by the Chinese Communists. The town was wrecked in 1979, but it has not been rebuilt — so that it can serve to demonstrate that a 2000-year-old conflict is still alive. It demonstrated to me, when I was there, that we were somehow in the wrong place if we were supposed to be containing Chinese Communism.

But how could we have known then? In early 1950, an official in the State Department's Far East division, Raymond B. Fosdick, warned against helping the French to fight their war. "There may be unpredictable and unseen factors in this situation that in the end will be more favorable to us than now seems probable," he wrote. "The fundamental antipathy of the Indochinese to China is one of the factors." In 1954, at the Geneva Conference, we surely should have known that the Chinese had cut off military aid to the Viet Minh to compel them to negotiate with the French on unfavorable terms. Pham Van Dong said at the time — or at least he told me he said at the time: "The Chinese have betrayed us."

In my estimation, therefore, the "lost opportunities" were diplomatic. And, along with all the other dismal superlatives about Vietnam, it may have been the most avoidable war in our history.

COMMENTARY: The Air War

by Alan Gropman

I find Pike's paper provocative for a number of reasons:

First of all, it's an axiom that all people and material being equal, the side with the better strategy will win. And it's also true that all people and material not being equal, the better strategy can win if it's much better. And that's what happened in this case. We lost in Vietnam because our military and political strategies were inferior to the adversary's. You can't have a valid strategy when your view is no longer than the next Congressional election or the next roll-call vote on the highway beautification bill.

There's no reality save one's perception of reality; reality is all perception in this business. And that's related to moral perceptions, too. The effect of U.S. intervention in 1965 on the morale of the South Vietnamese was undervalued by the North Vietnamese, writes Pike. It's true and the effect of U.S. withdrawal in 1973 was also undervalued by the North Vietnamese and by us, too. That's why the collapse in 1975 came so much faster than anyone thought it would.

Like the companion piece by Allan Goodman which tells us that we failed to understand the South Vietnamese ally, we even understood less of the North Vietnamese enemy. Richard Betts points out that we never even understood the nature of the struggle.

Therefore, we could not have understood why it could not be mediated. By we, we mean the American decision-makers — from Harvard or wherever.

Addressing specifically the air war, let's recognize that I'm an Air Force colonel. I agree with Dr. Pike's suggestion that had the 1972 bombing, which had been recommended by the Air Staff in 1964 and 1965, been visited upon the North Vietnamese, the complexion of the war would have changed sufficiently for the United States to build a South Vietnam able to withstand the Viet Cong.

Dozens of Rand Corporation conferences, dozens of Rand Corporation reports during the 1950s and '60s came to the conclusion that one cannot win against an insurgency unless one shuts off the outside aid. The bombing of whatever counted as strategic targets in North Vietnam (and North Vietnam of course was never "terror-bombed," not even in 1972), the electric grid, the oil, the manufacturing, etc., the mining of the harbors, the interdiction of as much of the transportation as possible — all of that, had it been visited upon them in 1965, would have made the problem in the South manageable.

The idea that North Vietnam could not have been bombed out of the war because of its fanaticism is folly; Japan was much more fanatic. The 1965 bombing was nothing like what had been recommended by the Air Force. Had it been carried out before the radar and the SAM and the conventional anti-aircraft weapons, before all those things had been brought in, it would have been cheap, relatively. Having talked to numerous American POWs who were on the ground while this was going on, I believe that the same effect could have been accomplished in 1972 and '73 had the Christmas bombing gone on.

I end with a question and a comment. The Viet Cong never recovered from the 1968 Tet Offensive, which was their battle, except for parts of I Corps. Is there not evidence today that this countrywide, ill-advised attack was ordered by North Vietnam and that the results, the defeat and virtual destruction of the Viet Cong as a fighting force and therefore as a political force, was desired by the North Vietnamese?

Finally, this war was not a nine-inning baseball game. And it didn't matter if, at the end of nine innings in 1969 or '70, the score was 264 to 6. It was an endless game, and the enemy set the terms of the length of the game. We couldn't kill them faster than they could birth them. Not with the limitations set by the White House. We must lose the attitude or the American naiveté that defines military success as a matter of toting up a score. We won't get on the path of wisdom in winning against revolutionary wars, not till we do that.

DISCUSSION

PIKE: [re the effect of the 1972 bombing] This is a tough thing to explain. It's as if your wife gives you love pats all these years and you get a general idea of her strength; all of a sudden she hauls off and she socks you and it knocks you across the room. That will cause you to re-evaluate her prowess; it doesn't mean you don't think you can lick her. It's just that what you believed all these years isn't any longer true.

WEBB: Until the Christmas bombing, no B-52s had ventured beyond the southern portions of North Vietnam, creating the illusion in Hanoi that they could handle whatever the Americans hit them with. After eight days of this bombing, with Haiphong blockaded, they lost their anti-aircraft capacity, and the bombing was very effective.

OBERDORFER: But how could doing it in 1965 possibly lead to an end of the war?

PIKE: The war *as we know it* would have been over. The North Vietnamese objective was unification of North and South Vietnam under their flag. They had in the Politburo two basic strategies with about two sub-versions of each. There was enormous argument all during the war about how best to achieve unification. The regular strategy they instigated in 1965 brought the American military power to bear. They felt that they could surmount this and achieve unification. If the price and the punishment [inflicted by U.S. bombing] had been increased, they would not have surrendered. They would have said, "Rationally, there is another way. . . .We're taking this punishment for nothing. It's gratuitous. We're not talking about capitulation or loss of honor, we're talking about another road to get to the same place."

 The Vietnamese determination and fanaticism was still there, but they were in many ways much more rational in attempting to achieve their objective than we were.

OBERDORFER: From what I know of their military strategy and thinking, when they ran into heavy American firepower, which they did on a number of occasions, they found, in a kind of trial-and-error and painful way, how to deal with it. That makes me very doubtful about the idea that you could just do it with iron bombs. The United States had rained down the bombs and they could have sent a tremendous expeditionary force to invade North Vietnam. I can see that having a decisive effect; we were going to occupy Vietnam. But I just can't see how you can think that even the heaviest bombing campaign [in 1965] was going to cause them to practically throw in the sponge.

PIKE: Not to throw in the sponge, but to adapt another strategy, another approach. "We have to do whatever we have to do to get the Americans out of here." If the bombing is punitive enough, in the end you pay whatever price on the grounds that once you get the Americans out, they're not going to come back. Once you get them out, things are going to be better. We want unification but not tomorrow, not next week; 50 years from now is fine. There was this notion of the indefinite duration.

What kept the North Vietnamese in the war was the perception that we couldn't hang on. Victory was over the next hill. It was almost as if the Nixon administration, particularly, designed a policy to keep them in the war. You don't think for one minute that if General Giap in 1960 could have known the full scenario and that he would still be in the war in 1975, he would have done it the way he did. Not on your life.

OBERDORFER: Whenever the North got hit hard, they managed to recuperate. I am especially skeptical that iron bombs alone, short of a U.S. invasion of the North, could have forced North Vietnam to concede. Bernard Fall said before 1965, "Americans do not like long, inconclusive wars, and this is going to be a long, inconclusive war."

ISAACS: I have a factual contribution to make. No one ought to be mistaken about what was achieved by the December 1972 bombing. If you are going to argue about what the effect of that kind of bombing was, the argument is made and a lot of people seem to believe that the bombing was decisive in forcing the North Vietnamese to sign the peace agreement that they signed at the end of January, three or four weeks after the bombing. The facts make that a little hard to support.

PIKE: [responding to prior questions] Did Hanoi maneuver to destroy the NLF in the 1968 Tet Offensive by throwing them into the breach?

This is widely believed among most Vietnamese on both sides, I would say, in South Vietnam. It says more about the kind of paranoid conditions of the mindset of the Vietnamese than it did about reality. I do not think that they did, but it's a moot point and you could build a case for it. It certainly looked like it on the surface.

Communist intelligence in the South? The reporting system of the Viet Cong and the North Vietnamese in the South was guilty in the pre-1968 period of over-optimistic reporting about the conditions in the South. They reported widespread anti-Americanism; they equated that with pro-Viet Congism. This over-optimistic reporting is not a phenomenon peculiar to the Communists; we suffer from it ourselves. They really believed this, but much of the Tet Offensive campaign was faulty because it was assumed in Hanoi that there was a ripeness in the South that really didn't exist.

On the issue of these three sides of the triangle: strategy, organization, and spirit, I will simply say that among those of us who write on the North Vietnamese, we all agree that the essence of their success was strategy, organization, and spirit; we quarrel on the shape of the triangle. Is it equilateral, is it right angle, is it isosceles, or what? It strikes me as a kind of precise argument. We all agree what the ingredients were, what the essence of their qualities was. What we quarrel over is the relative values and the relative dimensions and importance of them. Nobody says they won because they had spirit. Or they won because they had good organization. Or they won because they had good strategy. It's a mix and the only question is how you rank these.

Giap was clearly the architect of the campaign. He wrote a book, *Great Victory, Big Test*, which laid it out. It's virtually a blueprint, calls the shots right down the line. It's almost a scenario. His name is on it; you could argue that it was ghosted for him, but I don't believe that.

Giap's last hurrah was the 1972 Easter Offensive; he was on the decline. His strategic value was being questioned increasingly by younger PAVN officers. There is a question as to how good Giap was. Bernard Fall used to maintain that Giap was a logistics genius. He could move men and forces around the battlefield far faster than he had any right to expect. He did it with the French; he did it with us. But Fall maintained that Giap was a mediocre tactician and strategist. By the time of the Easter Offensive of '72, this had begun to catch up with him. Giap reached about the extent of what you could do with logistics, and he had not been able to deliver victory. There was a ghastly cost in terms of casualties, and it just caught up with him.

On the combat performance of PAVN and Viet Cong: In a word, I think they were pros. They took a very professional attitude toward their work; they had high standards which they imposed on themselves. They were professional in the sense that any professional imposes on himself a discipline and rigor and high standard of performance.

On Hanoi's attitude toward U.S. public opinion and the antiwar movement: They never really knew what to make of it. They started out by underestimating its importance and they wound up by overestimating it. You can build a case that every major enemy drive in Vietnam came in advance of a presidential election: 1964, 1968, 1972, and there was to be a 1976. You can also argue that was simply a coincidence. We tend to read into what they do in terms of what we're doing.

On Hanoi's view of Laos and Kampuchea: It was a single unit. They always regarded Indochina strategically as a package deal. What they did in Laos and Cambodia was almost entirely not for the sake of Laos and Cambodia, but was designed to serve the war in the South.

On support from the superpowers: There was no arms industry in North Vietnam; it was all underwritten first by the Chinese and later by the Russians. They made it possible. The Russians could have dried up the war any time they wanted to. It would have been a slow dry-out but they could have shut off the pipeline. The Russians made the war possible.

On Watergate and the end of the war: The answer is a visceral judgment. If there had been no Watergate, there would still be a South Vietnam today. The North Vietnamese were emboldened by the loss of U.S. presidential authority to make the moves that they did. I believe that the Christmas air attack in 1972 scared the bejesus out of them. A credible threat of that to return and they simply wouldn't have gotten the votes in the Politburo to resume an all-out offensive in 1975. Not that they would have capitulated, not that they were cowards or giving up their great dream, but the leadership would just have deferred to those at the table who said that there were other ways of doing this, we don't have to go that route and look at the price we paid in the past. This is another historical might-have-been; you can argue it.

THE DYNAMICS OF THE UNITED STATES–SOUTH VIETNAMESE ALLIANCE: What Went Wrong

by Allan E. Goodman

The failure to understand the capabilities and limits of our ally in Vietnam is probably the single most important explanation of what went wrong with U.S. policy there.

It is a key lesson of the largest, most costly, and least successful war in American history. This essay focuses on how the dynamics of our relationship with the South Vietnamese affected U.S. strategy both in the war and the efforts to end it by diplomacy.

At the corner of Lam Son Square in Saigon stood a monument to the ARVN (Army of the Republic of Vietnam). Two giant infantrymen were depicted rushing forward to attack. The object of their attack, however, appeared to be the ornate opera house that served as the National Assembly building in 1967–75.

The scene thus created was the subject of much cynical comment. Some American advisors (and Vietnamese opposition political leaders as well) saw the placement of the statue as deliberate, intended as a constant reminder of the disdain that Vietnam's generals had for the effort to create a civilian political alternative to the Viet Cong.

Other Americans said the statue depicted why Vietnamization would fail. The lead soldier, according to this version of the story, was actually a U.S. infantryman; the soldier cringing behind him was ARVN.

To me, the comments about the statue in Lam Son Square symbolized the basic trouble in our alliance with the Vietnamese. At the highest levels of national leadership, especially, neither side trusted or respected the other. As a result, U.S. military and diplomatic strategies were shaped by a profound misunderstanding of the Vietnamese, their political culture, and their attitude toward war and peace.

As with any stereotype, the misperceptions which influenced U.S. policy toward our ally in Vietnam appeared to be confirmed even by casual observation. Vietnam was the most open, accessible society, for example, in which I have ever worked. Reporters, academics, visiting official inquisitors (friendly and critical), and spies could see an enormous amount of the countryside and people. In part, this was possible because of the road and air network created by USAID and the decision of the GVN to let Americans operate as counterparts down to the district (and, in some cases, village) level. This meant that virtually wherever you wanted to go in Vietnam you could get there and find an American with whom to chat. But such access was also a product of Vietnamese motives as well. With its sixty-plus political parties and groups[1] and thirty-plus newspapers, every would-be Vietnamese political "leader" wanted to talk to the types of Americans mentioned above in the hope that the reported views might influence U.S. policy, which was constantly under review.

Access can breed contempt, and this was often what happened.

The more most Americans penetrated the Vietnamese scene, the less they liked about what they saw. Corruption was widespread. Many Vietnamese politicians were venal, vindictive, and petty. ARVN was run like a business and most commanders were generally reluctant to fight the Viet Cong. But the danger with these judgments was that they blinded U.S. policy-makers to the opportunities presented when Vietnamese behaved differently.

No Desertions To the Other Side

Many ARVN units, for example, were good fighters. This was proved both in the aftermath of the 1968 Tet and 1972 Easter Offensives, and is treated extensively in the military histories of the period.[2] Briefly, the key facts are these:

In virtually every battle of the 1968 offensive, including the retaking of the citadel of Hue, regular ARVN infantrymen, airborne troopers, and marines were at least as important to the outcome as U.S. forces.

In the much more powerful and serious attack by North Vietnamese forces in the 1972 offensive, the tide of battle on the ground turned almost entirely on the action of Vietnamese soldiers. In this case, ARVN proved far more reliable and effective than even its American admirers and supporters had hoped.

In contrast to the "living room war" image of the South Vietnamese soldier as cowardly and bumbling, ARVN paid dearly (nearly 200,000 dead, plus a half million wounded) for its campaign against the regular and guerrilla Communist forces. In contrast to, say, the Chinese Nationalists in 1945–49, few ARVN individuals and no organized ARVN units went over to the enemy, even at Tet 1968 or in 1972. ARVN desertion rates, like those of Union regiments during the U.S. Civil War, often ran high; but the deserters went home. They did not desert to the other side.

U.S. military strategy, however, was based on the premise that American soldiers could fight and win the war more cost-effectively than the ARVN. Hence ARVN was almost always assigned the mission of protecting the *flanks* of an allied attack or some other subsidiary role. If a victory ensued, the Americans received the credit. If the Viet Cong escaped, the ARVN was blamed for letting them get away.

Some Vietnamese political leaders were men and women of principle and charisma. But U.S. policy-makers were consistently unwilling to back them, ironically, for fear of intervening in the internal affairs of another country.

The open contempt for Vietnamese politicians and political institutions that pervaded much of the official American presence was also generated by frustration at having to fight a very unpopular war on behalf of an ally for which there was no sympathy in the United States, and against an enemy that was consistently portrayed by war critics as heroic, self-sacrificing, entitled to political control over some parts of South Vietnam, and less politically repressive than successive governments in Saigon.

Almost nothing the South Vietnamese did politically was the subject of positive press or other media coverage in the United States, and one colleague has suggested that by his reckoning not a single United States newspaper *ever* published a story depicting the heroism and courage of an ARVN unit. As I will suggest below, moreover, this contempt had very direct consequences not only for U.S. counter-insurgency programs in Vietnam, but also for our attitude toward the GVN in the

Paris negotiations.

What was not readily apparent to the casual or even sophisticated observer in Vietnam was how the culture operated beneath the surface of the stereotypes mentioned above. Here, a basic point must be made about American ignorance of the Vietnamese.

U.S. policy-planners never had the kind of anthropological or sociological analyses of South Vietnamese behavior and customs that the French had of the North Vietnamese, for example. The classic work from the French era — Paul Mus's *Sociologie d'une Guerre* (1952) — was never translated into English. A start toward the creation of base line data was made with the work of the Michigan State University Advisory Group (MSUAG) in 1959–62, but during the period of peak U.S. involvement (1967–70), few of the important studies done by the MSUAG had been updated, and the group's experts had either turned against the war or to other academic pursuits, or both.

Thin Scholarship

In the years during which our commitment to Vietnam was in the process of gathering momentum, there were no academic programs of language study or research in Vietnamese available in any U.S. university. Between 1965 and 1970 only twenty Ph.D. theses were done on Vietnam (out of some five thousand in the field of modern history and international relations). Throughout this period, moreover, Vietnamese studies were an orphan in American academia. And when in early 1970 AID offered $1 million to create a Vietnamese Study Center, there was only one taker.

In short, stereotypes gained great currency because there was little with which to counter them in training programs or policy-planning exercises. The field of Vietnamese studies never achieved the critical mass needed to change the antipathy with which we viewed our ally.

Did the sterotypes we held of our Vietnamese ally make much difference to the outcome of the war?

For some, the dénouement in Vietnam in April of 1975 is now and was then seen as something akin to original sin; the collapse of the ARVN and the Saigon government, according to this view, was inevitable. Because of the flawed nature of the U.S. commitment, including especially the lies we told ourselves about why we were there and what could be accomplished, the truth about what would really happen was always shrouded. To believers in this school of thought, therefore, even policies and programs premised on a realistic appreciation of the Vietnamese and their situation and outlook would at best postpone the collapse of the GVN.

I subscribe to the view that U.S. policies and programs in Vietnam were remarkably effective and accomplished a great deal toward the modernization of South Vietnam and the destruction of the Viet Cong. By January of 1973 (when the Paris Agreement on "Ending the War and Restoring Peace in Vietnam" was signed), South Vietnam had amassed one of the largest armies in the world, and its leadership presided over a capitalist, pluralistic society with an enormous stake in preventing a communist takeover.

This brings us to the basic intractability of the military and political problems our ally faced. No matter how effective ARVN became, it could never cope with the sanctuaries in Laos and Cambodia which permitted Viet Cong and PAVN forces to rest and resupply and from which they could launch a military offensive at the beginning of every dry season. North Vietnam was next door. Saigon's ally was 10,000 miles away and anxious to disengage. Militarily, the South would always face a substantial threat from the North.

Intractable Problems

Another key point consistently ignored by critics of U.S. policy was that, politically, South Vietnam was not North Vietnam. In terms of the socio-political complexity of the two countries, for example, the leadership in Hanoi faced nowhere near the difficulty that leaders in Saigon did in establishing a central political authority.

In retrospect, however, I think many policy advisors and analysts, including myself, gave too much weight to the phenomenon of local accommodation, the process by which ARVN outposts, companies, and entire villages made "live-and-let-live" deals with local Viet Cong.[3] The discovery of such accommodation led many in and out of government to conclude that by and large the South Vietnamese population did not contain a substantial enough anticommunist base on which to organize a political alternative to the Viet Cong. As this became accepted doctrine, U.S. policy tried to compensate by providing more resources; thus, the political participation component so essential to legitimizing civic action and counter-terrorism programs (such as pacification, "Revolutionary Development," "Phoenix") and to creating a sense of trust between the government and the population was given short shrift.

The U.S. government basically lacked a theory to explain the noncommunist opposition political behavior we observed in Vietnam (and in most LDCs at that time). Such a doctrine or theory is still missing today. The U.S. government, for example, has had considerable difficulty in dealing with pressures for political change that come from the noncommunist left and the Church in Central America or from radical religious elements in the Middle East.[4] And it is interesting to note that the development of such an operational doctrine is the first order of business for the bipartisan Institute for Democracy, created as a follow-up to President Reagan's 8 June 1982 speech in the House of Commons.

There was also a lingering sense that the South Vietnamese were so wracked by regional and ethnic factionalism that they were incapable of being nationalists. In addition to the many political groups and parties that existed (and flourished, despite the image of the Saigon government as a heavy-handed, repressive dictatorship), there were three major ethnic minorities (4.5 million Chinese, 700,000 Montagnards, and 500,000 Khmer, which together amounted to more than 15 percent of the population of the South) as well as a high degree of consciousness about the regional origins (north, south, center) of ethnic Vietnamese.

Regionalism, while often cited as an obstacle to national integration in Vietnam, actually played an important part in lending cohesion to army divisions and instilling them with a sense of mission (especially when it came to territorial defense). This was particularly true of the 1st (Central Vietnamese Buddhist), 7th, 9th (Northern Vietnamese Catholic), and 21st (Central Vietnamese Cao Dai) ARVN infantry divisions, all of whom played key roles in defeating Viet Cong and PAVN forces during the 1968 and 1972 offensives. Regional roots also proved important to assuring that the vast migration to the cities, as well as the existence of a huge refugee population, occurred with a minimum of the anarchy and psychological strains that usually accompany such phenomena. The principal entity here was the traditional, local "burial and self-help organization" that provided social welfare services to millions of people the GVN failed to reach effectively. Whole districts of Saigon, plus many provincial cities and refugee camps, were virtually run by these organizations.

Autonomy Versus Collectivism

With respect to the rural population, the social and regional organizations mentioned above contributed importantly to the maintenance of a corporate life and to agricultural production in ways that made relatively little demand on the central government for resources.[5] Unlike the "hydraulic society" of the North, which required vast amounts of collectivized labor to maintain the dikes, rural society in the South was able to prosper more autonomously. When intervillage cooperation was required, this was usually organized by such religious organizations as the Hoa Hao or Cao Dai or along lines established by the local Vietnamese and Khmer Buddhist hierarchies.

In terms of mobilizing the political groups spawned by religions or regionalism, there were in my view two critical periods of lost opportunity for the GVN and the United States, one in 1966 and the other in 1968–70. The GVN's harsh response to demands by these groups for the expansion of political participation had the effect of alienating the population from its cause. Had the GVN been more accommodating, it would have derived two key benefits: It would have inherited (from the religions) an already legitimate anticommunist ideology, and it would have been able to support ongoing social welfare and self-help programs rather than appear in competition with them. Instead, the leaders of the GVN viewed such political and social activism as a threat to their own survival.

In early 1966, the government of Nguyen Cao Ky committed itself to organizing elections and drafting a constitution as a consequence of the U.S.-GVN summit meeting in Honolulu that February. Ky pledged "to formulate a democratic constitution in the months ahead, including an electoral law; to take that constitution to our people for discussion and modification; to create on the basis of elections rooted in that constitution, an elected government." Ky's return from Honolulu, however, brought little subsequent progress in either drafting a constitution or preparations for holding elections. Instead, Ky continued to focus on consolidating his support within the coalition of generals in the national Leadership Committee (the Directory) that ran the GVN.

As part of his strategy, in early March, Ky called for the resignation of General Nguyen Canh Thi, the popular commander of the I Corps region and one of Ky's principal rivals within the Directory. Within two days of the resignation order, riots and demonstrations calling for the reinstatement of General Thi and tangible progress toward free elections broke out in Da Nang (the administrative capital of I Corps), Hue, and other major urban centers. Ky, in turn, declared martial law, and ordered army troops to occupy Buddhist pagodas and to arrest Buddhist leaders.

Ky regarded this struggle movement primarily as a demonstration of support for General Thi rather than for elections. As such, he responded in military rather than political terms.

The Hue Massacre

The demand for reinstatement of General Thi, however, was rapidly over-shadowed by the demand for a new constitution and elections, and reflected the desire of the Buddhists to participate in the process of government rather than to overthrow it. This is a key point that the GVN and most U.S. policy-makers failed to realize. While a constitution was subsequently drafted and elections held in which some Buddhist political leaders participated, throughout the period government security forces continued to arrest leaders of the demonstration. The result was that the government system created in 1966–67 lacked legitimacy from the outset.

This made the political developments of the 1968–70 period even more striking. The Communists' Tet Offensive turned Americans off the war.[6] It had the opposite effect on large segments of the South Vietnam population. Urban residents, espe-cially, turned decidedly against the Viet Cong, in sharp contrast to the predictions of Communist strategists that conditions were ripe for a general uprising against the GVN. In fact, it was the cooperation of civilians — who often risked destruction of their own homes and neighborhoods — that allowed ARVN units to pinpoint where Viet Cong were hiding and then dislodge them. And it was in the wake of Tet that the GVN mobilized with surprisingly little resistance more than 500,000 draftees, many of whom helped turn back the 1972 Communist offensive.

As I have noted in detail elsewhere, moreover, Tet — especially the massacre of between 1000–1500 persons during the seige of the Hue citadel — convinced many Vietnamese political leaders that their principal enemy was the Viet Cong, not each other.[7] To this end, after the Tet Offensive the leaders of even opposition political organizations appeared to rally behind major GVN pacification programs. They also sought to accelerate the establishment of local self-defense forces and to work closely with provincial government authorities in social welfare and community develop-ment projects. At the national level, moreover, even those members of the oppo-sition who had been imprisoned by the Ky government or its predecessors were seeking to run for election to the National Assembly.

Perhaps the most dramatic example of this change in attitude appeared within militant Buddhist political organizations. All of the members of the 1966 Struggle Coordinating Committee, for example, were, by 1969, leaders in Buddhist social welfare services. The order of the day for these social welfare organizations and local Buddhist hierarchies in general was cooperation with the government.

In only rare cases, however, was such cooperation welcomed by Saigon and used as a means of bridging the gap between the government and the population. All too often, Thieu and his close circle of advisors evaluated such actions on the part of other politicians in terms of the impact they might have on Thieu's ability to remain in power rather than on what they could contribute to the war effort. Thus, most who sought a stake in the GVN even on Thieu's terms were denied it.

Ally or Burden?

U.S. policy suffered in both of these periods through the reluctance of the administration in Washington either to disassociate itself with the leadership of the GVN or to put significant pressure on it to expand opportunities for political participation. This reluctance is all the more striking given the low regard that

American Presidents had for their Vietnamese counterparts, and the crucial role the latter played in determining the effectiveness of U.S. policy. In retrospect, at least, I think it fair to argue that the U.S. commitment was so extensive and costly that breaching Washington's self-proclaimed policy of nonintervention was essential.

The fundamental difficulties in our alliance with Saigon also plagued efforts to achieve a negotiated settlement of the war.

The image of Saigon's role in the Paris talks was extremely poor. The refusal of then Vice President Nguyen Cao Ky to sit at a four-sided table in 1968, the 100-plus objections raised by President Thieu to the Kissinger—Le Duc Tho draft treaty in October 1972, and the GVN's ignoring of the Paris Agreement's political provisions only a few months after it was signed all created the impression that our ally (a) did *not* want to end the war by negotiation; and (b) was repeatedly the main obstacle to a reasonable agreement. What was not reported or grasped was that for Saigon the outcome of the negotiations was a matter deeply affecting the *survival* of a noncommunist government in the South. U.S. policy makers did not want to deal with this issue; America wanted out of the war and our leaders believed that the survival of the GVN could be decoupled from the negotiations.

The reality was that most South Vietnamese did not want a negotiated settlement, because they did not trust Hanoi to observe its terms. Subsequent developments, of course, proved Saigon right. By the fall of 1974, for example, there were more regular North Vietnamese Army troops operating in the South than at any time before. Nearly a thousand kilometers of all-weather roadways had also been constructed by the NVA inside South Vietnam, and Hanoi had by early 1975 deployed more than 600 tanks and 200 130mm field guns, weapons systems which were substantially better and more lethal than those available to the ARVN.

South Vietnamese leaders privy to the Kissinger-Tho draft agreement, moreover, did not think the October 1972 version a good one. But in virtually all cases, the U.S. government chose to ignore or downplay our ally's objections until the eleventh hour.[8]

In this respect, Washington appeared to act toward Saigon as it had generally done with smaller wartime allies. As Henry Kissinger observed of this pattern of behavior in a footnote, ironically, to his famous *Foreign Affairs* article on "The Vietnam Negotiations":

Clashes with our allies in which both sides claim to have been deceived occur so frequently as to suggest structural causes (see Skybolt, the Non-Proliferation Treaty, now the bombing halt). . . .When an issue is fairly abstract — before there is a prospect for an agreement — our diplomats tend to present our view in a bland, relaxed fashion to the ally whose interests are involved but who is not present at the negotiations. The ally responds equally vaguely for three reasons: (a) He may be misled into believing that no decision is imminent and therefore sees no purpose in making an issue; (b) he is afraid that if he forces the issue, the decision will go against him; (c) he hopes the problem will go away because agreement will prove impossible. When agreement seems imminent, American diplomats suddenly go into high gear to gain the acquiescence of the ally. He in turn feels tricked by the very intensity and suddenness of the pressure while we are outraged to learn of objections heretofore not made explicit. This almost guarantees that the ensuing controversy will take place under the most difficult conditions.[9]

Such "structural" problems still bedevil U.S. foreign policy today, especially in the Middle East, and suggest how little the Vietnam experience has changed the way we manage our alliances.

Post-mortems

Post-mortems on the fall of the GVN generally stress the impact of Communist violations of the Paris Agreement in 1973 and 1974 (which made possible the prepositioning of Hanoi's troops and supplies for the 1975 offensive) and the waning political will in the United States to counter these violations.

Such assessments obscure the fact that the GVN collapsed from within despite nearly two decades of massive American support and the steady erosion of Viet Cong control over and support in the countryside. However creative Vietnamese (and, later, American) politicians and advisors were throughout the period, the GVN never outgrew its cabal-like and repressive character. Each of South Vietnam's nine governments (between 1954–75), thus, basically depended for their support on a faction of the military officer corps.

There was a time in the life of each of these regimes, nevertheless, when its authoritarianism seemed a welcome relief from the instability generated by waves of street demonstrations and successive coups. It is important to keep in mind that societies can be immobilized either by anarchy or by the response to it (i.e., repression by police and other security forces). Eventually, there is stagnation, and with it, the tendency for government to come to rest in the hands of an elite group that possesses a monopoly on force. The intervention of the military into politics under these conditions is far from a temporary expedient; hence the "staying power" of such juntas as those in Chile today or in Brazil and Nigeria in the 1970s, and the tendency of "martial law" administrations elsewhere (e.g., Argentina, Turkey, Ghana, the Philippines) to become institutionalized.

For such regimes, stability is an end in itself. Public order — rather than widened political participation — becomes the gauge of its strength. The regime holds on to power by divide-and-conquer tactics; this means that its survival depends on keeping all other political forces weak.

Loyalty First

That President Thieu remained in office so long is, from one perspective, a testament to his effectiveness as a divide-and-conquer tactician and his ability to control the military. But such an approach also prevented Thieu from creating a professional military high command (for fear he would be displaced by it) and required him to assure that all promotion (and access to the perquisites of rank) deepened officers' personal loyalty to him and his most trusted assistants. Thus, despite all the training and support the ARVN got from the United States, its leadership was essentially determined by short-term political considerations and loyalties rather than competence.[10]

Over the long haul, however, countering insurgency requires more than the capacity to maintain public order and prevent coups. In such situations, governments require the active support and cooperation of the people to defeat the insurgent politically and militarily. For the insurgent and his outside allies make two claims that the government cannot refute as long as it refuses to expand political participation: first, that the government lacks legitimacy and second, that it cannot draw support (political, economic, or military) from the population it claims to govern. In such situations, counter-insurgency depends both on what the government can do to prevent the insurgent from making headway through unconventional warfare and on the degree to which the population can be effectively mobilized to the government's cause. The latter task often conflicts directly with what the regime feels it must do to survive against its domestic political rivals. Nowhere was this tension more acute than in Vietnam.

There are limits to the lessons that can and should be learned from Vietnam. The U.S. is unlikely ever to be as deeply involved in a Third World conflict as it was in Southeast Asia in the 1960s. Consequently, much of the operational lesson-learning that has been undertaken by the Pentagon and defense-oriented think tanks will probably not be of great relevance to American policy-makers (and even generals) in the 1980s. But the problem of how to manage our alliances with small states who are threatened by internal struggles (in which external troublemakers are involved) will persist. So also will the question of how we can determine those local conflicts in which U.S. policy and modest actions could make a difference to the outcome.

The Vietnam experience suggests that for a strategy of revolutionary war to succeed, what is required beyond an organized armed struggle movement is massive external support plus the unwitting cooperation of a government that refuses to expand its political base. There are few instances in which the leaders of governments of the type described here find it in their immediate interest to respond positively to demands for the expansion of political participation.[11] Resistance to expanding political participation, instead, has a tendency to become institutionalized. If it does, this could virtually assure that movements of the type Hanoi created will succeed, provided their time horizon (and aid pipeline) is long enough. So the answer to the question of whether U.S. actions can make a difference in internal struggles may well depend on the level of political participation that presently exists in the societies where insurgencies are under way or in prospect.

If this finding is correct, the need for understanding the political capabilities of the ally as well as the enemy may be as important today for U.S. policy-makers planning for contingencies in Central America or the Middle East as, in retrospect, it should have been when the struggle over South Vietnam began. For the U.S. experience in Vietnam suggests that to Sun-Tzu's classic dictum on the "art of war" — "Know yourself; know your enemy. A thousand battles; a thousand victories" — should be added, "Know your ally."

Notes

[1] For a survey of the South Vietnam's major political parties and groups, circa 1969, see Allan E. Goodman, "South Vietnam: Neither War nor Peace," *Asian Survey*, X (February 1970), pp. 124–131.

[2] See Col. Hoang Ngoc Lung, *The General Offensives of 1968–69*, (Washington, D.C.: U.S. Army Center of Military History, 1981) and Lt. Gen. Ngo Quang Truong, *The Easter Offensive of 1972*, (Washington, D.C.: U.S. Army Center of Military History, 1980).

[3] For descriptions of how accommodation worked, see Samuel P. Huntington, "Vietnam: The Bases of Accommodation." *Foreign Affairs*, 46 (July 1968), pp. 642–656, and Allan E. Goodman, "Government and the Countryside: Political Accommodation and South Vietnam's Communal Groups," *ORBIS*, XIII, (Summer 1969), pp. 502–525.

[4] David D. Newsom, "The Challenge of Political Change," Address before the American Whig-Cliosophic Society, Princeton University, March 22, 1979. Mr. Newsom was Undersecretary of State for Political Affairs at the time.

[5] See Robert L. Sansom's study of *The Economics of Insurgency in the Mekong Delta of Vietnam*, (Cambridge, Massachusetts: MIT Press, 1970), especially pp. 160–163.

[6] See Peter Braestrup, *Big Story: How the American Press and Television Reported and Interpreted the Crisis of Tet 1968 in Vietnam and Washington*, (Boulder, Colorado: Westview Press, 1977).

[7] *Politics in War: The Bases of Political Community in South Vietnam*, (Cambridge, Massachusetts: Harvard University Press, 1973), pp. 188–222.

[8] For details, see Allan E. Goodman, *The Lost Peace: America's Search for a Negotiated Settlement of the Vietnam War*, (Stanford, California: Hoover Institution Press, 1978), pp. 132–138 and 147–151.

[9] *Foreign Affairs*, 47 (January 1969), p. 22.

[10] The cost of tolerating a politicized officer corps is a very key point that emerges especially in South Vietnamese post-mortems. See, for example, General Cao Van Vien, et al., *The U.S. Advisor*, (Washington, D.C.: U.S. Army Center of Military History, 1980), especially p. 75.

[11] Such examples would include the experiences of Gandhi and Nehru in India, Mao in China, Magsaysay in the Philippines, Nyerere in Tanzania. For a systematic discussion of the pros and cons involved in expanding political participation, see Samuel P. Huntington and Joan M. Nelson, *No Easy Choice: Political Participation in Developing Countries*, (Cambridge, Massachusetts: Harvard University Press, 1976).

COMMENTARY: The Americans in Saigon

by Vincent H. Demma

I don't think anyone would disagree with Goodman's exhortations to "Know your ally." Few, if any, would contest his assertion that our knowledge and perception of South Vietnamese politics was not always the best informed. But I think it is more debatable whether it follows that our failure in South Vietnam stems in a large measure from our inability or perhaps unwillingness to understand South Vietnamese culture and the limited political capacities of the various leaders in the South who were American-supported. According to Goodman, "lack of American understanding of South Vietnamese political dynamics and culture is probably the single most important explanation of what went wrong with U.S. policy there since our overall strategy and policy, military and diplomatic, was shaped by this ignorance and misunderstanding."

I think there is a kernel of truth in these assertions.

But let me suggest that despite the lapses of our understanding of South Vietnamese political scene and their culture, we did know our ally somewhat better than Goodman suggests, and we were acutely aware of the political limitations of those we allied ourselves with. There is an avalanche of reporting filled with the minutiae of the political life of Saigon and the provinces. Washington was peppered with information detailing the political, familial, religious, regional, professional, ethnic influences impinging on South Vietnamese political dynamics. Close tabs were kept on the activities of Buddhists, students, labor organizations, the sects, and any other grouping in South Vietnam that had the potential for political mischief. General Lansdale submitted eloquently gossipy reports on the comings and goings of South Vietnamese politicians both in and out. American provincial reporters, monthly and quarterly, assessed local political trends.

Rather than an absence of information, let me suggest that the mass of information may well have been indigestible. What might well be the task for students of the Vietnam War now is a more systematic examination of what we did know and perhaps, more important, to what use that information was put, what was available to policy-makers, how much did they know and how much did they use it.

I tend to agree with Goodman that no small measure of American perception of Vietnamese inferiority, or lack of confidence in their military ability, our doubt about their political capacities, did give impetus and help shape up policies and strategies both military and diplomatic.

But I think we might want to explore further whether the influence attributed to these perceptions in the long run was as significant as the degree to which American policies, strategies, and activities in the South influenced and helped foster and reinforce the very political attitudes, traits, and behaviors displayed by the South Vietnamese leaders that militated against broadening political participation and representation.

Although it is somewhat fashionable to talk about the tyranny of weak states over their more powerful allied partners, it may be profitable to examine a bit more closely than did Goodman the degrees to which South Vietnamese policy and strategy were fashioned by American actions, and how American activities exacerbated divisive forces in Vietnamese society. Certainly the operations of American Special Forces among the Montagnards, for example, or the Khmers, only aggravated the tensions that already existed between South Vietnamese officials and these ethnic groups.

No matter how recalcitrant and stubborn the South Vietnamese might have been, in general I think we can say that they were overwhelmed by the American military presence. Their military forces operated on the strategic guidelines and concepts formulated by Americans. And to a large degree, there were Vietnamese leaders who were only too eager to adapt to a style of combat, and to some degree, a managerial style of governing and politics and administration that suited their American patrons. South Vietnamese military and political leaders of whom Goodman speaks may well have been "our" Vietnamese, as Stan Karnow suggests, but they were quite willing to jump into bed with us since American support was a substantial insurance policy against domestic political challenges. As an aside, even with the Vietnamization policy, a policy allegedly turning the war back to the Vietnamese, according to one Vietnamese general who wrote a study of the Vietnamization policy, Vietnamization was a misnomer. That in essence it was really the last stage of the Americanization of the war.

If Americans lacked understanding of Vietnamese political dynamics, Goodman assures us that the Vietnamese leaders at times were equally in the dark about the political aspirations of their own countrymen. And he suggests that there were two lost opportunities when South Vietnamese leaders might have broadened their base of political participation in the South. But the discussion of at least one of these opportunities is incomplete; namely, the Saigon government's response to the Buddhist crisis in the northern provinces in the spring of 1966.

What is lacking here, and I think elsewhere throughout the paper is the instrumental role played by American advisors in fashioning the response to the key governments. Exhorted by Americans to act forcefully and decisively to quash what Americans perceived as a serious if not potentially fatal challenge to Saigon's central authority and the war effort, the South Vietnamese leaders, abetted by American military authorities, took the actions described by Goodman to neutralize the Buddhist struggle movement in northern South Vietnam. Even though we may agree that the Saigon government misread the import of that movement, the government nevertheless responded in a manner that it did under some very intense American pressure. This episode suggests as well the need to further explore the mechanisms through which American advice was proffered to the South Vietnamese.

Goodman is silent on this subject. But it is part and parcel of any attempt to understand the dynamics of our relationship, both military and political, with our ally in Saigon.

I've been enjoined to talk about two of these vehicles.

The consideration to establish a joint command illuminates not only our perceptions of the Vietnamese capabilities, but sheds some light on some aspects of South Vietnamese politics itself.

In all these advisory and joint command arrangements proposed in 1964–65, they all would tend, under certain circumstances, to reduce American flexibility of action, inhibit our disengagement from the South should that be in our national interest. Remember that at that time there was a feeling that another political upheaval might even bring to Saigon a government which was critically anti-American, which might disinvite the Americans out of Saigon; but more important, place the burden of possible failure even more squarely on American shoulders. What was rejected in many instances is even more interesting than what did take place in the U.S. advisory effort.

The American advisory influence for the most part from 1961 to 1967, except for bigger numbers and overcoming earlier Vietnamese resistance to accepting U.S. advisors at the low echelons and at the critical district level, did not change very much. But throughout this period, the advisory efforts tended to be overshadowed, in 1965–67, by the commitment of American ground forces. Let me add that with the advent of new American command arrangements in 1967 for the pacification program, top-level U.S. interest in the advisory effort was revived, but that is another and a much more substantial story.

COMMENTARY: The Village War

by Samuel Popkin

As a political scientist who lived in South Vietnam for several years in villages, studying the war from the bottom up, I would say we should also realize that equally subject to criticism is the whole notion of nation-building as it was practiced in Vietnam, or the way it was taught.

With some embarrassment now I remember all of my innocent zeal when I first got to Vietnam, because I was an undergraduate at MIT when John Kennedy was elected President, and by coincidence, the next day Walt Rostow was scheduled to talk to all the sophomores who were studying sophomore-level social science. To this day I remember how he fired us up when he came into the room and, like an officer getting his troops ready, walked around the room and said, "Right now those communists are out there coming out with new ideas, and if you want to beat them, you'd better hit those books." There was a sense that we'd better work an hour later every night because the Cold War was heating up and we'd better come up with better ideas.

After my first year of living in Vietnamese villages, I came back home with a certain amount of shock and people said to me, "What is the first thing you learned in Vietnam?" And I answered that "baby countries do not have baby politicians." They were not a bunch of innocents waiting to be filled with wonderful American ideas about orderly central government and how things were done. They were people who had their old grudges and their old views and their old ideas and most of the time had intelligent, complicated reasons for doing things.

I lived in a set of villages throughout the Delta and some dangerous areas for a year before the Communists' 1968 Tet Offensive, and for eight months in two different areas after the Tet Offensive. There was a really extraordinary change of attitudes that occurred in the countryside. By the time of the Tet Offensive, most villages in the Delta had TV sets. So besides seeing (later) the first American walk on the moon, and besides seeing a certain amount of soap opera, people saw a certain number of piles of bodies laid out like cordwood around the streets of Saigon. And basically, the attitude in the villages where I lived was that this was a total collapse on the part of the Communists. And as one village chief put it to me: "The Communists caught ARVN with their pants down, and they caught the Americans napping, and they still couldn't pull it off."

Before the Tet Offensive, 18-year-old villagers would lie and say they were 13 to get out of the draft; after the Tet Offensive, 13- and 14-year-olds would lie and say they were 18 to get into the draft before the Communists got to them. The perceptions of the craziness of what the Communists were doing was increased, and the idea that they were inevitable winners was so deflated that people changed very much how they felt.

At the very end, in 1975, when researchers talked with the refugees fleeing from the North — a work, interestingly enough, commissioned by the *Washington Post* which they then never published [but was published later as a book under the title

Why They Fled], it was total fear of the Communists and the way they behaved during the Tet Offensive that occasioned most of the refugee flow from northern South Vietnam.

There was a tendency on the side of Americans to think about land reform or economic reform, little bits of change. When you've had a war that's gone on for 10, 15, 20 years, the important political issue is the war. How you fight the war is the main political issue. More important than whether you get a little more land or a little less land is who's being bombed, who is being drafted, who's being arrested, who's being interrogated, who interrogates whom. All this is much more of a political issue in the villages than an economic issue.

It is part of the cultural condescensions or almost racism sometimes on the American side, that we are willing to give the peasants only credit for being concerned with bread and their bowl of rice. But the overwhelming repudiation of Indira Gandhi in India, or the reaction of the Chinese peasantry to the relaxation after the cultural revolution, showed that peasants in their way, as much as anybody else, have deep concerns that would be best called civil liberties or human rights.

They may not care about how many parties there are, they might not care about the shape of the government, but the ability to move around, the ability to talk openly and freely, these issues of civil liberties are as important there as they are anywhere in the world.

Our Army has ignored, and still does in its training, all the way in which how wars are fought affect governments of both sides in an internal war. Very briefly, how you fight a war, in an internal war as opposed to a war between nations, has tremendous implicatons for the ability of your enemy to recruit. Something that never dawned on our strategists: The ability of NLF, the ability of the North Vietnamese to mobilize, was greatly affected by how we fought the war.

Even more important, how we fought the war had tremendous implications, still not fully realized, for the kinds of governments that could be built, or the kinds of political issues that needed to be considered in Vietnam for the government of Vietnam to be legitimate. If America had fought the war in Vietnam as if defending peasants was as important as killing Communists, we would have done better at both.

When it comes to the advisory effort and the way we looked at the government of Vietnam, I would say that from top to bottom, and especially on the military side, we generally confused what looked to us like technical recommendations with political recommendations. We never understood the politics behind why there were or were not battlefield promotions. Or why there were or were not local troops allowed into field hospitals, or who became an officer and why.

We never understood the contradiction between South Vietnamese individuals' desire to stay in power in Saigon and our not caring who was in power as long as somebody was in power other than the Communists.

Let me mention the dogs that didn't bark — some of the unobtrusive things that give some interesting perspective on Vietnam compared to Afghanistan, El Salvador, or some other revolutionary wars. In Afghanistan, it's commonly noted in the press that if a Russian soldier goes to a bar and gets drunk, and then goes out behind the bar to relieve himself, he's likely to get his throat slit.

In contrast, during the Tet Offensive in Vietnam, hundreds if not thousands of Americans got trapped in civilian neighborhoods all over Vietnam and, literally without exception, these people were protected and hidden, and were never found by the NLF or the North Vietnamese during the offensive. In Vietnam, villagers with impunity could talk freely about their criticisms or their dislike of the government, the ways they disapproved about what the Americans were doing. They could stand up and talk openly. In contrast, in Central America today, if anybody stands up in a village and says something nasty about the government, he's likely to have a bullet through his head before he can sit down. There were no death squads in Vietnam.

In the 1945–49 Chinese civil war, it was common for whole government units to defect to the Communist side. No ARVN unit defected in Vietnam, although a few times an NLF unit opened tentative negotiations to consider defecting the other way.

There were very few times that American civilian offices (e.g., the USIA building in Hue) were ever attacked by rampaging mobs in any show of real displeasure.

All of this suggests that the notion of popular support for the communist revolution, or popular opposition to some American presence, was vastly overstated during the war. That doesn't suggest necessarily that the war was winnable, but it suggests perhaps how small a factor in the end, if you're going to have a viable political system, is the support of the masses as opposed to the kind of local elite you have running things.

The only leader I see having legitimacy in the Indochinese refugee community in America who was the darling of the Americans during the war is General Van Pao [the leader of the Meo irregulars in Laos], whose speeches on cassettes are passed around through the mail, whose attitudes on how to adapt marriage practices to life in the United States are taken seriously throughout the Laotian emigre community. I see former South Vietnamese Vice President Nguyen Cao Ky with his liquor store a few miles away in the Los Angeles area not exactly welcome. I don't see young teenage Vietnamese going to sit at his feet and learn wisdom about the future — which says something about some of our problems with allied politicians.

We have not fully appreciated how hard it is to lead when you're having explosions of demands for political participation in a country and these are simply inevitable, given the pressure that war produces. In Vietnam, the overthrow of the social system, the U.S. money coming in. Anybody who was going to be a putative leader in a situation like that had the extraordinary burden, with no real experience, of having to satisfy two constituencies. In effect, you had to run for election both in South Vietnam and in Washington. That's extraordinarily difficult, and very often maybe Washington had too many votes.

DISCUSSION

DIEM: The American objective in building a South Vietnamese political structure was always to win the war; everything was subordinated to this. The American intervention was indeed overwhelming. As a friend of Ambassador Bunker, we often talked about the political situation in South Vietnam, and he would suggest necessary reforms which the GVN should carry out in order to survive. I agreed with many of his ideas, but he never understood why I could not prevail upon Thieu as he might influence Washington in his consultations with American officials. But while I was aware of Washington's perspective on the internal situation in South Vietnam, as Thieu's appointee, I had absolutely no independent status as an advisor, and Saigon would not listen to me.

KARNOW: We were in Vietnam for our own purposes. On many occasions, perhaps most occasions, our purposes were different from the purposes and the goals of the South Vietnamese government. That conflict of goals persisted and when we finally decided that we had to get out of Vietnam, we got out, because that's when our goals, our imperatives, prevailed. This is the basis for the constant conflict that was going on between South Vietnamese sovereignty and American interests. It raises the question of how does one face this sort of problem in the future?

LOMPERIS: Given Thieu's inability to handle the insurgency, should the United States in the future be more reluctant to intervene in internal wars?

MURRAY: We not only baffled the Vietnamese, we baffled ourselves. With the cease-fire, we offered the Vietnamese inferior military equipment under the ENHANCE-PLUS program, which the ARVN did not want.

AVERY: In what way did the 1963 Buddhist rebellion and the overthrow of Diem influence American perceptions and reactions in 1966?

BLAUFARB: What could the United States have done to convince Thieu that broadening his government did not mean political suicide?

WEBB: Contrary to Popkin, I never saw any televisions, let alone electricity or plumbing, in my year in Vietnamese villages from which peasants could have received impressions of the Tet offensive. What really motivated the peasantry was fear.

GOODMAN: As I concluded the paper, I suggested that one of the most important foreign policy challenges that the U.S. government will face in the 1980s is how to conduct the relationship with the smaller ally in such a way that, if the leader falls, we don't.

To relate that thought to the questions raised is perhaps the least-studied part of the whole Vietnam experience since 1975 and may be the most significant, namely, the relationship between us and our partner, ridden with clichés though it may be.

I remain skeptical, but not entirely skeptical, that even if there had been effective political leadership at any point in Saigon, and effective military leadership in all of the ARVN divisions throughout the countryside, that would have been sufficient for a different outcome or for the achievement of either our objective or the South Vietnamese objective.

I'm still struck by the intractability of political problems presented by a society as complex as South Vietnam, and the military problems presented by a situation where your adversary has basically unlimited time horizons, unlimited external support, and two entire countries as sanctuaries to conduct a 10-year offensive, a 50-year offensive, but he won't give up, whereas we will.

Nevertheless, I think that the [American-Vietnamese] relationship is a very important element of what went wrong with our policy. I would suggest that maybe a way to focus in the research is to look first of all at the divisions that existed with the U.S. government over the issue of accommodation by the Saigon government to its non-communist opponents in the pre-Tet 1968 period. And whether that problem so influenced our outlook that we thought maybe we ought to take the effort over, the effort of nation-building, the effort of winning the hearts and minds because "it's obvious that Saigon can't do it."

Similarly, to the question of whether or not there were differences in outlook between levels in the U.S. government over the relations with Saigon and the Vietnamese in general, I suggest that another fruitful period to look at would be the post-Tet, new optimism period [in late 1968]. Some of the statistics were read to us yesterday. What impact the new optimism, the new statistics, the rise of John Paul Vann, his access to LBJ in certain critical moments, whether that also had the kind of impact that could explain the policies we adopted. There was a non-communist political base out in the villages in which Popkin and I lived, and the GVN wasn't capturing them, and that was the fundamental problem that we faced on the political score.

The Buddhist question — how Saigon and Washington dealt with Buddhist dissidents in 1965–67 — is something very important for the 1980s, not just the '60s. We have to learn to work overseas with religious fundamentalists, radicals, fanatics, whose objectives in certain levels and certain senses may be very different than our own. We have a precursor here of the kinds of situation we might find ourselves faced with in the future.

I think the problem all along was less a problem of what we could have said or done to Thieu or to Ky than the fact that at the top, we picked or were associated with or were over-identified with the wrong guys, the wrong leaders. We had the persons who didn't have what it took to achieve either their objectives, beyond staying in power, or our objectives: withdrawal, a decent interval, the winding down of our commitment. This goes back to the question of how do we work in countries where leaders like that have to fall, or will fall, or should fall, so that we don't fall with them.

What really deserves a new look is the concept of nation-building simultaneously with the concept of counter-insurgency. Maybe the terms are wrong. The phenomena that we're talking about are no less relevant today than they were when the struggle for Vietnam began. The two efforts have to be related, to respond to Ambassador Diem's point, and I don't think we have much in the way of inside wisdom to apply to that problem.

III LESSONS AND NON-LESSONS OF THE U.S. EXPERIENCE IN VIETNAM

PAPERS AND DISCUSSIONS

LESSONS: A SOLDIER'S VIEW

by Harry G. Summers, Jr.

A story made the rounds of the Army during the closing days of the Vietnam War. When the Nixon administration took over in 1969, so the story goes, Pentagon officials fed all the data on North Vietnam and the United States into a computer: population, gross national product, manufacturing capacity, size of the armed forces, and the like. The computer was then asked: "When will we win?" It took only a moment to answer: "You won in 1964!"

From the American professional soldier's perspective, the most frustrating aspect of the Vietnam conflict is that the U.S. armed forces did everything they were supposed to do, winning every major battle of the war, yet North Vietnam, rather than the United States, triumphed in the end. How could U.S. troops have succeeded so well, but the war effort have failed so miserably?

Some historians, notably Herbert Y. Schandler, have blamed President Lyndon Baines Johnson's refusal to curtail his Great Society programs to meet the needs of wartime. That is only part of the answer. Even if Johnson had chosen between "guns and butter," Schandler himself observes, no amount of men and firepower could have won the war without a coherent White House war strategy.

Others, such as historian Russell F. Weigley, argue that America's failure was tactical, an attempt to apply conventional military doctrines to a "revolutionary" war. But the U.S. and South Vietnamese forces decimated the Viet Cong guerrillas after Hanoi's 1968 Tet Offensive, and the Communists emerged victorious only in the spring of 1975, after the Americans went home, when Hanoi launched a conventional armored assault upon the South.

Few Army officers who served in Vietnam accept the simplistic explanation that a collapse of national will, or a home-front "stab in the back" fostered by the New Left and the news media, made this country lose the war. Older officers tend to blame civilian leaders, notably Defense Secretary Robert S. McNamara, while younger men criticize senior generals, notably General William C. Westmoreland, the U.S. field commander.

The causes of U.S. failure, in my view, are more complicated. And they start at the top.

First of all, President Johnson made a conscious political decision not to mobilize the American people for war. This was a fundamental mistake. (Among other things, Johnson had forgotten that the attempt to fight a war in Korea in 1950–53 without a congressional declaration of war had helped to cripple the Truman Presidency.) This misjudgment of the nature of limited war was highlighted by McNamara, who was quoted as saying that Vietnam was "developing an ability in the United States to fight a limited war, to go to war without the necessity of arousing the public ire."

Why was this approach adopted?

Civilian limited-war theorists such as Robert Osgood and Thomas Schelling had (falsely) postulated that the existence of nuclear weapons had entirely changed the nature and conduct of warfare and that all past battlefield experiences were thus irrelevant. Political leaders, the academic theorists seemed to contend, should tightly control the conduct of a limited war, "fine-tuning" while ignoring public opinion and the demands of the fighting men if necessary. As defense analyst Stephen Peter Rosen observes, such arguments, widely echoed, helped to persuade the Vietnam-era generation of policy-makers — particularly McNamara, National Security Adviser McGeorge Bundy, and President Johnson himself — to think of limited war as an *instrument* of diplomacy, of bargaining with the enemy, rather than as a bitter struggle in which the nation invested blood and treasure to secure important goals.[1]

War as Theory

Largely accepting this approach during the 1964–66 build-up in Vietnam, LBJ and his civilian advisers stressed the dispatch of "signals" to the enemy rather than military measures to win the war. They avoided seemingly risky strategic decisions that could have ended the war.

"I saw our bombs as my political resources for negotiating a peace," Johnson later explained to political scientist Doris Kearns. "On the one hand, our planes and our bombs could be used as carrots for the South, strengthening the morale of the South Vietnamese and pushing them to clean up their corrupt house, by demonstrating the depth of our commitment to the war. On the other hand, our bombs could be used as sticks against the North, pressuring North Vietnam to stop its aggression against the South."

Washington's overall defensive stance in Indochina surrendered the long-range initiative to the enemy and, inevitably, alienated the American public. In effect, Lyndon Johnson limited not only his objectives in the war, but the military and political means employed to attain them. Fearing Communist Chinese intervention,[2] the President variously declared that he would restrict the bombing to the southern portions of North Vietnam, that U.S. troops would never invade the North, and that the United States would under no circumstances use nuclear weapons. He forbade U.S. ground commanders to interfere with crucial Communist base areas and reinforcement routes in neighboring Laos and Cambodia; in short, he chose to treat South Vietnam as an "island."

Johnson did not apply political pressure upon the Soviet Union to stop its materiel support of North Vietnam, without which the war would have soon ended. His successor, Richard Nixon, took firm action during Hanoi's 1972 Easter Offensive, sharply increasing the bombing against the North and mining Haiphong harbor. But he refused to take such decisive steps in 1969 to end the war, partly because he feared such bold action would endanger the budding U.S. rapprochement with China and détente with the Soviet Union. (He secretly bombed Hanoi's bases in Cambodia instead.)

In sum, the civilian policy-makers failed to understand what most ordinary Americans know in their bones: *War*, whether limited or not, imposes a unique national effort. It has its own imperatives, its own dynamic. It requires the undivided attention and dedication of the President, the Congress, and the citizenry. The President, in particular, has the duty to define the aims of the war, to fix a military strategy for success, and to clarify for the American people why they and their sons should be willing to make major sacrifices.

As Dean Rusk stated in 1976, "We never made any effort to create a war psychology in the United States during the Vietnam affair. We didn't have military parades through cities. . . .We tried to do in cold blood perhaps what can only be done in hot blood, when sacrifices of this order are involved."

Unlike North Vietnam, the United States never focused its full attention on the war. President Johnson believed that destiny had chosen him to transform America through his Great Society programs, and that the country could simultaneously afford guns and butter. "I knew from the start," Johnson confided to Kearns in 1970 about the early weeks of 1965, "that I was bound to be crucified either way I moved. If I left the woman I really loved — the Great Society — in order to get involved in that bitch of a war on the other side of the world, then I would lose everything at home. All my programs. All my hopes to feed the hungry and shelter the homeless. . . .I was determined to be a leader of war *and* a leader of peace."

Don't Alarm The Home Folks

In addition to refusing to cut back his domestic programs as the war began, the President failed to seek a congressional declaration of war against North Vietnam, to call up the reserves, or to ask for a tax increase until 1967.[3]

The Johnson administration also sought to disguise the cost and impact of the Vietnam effort by engaging in a slow and incremental build-up of the air war and U.S. combat forces. Demonstrating strength and determination to the enemy — without alarming the home folks — became the primary aim of Washington's early policy in Vietnam.

By increasing air sorties over the North from 55,000 in 1965 to 148,000 in 1966, for instance, U.S. policy-makers entertained few illusions about turning the tide: In 1966, the bombing cost the United States $9.60 for every $1 of damage inflicted upon the enemy, to say nothing of American pilots lost in action. Rather, they thought the growing air effort would convey the strength of the U.S. commitment to South Vietnam.

Similarly, William Bundy, then Assistant Secretary of State, favored sending U.S. troops to the northern provinces of South Vietnam in January 1965 because "it would have a real stiffening effect in Saigon, and a strong signal effect to Hanoi." But gradualism in the air and on the ground proved poor psycho-strategy. It was also poor politics: Congress and the public never mobilized for war.

The Vietnam War made clear that Congress should declare war whenever large numbers of U.S troops engage in sustained combat abroad. As General West-moreland later wrote, "President Johnson. . .should have forced the Congress to face its constitutional responsibility for waging war." Following Communist attacks against U.S. bases (at Pleiku, in February 1965), Johnson probably could have obtained a congressional declaration of war against North Vietnam, thereby slowing the rise of later opposition from Congress. And if Johnson had failed to win a congressional mandate, he at least would not have felt compelled by fears of right-wing criticism to commit U.S. combat troops to South Vietnam's defense. In both cases, the country would have shared in the debate and in the decision.

By failing to bring the public and the Congress into the war effort, Johnson drove a wedge between the Army and large segments of the populace, notably intellectuals and college students. Even in the eyes of many moderate critics, the armed forces and the GIs in combat soon became the executors of "Johnson's war," rather than the instruments of the national will. For future presidents, the War Powers Act of 1973, which bars presidential commitment of U.S. troops in combat beyond 90 days without congressional approval, partially solves this problem. But only partially. It does not necessarily force the President to mobilize the entire nation.

Back to Basics

Thus, as the Constitution envisions, the civilian leadership — the President and the Congress — must make the basic decisions about going to war and define the war's objectives. For their part, the nation's senior military leaders have the obligation to devise the strategy necessary for success — as they did in World War II and Korea. During the Indochina conflict, the U.S. Joint Chiefs of Staff (JCS) did not play this role. Unlike all his wartime predecessors, the President allowed civilian strategists with little or no combat experience to take charge, as if their "cost-benefit" or "psychological" approaches were superior to the insights of the military commanders. One result: From June 1965 to June 1966, as U.S. troop strength in Vietnam grew from 60,000 to 268,000, the President met privately with his Army Chief of Staff, General Harold K. Johnson, only twice.

Seeking always to "keep their options open," the civilian leaders never determined the maximum number of troops that the United States *should* commit to Vietnam, let alone a plan to win the war. For example, despite strong reservations expressed by Under Secretary of State George W. Ball and National Security Adviser Bundy, McNamara persuaded Johnson in July 1965 to approve a build-up of U.S. troops in South Vietnam to more than 200,000 men without any assurance that that number would suffice to shore up the beleaguered Saigon regime, let alone to defeat the Communist forces decisively on the battlefield. At the Pentagon, during the Tet 1968 crisis, Defense Secretary Clark M. Clifford discovered that he "couldn't get hold of a plan to win the war. [When] I attempted to find out how long it would take to achieve our goal, there was no answer. When I asked how many more men it would take. . .no one could be certain."

Westmoreland, despairing of winning White House approval of the higher troop levels that he believed necessary to win the war, had received much the same impression in Washington in late 1967 when he proposed — and proclaimed — a strategy for Vietnamization. "The [Johnson] administration was totally noncommittal on it," he later wrote. "They kind of nodded their heads and did not disagree."

The Joint Chiefs, led by General Earle Wheeler, strongly questioned the White House's approach in private, but Johnson (and Nixon) rarely consulted them directly. The Chiefs acquiesced in presidential mismanagement of the war, even allowing Johnson to set weekly bombing targets in North Vietnam; they hoped for better days. But the military leaders could have best served their country in early 1965 by dramatically protesting against the President's policies. By quietly threatening to resign, for instance, the Chiefs might have forced the Commander-in-Chief to adopt a winning strategy in Indochina — notably, by cutting the Ho Chi Minh Trail and isolating the southern battlefield. Or, failing that, the JCS could have brought the dispute before the American people and spurred a national debate on the war *before* a major commitment put a half-million U.S. troops into battle *without* a strategy.[4]

In any event, the military leaders should not have echoed Washington's euphemisms — "kill ratio," "neutralize," "incursion" — to disguise the bloody realities of combat. General Fred Weyand argued in 1976 that as

> military professionals we must speak out, we must counsel our political leaders and alert the American public that there is no such thing as a "splendid little war." There is no such thing as a war fought on the cheap. War is death and destruction. The American way of war is particularly violent, deadly and dreadful. We believe in using "things" — artillery, bombs, massive firepower — in order to conserve our soldiers' lives. The enemy, on the other hand, made up for his lack of "things" by expending men instead of machines, and he suffered enormous casualties. . . .The Army must make the price of involvement clear *before* we get involved, so that America can weigh the probable costs of involvement against the dangers of uninvolvement. . .for there are worse things than war.

In the field, the military's role is to destroy the enemy's forces and its will to fight, even in an allegedly "revolutionary" conflict, as the North Vietnamese proved conclusively in their spring 1975 blitzkrieg. In my view, the U.S. Army should never have become so heavily engaged in "nation-building," pacification, and, thus, local politics as it did in South Vietnam. The South Vietnamese Army and the Saigon government, perhaps with the aid of the U.S. Embassy, could have conducted the struggle for the "hearts and minds" of the South Vietnamese people. In any case, this struggle, so heavily publicized by Washington, was *secondary*. As events made abundantly clear, the troops of the North Vietnamese Army, not the southerners of the Viet Cong, posed the primary threat to South Vietnam's independence, and eliminating that danger should have been the chief concern of both the U.S. Army and the White House from the start.

Empty Threats

Even as it alienated or confused Americans at home, the gradualist and almost timid manner in which the United States had waged the war surely eroded its diplomats' credibility when talks began in Paris in 1968. The Americans and their allies could not conduct successful negotiations — successful in the sense of securing a withdrawal of Hanoi's troops from the South with residual U.S. air power serving as a deterrent against future invasion from the North — from a position of weakness. No one could. President Johnson's nine unilateral U.S. cease-fires and 10 bombing halts during 1965–68 had only earned the enemy's contempt, as Hanoi's repeated cease-fire violations and accelerated transport of supplies over the Ho Chi Minh Trail during these episodes demonstrated.

And by announcing in June 1969 that the United States would begin withdrawing its troops without any *quid pro quo* from the enemy, President Nixon similarly signaled a lack of resolve to Hanoi that probably encouraged the enemy to stall the negotiating process, in the expectation of an eventual total American pullout.

Predictably, "Vietnamization" proved an empty threat since no President could guarantee perpetual U.S. aid to the vulnerable South Vietnamese, let alone the re-entry of American naval and air power into the region in the event of renewed North Vietnamese aggression from Laos and Cambodia.

In war, negotiations with the adversary cannot be a *substitute* for a coherent military strategy. To Americans, weary of bloodshed, negotiations with North Vietnam seemed to promise an end to the war. But Hanoi's unwillingness in 1968–72 to reach a compromise with Saigon, rather than the presence of U.S. ground troops or Saigon's intransigence, posed the key obstacle to a peaceful settlement in South Vietnam. Always hoping that a "reasonable" (i.e., painless) settlement was possible, the Johnson and Nixon administrations sought "honorable" conditions for American extrication, which, in the end, amounted only to the release of Americans held prisoner by Hanoi and a "decent interval" for the South Vietnamese ally we left behind.

War may be too serious a matter to leave solely to military professionals, but it is also too serious a matter to leave only to civilian amateurs. Never again must the president commit American men to combat without first fully defining the nation's aims and then rallying Congress and the nation for war. Otherwise, the courageous Americans who fought and died in the defense of South Vietnam will truly have done so in vain.

NOTES

[1] "Vietnam and the American Theory of Limited War," *International Security* 7, Fall 1982.

[2] But CIA estimates in 1965–67 belittled this possibility: Little love was lost between Hanoi and Beijing, and the Chinese would only enter the war if the U.S. invaded North Vietnam.

[3] Truman did not ask for a declaration of war against North Korea in 1950, but he did mobilize reserves, seek price controls, ask for tax increases, and curb domestic programs.

[4] LBJ worried about keeping the generals in line. Indeed, he once told Westmoreland, "General, I have a lot riding on you. . . .I hope you don't pull a MacArthur on me." Westmoreland, *A Soldier Reports*, Doubleday, 1976, p. 159.

REFLECTIONS ON "LESSONS" FROM VIETNAM

by Russell F. Weigley

Military men, we have so often been told, are forever preparing to refight the last war. It would be more accurate to charge them with preparing to refight the last *satisfactory* war.

However often it may be claimed that the American armed forces were not defeated in Indochina and that it was the political and not the military phase of the war that the United States lost, the conflict in Indochina was hardly a satisfactory one for the American military. Even the Korean War has been much more pleasant for American soldiers to contemplate in retrospect; whether the outcome in Korea was victorious may be debatable, but at least the conflict was readily understandable in terms of conventional American military education and theory. The last fully satisfactory war that American military men fought, however, was World War II, a conflict in which the conventional, preferred American tactics and strategy led to an indisputable triumph, the surrender of our adversaries.

In using the study of past wars to seek lessons for the tactics and strategies of future wars, the American military have displayed a strong tendency to shunt aside the unpleasant Indochina experience and the doubtful Korean experience as aberrations, and to return to the study of World War II in the hope that the next war may prove to be World War II writ large, presumably equally satisfactory in methods of combat and in outcome.

In suggesting much this same argument more tentatively as long ago as 1977, I surveyed the pages of *The Professional Journal of the U.S. Army*, as *Military Review* subtitles itself, for the then-preceding year, 1976. I found that so soon after the close of the Indochina War, *Military Review*, as the army's professional journal and more specifically as the organ of the Command and General Staff College at Fort Leavenworth, published almost no critical assessment of unconventional war throughout the year, while in contrast there was a major emphasis on historical and prospective studies looking toward large-scale conventional conflict on the World War II model.[1]

The emphasis in *Military Review* has not changed: In 1981 and at the time of this writing in 1982, again the focus of the army's professional thought as reflected in this journal — and less systematic surveys of other professional military journals suggest the same conclusion — has been on types of conflict reminiscent of World War II, while there has been remarkably little critical study of the Indochina War or acknowledgment of the possibility of similar wars in the future. The troubles of Central America seem to have exerted only the slightest push toward rethinking unconventional or counter-insurgency war. Military thinking about possible intervention in the Middle East has tended to emphasize logistical issues that, difficult though they are, bear a comforting similarity to the problems of long-distance warfare in the Pacific Ocean in 1941–1945.[2]

The brief American romanticization of guerrilla warfare, counter-insurgency warfare, the Green Berets, and all that during the Kennedy administration no doubt had its simple-minded and even ludicrously faddish aspects. Is it not equally faddish, however, equally a surrender to the fashions of a particular time, to neglect serious military study of the Indochina experience with unconventional war in the hope that such a war will never recur for the United States?

One recalls with dismay that long before the Indochina War, the United States Army's institutional memory had virtually expelled from recall the Philippine Insurrection of 1899–1902, apparently on the ground that this kind of guerrilla war of national liberation waged in a tropical climate and across rugged terrain was not likely to recur for Americans anyway. The experiences of the Philippine Insurrection eventually proved to resemble those in Indochina closely enough that a modicum of familiarity with their history might have been useful to our military planners during the 1960s, but the modicum was scarcely to be found.

Forgetting the Past

Still, such deficiencies in the U.S. Army's institutional memory are not new: The military leaders confronting the Philippine Insurrection might in turn have benefited from a knowledge of the counter-guerrilla operations of the Second Seminole War of 1835–1842, but they possessed little such knowledge. The U.S. army has persistently, over generations, refused to contemplate seriously the prospect of any kind of war except conventional warfare in the European style. When the Army has nevertheless had to participate in unconventional, insurrectionary, or guerrilla wars, the experiences have soon been dismissed as aberrant. Indeed, throughout a long history of warfare against the North American Indians, the Army never bothered to develop a doctrine fitted to the particular problems of Indian war as such conflict differed from European war; even in the wake of George Armstrong Custer's disaster on the Little Big Horn, the preoccupation of the Army's nascent professional school system was with Europe.[3]

At first viewing, Colonel Harry G. Summers's book *On Strategy: A Critical Analysis of the Vietnam War* certainly seems to run counter to these tendencies to evade the military problems raised by unconventional wars in general and by the Indochina War in particular.[4] Here we have a member of the Strategic Studies Institute of the Army War College, manifestly working with the encouragement of his associates in that and other centers of official Army strategic thought, attempting not only to come to grips with the strategic and operational issues posed by the American experience in Indochina, but to assure the fullest and most enduring understanding of that experience by placing it in the mainstream of military history through the application to it of the perspectives and insights of Clausewitzian strategic thought. Summers has taken upon himself a task as formidable as it is potentially useful if we are to reject the temptation to think only about past satisfactory wars. Unfortunately, the reader of *On Strategy* has to question whether Colonel Summers has not produced yet another evasion of unpleasant truths, albeit the evasion is this time obscured by the trappings of a tough-minded, unblinking analysis.

Colonel Summers's most fundamental contention is that the strategic and operational errors committed by the United States in Indochina sprang from a misconception of the very nature of the war. Carl von Clausewitz's advice for statesmen and military commanders in any war is "to establish. . .the kind of war on which they are embarking; neither mistaking it for, nor trying to turn it into, something that is alien to its nature."[5] Summers believes that American statesmen and soldiers failed to establish correctly the kind of war on which they were embarking in Indochina.

By the beginning of the 1960s, he argues, the concept of massive nuclear retaliation as the basis of American strategy had created a "doctrinal vacuum" within the army; army leaders grappled unsuccessfully with the problem of finding a role for their service under the umbrella of massive retaliation.[6] Into this doctrinal vacuum both our Communist adversaries, with N. S. Khrushchev's promise of Soviet support for "wars of national liberation," and various influential Americans, notably President Kennedy, thrust the idea of communist revolutionary war as the nuclear-age military threat with which the army remained particularly fit to deal. Not only was revolutionary war, however, a threat seemingly appropriate to counter-action by the army, and thus a concept able to restore a major role for the army. More than that, many American statesmen and soldiers regarded countering communist revolutionary struggle as waging a "new kind of war."

Misperceptions

To this type of struggle, traditional principles of war did not necessarily apply. President Kennedy insisted "that guerrilla fighting was a special art," and also "that future promotions of high-ranking officers would depend upon their experience in the counter-guerrilla or sub-limited war field."[7]

With the rejection of previous military experience and principles to fight the "new kind of war," Summers contends, "Counter-insurgency became not so much the Army's doctrine as the Army's dogma, and (as nuclear weapons had done earlier) stultified military strategic thinking for the next decade."[8] Yet it is Summers's conviction that the war the United States entered in Indochina was not a new kind of war and not primarily a distinctively revolutionary struggle. At the outset, therefore, Americans misperceived the nature of the Indochina War, and a host of further debilitating errors flowed directly from that initial error.

". . .the basic mistake [of the Americans]," says Summers, "was that we saw their [the enemy's] guerrilla operations as a strategy in itself."[9] In fact, he argues, after the assassination of President Ngo Dinh Diem in November 1963, North Vietnam altered the strategy of the war. It transformed the conflict from revolutionary struggle into essentially a conventional war, in which the guerrilla forces would be only auxiliaries. Summers quotes with approval from Brigadier General Dave R. Palmer, who said, "By committing its regular forces to a cause which had previously been cloaked in the guise of an internal war, Hanoi dramatically altered the entire thrust and scope of the conflict."[10]

At this point in the war, Summers contends, the United States should have countered conventional war by means of classical strategy and taken the offensive against the new backbone of the enemy's strategy, which was the North Vietnamese regular army. At best, the United States should have mounted a strategic offensive into North Vietnam; but since such a strategy would not have been consistent with the American policy of containment rather than destruction of Communist power, at least the United States should have taken the tactical initiative to isolate the battlefield. Instead, "We thought we were pursuing a new strategy called counter-insurgency, but actually we were pursuing a defensive strategy in pursuit of a negative aim. . . ."[11]

Vietnam as World War II?

Not least among the advantages that Summers believes would have accrued from a proper conception of the war would have been the ability of the American government and armed forces to sustain support for the war among the American people. Not only did the concept of Communist revolutionary war as a new kind of war, says Summers, "fail to fit the realities of the war, it did not fit the perceptions of the American people. To the man in the street, taking and holding terrain was winning; abandoning terrain to the enemy after it had been won at great cost (as at Khe Sanh), was losing. Their intuitive feelings toward war ultimately proved more accurate than the more sophisticated models of their leaders. For North Vietnam's final blitzkrieg in 1975 more closely resembled the fall of France in 1940, with its disintegrating armies unable to regroup or maneuver because of refugee-packed roads, than it did any model of revolutionary war."[12]

Part of this assessment is uncomfortably on target — especially the remark about the futility of the Khe Sanh battles. Another part of it, however, goes astray by confusing two different wars — the final North Vietnamese onslaught against the South, and the American war in Indochina from 1965 to 1973; here Summers betrays again the military tendency to want to think once more in terms of World War II. But more than that, it is with his argument about the possibility of sustaining American public support that we can find Colonel Summers's analysis becoming an evasion of the truth about the Indochina War rather than the tough-minded critique it claims to be.

Colonel Summers wants to persuade us that with the right kind of American strategy, the Indochina War could have been won. To make that argument, he has to persuade us also that the American government could have prevailed upon the public to stay the course, to support the war consistently and long enough to see it to a successful conclusion. To that end, he argues that public support was lost largely because the government had engaged in a misguided effort to sugarcoat the war, to make it appear that war can be waged without cruelty and almost without pain. When nevertheless the American people inevitably became aware of the true ugliness that the Indochina War shared with every other war, they felt a deep revulsion and their support for the war flagged.

> We did not kill the enemy, we "inflicted casualties"; we did not destroy things, we "neutralized targets." These evasions allowed the notion to grow that we could apply military force in a sanitary and surgical manner. In so doing we unwittingly prepared the way for the reaction that was to follow.
>
> We had concealed from the American people the true nature of war at precisely the time that television brought its realities into their living rooms in living color.[13]

This interpretation drastically oversimplifies the problem of maintaining public support for war. It ignores the broad and deep opposition that developed against every prolonged American war except World War II. It repeats the error, so common during and after the Indochina War, that regards the relative unanimity of American public support for World War II as the norm, and a public opinion divided over the issues of war as abnormal. In fact, it was the manner of our involvement in World War II — the seemingly unprovoked Japanese attack on Pearl Harbor — and the undoubted monstrousness of the enemy (at least of Hitler and the Nazis) that made the war of 1941–45 the exception to a historical pattern of major political opposition to every other American war that lasted more than a few months and imposed heavy casualties.

Let's Pretend

The Revolution, the War of 1812, and the American Civil War all came close to being lost by the United States because public support nearly collapsed. Only the weakness of the enemy prevented the Mexican War from falling into the same category. The rule that applies is John E. Mueller's dictum that the longer the war and the more the American casualties, the less public support remains.[14] Equally applicable is General George C. Marshall's dictum that "A democracy cannot fight a Seven Years' War."[15] Marshall offered that rule for World War II; even a war begun with the Japanese attack on Pearl Harbor and waged against Hitler could not, in Marshall's judgment, have remained popular if it had become unduly prolonged. To believe that public support for the Indochina War could have been assured by more astute manipulation of information is to pursue a chimera.

To be sure, Colonel Summers also argues that if his strategic and tactical prescriptions had been followed, the war in Indochina need not have been prolonged. But his reasoning here depends on his contention that from the time of the assassination of President Diem onward, and certainly throughout the large-scale American involvement, the Indochina War was already mainly a conflict of regular armies, more closely resembling World War II "than it did any model of revolutionary war." Is not this contention, however, precisely an example of focusing military study not on the last war but on the last satisfactory war? If the Indochina War was not the war we wanted it to be, then let us refashion it in retrospect to make it the kind of war we should have been able to win. If our efforts to combat communist revolutionary war did not produce a satisfying conclusion, then let us pretend that the conflict was not a communist revolutionary war.

Summers suggests that American strategy went wrong because we thought we were fighting a "new kind of war."

But just as American interest in counter-insurgency warfare during the John F. Kennedy administration was not merely faddish, so similarly no serious military analyst at that time contended that wars of national liberation represented a completely new kind of war to which traditional strategic concepts did not apply at all. Consistently, American strategic planners were willing to draw on the experience of past wars to deal with the problems of conflict in Southeast Asia, acknowledging that those problems were not altogether new or unique.

The best of the analyses of the challenges facing the United States in such arenas as Vietnam written *before* the American involvement became large continue today to have a value for military study that compares favorably with Summers's own book — and they do so because they display as large a regard for the relevance of classical principles of strategy as Summers's own.

Such a work, for example, is *Guerrillas in the 1960's*, by two academic military historians, Peter Paret and John Shy, written in 1961 and revised in 1962. These writers, one of whom was later to be a translator of Clausewitz's *On War*, grounded their assessment of communist revolutionary war at least as much in Clausewitz's precepts as Summers does. But where Summers presents a mainly military analysis — except for his concerns about generating and maintaining American public support — Paret and Shy based their discussion of communist revolutionary war on the principle that "A full understanding of Clausewitz's famous dictum on the interaction of war and politics is the key to successful modern guerrilla operations."[16]

Assessing Ho

To Paret and Shy, communist revolutionary war was a combination of guerrilla warfare with political mobilization, the latter achieved by using communist theory and propaganda. Often, as in Vietnam, the political side of communist revolutionary war involved also the enlistment of nationalism in the Communist cause; when Paret and Shy wrote, there had already been ample opportunity to discern that Ho Chi Minh's strength was largely that of being the incarnation of Vietnamese nationalism. Paret and Shy discerned, too, that a guerrilla insurrection almost always needs the support of substantial conventional or regular armed forces if it is to succeed. Neither they nor most other writers on revolutionary war at the beginning of the 1960s would have been surprised at Summers's stressing the importance of the North Vietnamese regular army in the Indochina War; only the idea that the regulars represented the heart of the Communist war effort would have seemed surprising and questionable — and rightly so.

For Paret and Shy, in describing the most difficult problems of military forces attempting to suppress revolutionary war, stressed as most intractable the difficulties not of contending against the enemy's regulars, but of coping with a situation in which that "taking and holding terrain," which Summers says would have been so desirable, simply could not be accomplished by the conventional means that Summers advocates. Writing before there was any major American involvement in Indochina, Paret and Shy presented a description of the basic problems faced by anti-revolutionary, anti-guerrilla forces in the past that could well stand now as a description of what Americans confronted in Vietnam later:

> Constant disorder and insecurity put their own authority in doubt. The population's fear or antagonism made the collection of information difficult. The frequent impossibility of distinguishing between terrorists and peaceful villagers led to inevitable brutality and injustice on the part of the police and troops, which in turn alienated the people still further.[17]

This last sentence of course points again to the political dimension inextricably entwined with the military dimension of communist revolutionary war — the dimension not accounted for in the prescription for seeking a conventional kind of military victory against the enemy's regular forces, but the dimension that so much explains that weakness of the Saigon regime which eventually permitted the Communists to turn the final phase of the war, after the Americans had departed, into a blitzkrieg-style campaign.

The Blitzkrieg Issue

But as for the suggestion that the Americans should have essayed a blitzkrieg of their own as the appropriate strategy for the kind of war that developed in Indochina after 1963, that method had already been attempted before us by both the French in Indochina and, against similar opposition, the Chinese Nationalists attempting to squelch Mao Zedong. Admittedly, neither the French nor certainly the Kuomintang had the wherewithal of the Americans to mount a lightning war. But they had ample hardware for the purpose in contrast with their enemies.

It was not lack of modern military paraphernalia that caused the principal difficulties when the French against the Viet Minh and Chiang Kai-shek's Nationalists against the Chinese Communists relied upon conventional Western offensive strategy, advancing along highways and railroads to capture cities and terrain. The French and the Kuomintang had sufficient mobility and firepower that the Communists melted away before their blitzkrieg advances. The Communists did not even attempt to defend most cities and most terrain — not even the Chinese Communist capital of Yenan. Instead, employing Mao's concept of "mobile war" as an element of guerrilla war, the Communists retreated from superior weaponry — only to reappear to harass their enemies' flanks and rear. They would not allow themselves to be pinned down in battle until they considered the circumstances right.

If it be objected that after 1963 the Communists in Indochina had already left behind the stage of Maoist-style mobile war, there was nothing to prevent their returning to it in the unlikely event that American blitzkrieg strategy had forced them back to such methods. Something similar to that sequence in fact occurred following the 1968 Tet Offensive.

Again, well before America's Indochina involvement, Paret and Shy knew the correct rejoinder to the prescription for a blitzkrieg strategy as the means of countering revolutionary war:

> The worst military mistake in fighting guerrillas is to treat them as if they were conventional opponents. In the long run, the ability to control certain pieces of ground, or to mount periodic expeditions into and out of a particular area, means little in this sort of warfare. Instead, the security of one's own base and rear is essential; the strategic offensive must be deliberately cautious and carefully coordinated, although tactical movement can be rapid, even daring.[18]

The security of one's own base and rear is another fundamental factor that Colonel Summers's analysis neglects. To have provided adequately for that security would have entailed coping with the political dimensions of communist revolutionary war well enough that a stable, self-sustaining regime would have appeared in Saigon; but how we could thus have overcome our political predicaments is something that Summers's military critique never tells us.

A Conventional Approach

My discontent with Colonel Summers's analysis of the Indochina War has nothing to do with any lack of serious purpose in the work. On the contrary, it is its very seriousness and thoughtfulness that make the book finally a disappointment. Together with Dave R. Palmer's *Summons of the Trumpet*,[19] Summers's *On Strategy* is one of the two military assessments of the Indochina War written by soldiers with which any student of the war must come to terms.

Palmer's book is the best effort so far to shape the battles and campaigns of the war into comprehensible military history, to fashion for the Indochina War the kind of narrative history that has customarily provided the foundation of our retrospective judgments on all other wars.

Summers's work is, its flaws notwithstanding, the most searching military-historical criticism of the conduct of the war we have yet received. These two otherwise impressive military studies nevertheless share that basic fault to which I adverted at the beginning. Both, finding the course of the Indochina War unsatisfactory, claim that the way to have made it a more acceptable conflict would have been to force it into the mold of a different kind of war. Palmer claims that the United States fought the war with no strategy at all that was worthy of the name.[20] Summers contends that such strategy as the United States applied was irrelevant to the true nature of the war. Both suggest that the application of a conventional, European-style strategy, much like that of the American armed forces in World War II, could have led the way to forcing the war into the desired mold and winning a World War II-style victory.

Profound Differences

Ultimately, the differences between the war in Indochina and any earlier American war, World War II or any other, ran still deeper than those involving a conventional versus an unconventional strategy. To contend against the forces of revolutionary war in a situation in which those forces had succeeded in making themselves the embodiment of nationalism in the country where the war was waged meant that the United States was taking on a military task new to it. For the first time, American ground forces were attempting in Indochina to impose upon a foreign people possessing a well-developed sense of their own national identity a vision of that people's future different from their own.[21] The point has often been made, and yet tends to elude too many military analyses, that Indochina was the Indochinese peoples' country, not ours. Eventually the Americans would have to leave and the peoples of Indochina would remain.

Here was the final, most intractable problem of securing our rear areas and of the political dimensions of the war. Even if American strategy had achieved more than it ever did — or was likely to — in quelling insurgency behind our lines and within South Vietnam's borders and sealing the borders against incursion from outside, how long could the Americans have stayed to maintain the suppression and the sealing? As Colonel Summers rightly points out in evoking comparison with the German blitzkrieg of 1940, the climactic enemy drive that captured Saigon in 1975 did come from outside; but the ease with which the North Vietnamese blitzkrieg slashed forward nevertheless confirmed that it was the political war that the Americans had failed to win.

The fragility of the Republic of Vietnam had never been remedied; Vietnamese nationalism continued to find its incarnation elsewhere. A Saigon regime genuinely embodying its country's national consciousness might have been able to build an army that could resist Hanoi's blitzkrieg. The actual Saigon regime could not. To the end, the Republic of Vietnam was too much the creation of the Americans, and by 1975 the Americans had departed as sooner or later they had to.

As long ago as 1926, a writer in the *Proceedings* of the United States Naval Institute had discerned the likelihood of such an outcome should the United States some day grapple militarily with an Asian nationalism inside Asia. Such a contest, the writer had warned, could not be won by military strategy alone, not by any military strategy:

> There is great importance in the fact that in a war between the United States and an Asiatic power the latter's aims would seem distinctly "limited" to Americans, whereas, in order to maintain our position in Asiatic affairs, we might have to aim at "unlimited" reduction of the enemy's country, though not necessarily by invasion in force. In other words, the geographic distribution of interests is such that the inauguration of a "limited" war by an Asiatic power would be likely to compel us to carry through an "unlimited" war to victory as the only alternative to accepting defeat. Consequently, the enemy's combativeness would be aroused to the utmost while some among us probably would rather yield than continue the war.[22]

To have invoked World War II-style strategy in Indochina was to inaugurate the very kind of war likely to arouse the enemy's combativeness to the utmost. And in the end, some Americans were bound to prefer yielding to continuing the war — recognizing that the United States simply could not garrison somebody else's country forever.

Any strategic critique that continues to depict the Indochina War as a suitable arena for traditional American methods of war repeats the basic American military error during the war itself. Any strategic critique contending that the Indochina War was essentially a conflict on the model of World War II repeats the fundamental and chronic military error of preparing for the next war by refighting the last satisfactory war.

NOTES

[1] Obviously there can be disagreement about whether a particular article concerns principally the Indochina War or unconventional war in general on the one hand, or European war either in the future or during World War II on the other, so this assessment is less precise than the following numbers may make it seem. By my count, however, of 124 articles in *Military Review* in 1976, only 13 focused on the Indochina War or unconventional war more generally, while 31 focused on the military problems of the North Atlantic Treaty Organization or on World War II in Europe.

[2] In 1981–1982, of 190 articles in *Military Review* only 9 dealt with the issues of unconventional war as a primary topic; 48 focused on NATO, the Soviet armed forces likely to be involved in a NATO war, or World War II in Europe.

[3] On the failure of the United States Army to think seriously enough about the special problems of its Indian wars or to develop an appropriate doctrine, see Robert M. Utley, *Frontier Regulars: The United States Army and the Indian, 1866–1890* (New York: Macmillan, 1973), Chapter Three, "The Problem of Doctrine," pp. 44–58, and the same author's "The Contribution of the

Frontier to the American Military Tradition," in James P. Tate, ed., *The American Military on the Frontier: The Proceedings of the 7th Military History Symposium, United States Air Force Academy 30 September–1 October 1976* (Washington: Office of Air Force History, Headquarters USAF and United States Air Force Academy, 1978), pp. 7–13. On fighting the Seminoles in particular, see John K. Mahon, *History of the Second Seminole War, 1835–1842* (Gainesville: University of Florida Press, 1967). On the Philippine Insurrection, see John Morgan Gates, *Schoolbooks and Krags: The United States Army in the Philippines, 1898–1902* (Westport, Conn.: Greenwood Press, 1973), and Russell Roth, *Muddy Glory: America's Indian Wars in the Philippines, 1899–1935* (West Hanover, Mass.: Christopher Publishing House, 1981).

[4] Harry G. Summers, Jr., *On Strategy: A Critical Analysis of the Vietnam War* (Novato, Calif.: Presidio Press, 1982). Essentially the same work was also published for limited distribution as Harry G. Summers, Jr., *On Strategy: The Vietnam War in Context* (Carlisle Barracks, Pa.: Strategic Studies Institute, U.S. Army War College, n.d.). All subsequent citations refer to the Presidio Press edition.

[5] Quoted *ibid.*, p. 83, from Carl von Clausewitz, *On War*, Michael Howard and Peter Paret, eds. and translators (Princeton: Princeton University Press, 1976), Book I, Chapter One, p. 88.

[6] Summers, *On Strategy*, pp. 68–69 and, for the quoted phrase, p. 72.

[7] *Ibid.*, pp. 71–76, quotations from p. 71 ("new kind of war") and p. 73.

[8] *Ibid.*, p. 73.

[9] *Ibid.*, p. 86.

[10] *Ibid.*, p. 87, quoting from Dave Richard Palmer, *Summons of the Trumpet: U.S.-Vietnam in Perspective* (San Rafael, Calif.: Presidio Press, 1976), p. 62.

[11] *Ibid.*, p. 88.

[12] Harry G. Summers, Jr., "Vietnam Reconsidered," *The New Republic*, July 12, 1982, p. 25.

[13] Summers, *On Strategy*, pp. 35–36.

[14] John E. Mueller, *Wars, Presidents, and Public Opinion* (New York: Wiley, 1973). See also my article, "Dissent in Wars," in Alexander DeConde, ed., *Encyclopedia of American Foreign Policy: Studies of the Principal Movements and Ideas* (3 vols., New York: Scribner's, 1978), I, pp. 253–267.

[15] Quoted in Maurice Matloff, *Strategic Planning for Coalition Warfare, 1943–1944 (United States Army in World War II: The War Department*, Washington: Office of the Chief of Military History, 1959), p. 5, from Interview, Dr. Sidney Mathews, Major Roy Lamson, and Major David Hamilton with Marshall, July 25, 1949, OCMH Files.

[16] Peter Paret and John W. Shy, *Guerrillas in the 1960's* (Revised Edition, New York: Praeger, 1962), p. 19.

[17] *Ibid.*, p. 30.

[18] *Ibid.*, p. 41.

[19] See note 10, above.

[20] Palmer, *Summons of the Trumpet*, especially Chapter Eight, "The Search Fails," pp. 147–160.

[21] To be sure, the conquest of the Philippines had been an earlier, similar effort; but amidst the ethnic and linguistic diversity of the Philippines, there was not yet a well-developed Filipino sense of national identity at the time of the Philippine Insurrection — and furthermore, the Americans never altogether suppressed insurrectionary activity, and eventually departed from the Philippines. As for the conquest of the North American Indians, they too lacked a well-developed sense of national identity at the time of the Indian wars, and in any event the white Americans were also in North America to stay.

[22] William Howard Gardiner, "National Policy and Naval Power," United States Naval Institute *Proceedings*, LII (Feb. 1926), p.238.

COMMENTARY: The Paradox of Vietnam

by Ernest R. May

In crude summary, not strictly fair to either, one can say that Colonel Summers blames political authorities for America's debacle in Vietnam, while Professor Weigley blames soldiers.

Colonel Summers argues that the military acquiesced in doctrines developed by civilian theorists and imposed by Presidents and their appointees. These doctrines supposed "revolutionary war" or "counter-insurgency" to be separate and distinct from war as usually understood. Applying them, the Kennedy and Johnson administrations employed America's armed forces as pieces in a game, failed to assert or pursue a goal justifying or excusing the consequent costs, and, as a result, bought the nation an expensive and humiliating defeat.

Professor Weigley retorts that, in reality, the armed forces fought in Vietnam according to their own traditional doctrines, not those of the civilian theorists, and that, in fact, their failure to acknowledge the special requirements of "revolutionary war" accounted in large part for the losses and sacrifices which eventually deprived the effort of adequate public support.

We have here a textbook case of the divergent results obtainable from analysis by historical analogy, when that analysis is pursued only through a single stage. As Professor Weigley contends, the paper by Colonel Summers can be read as one comparing the Vietnam War with World War II. It is solely concerned, however, with identifying the respects in which the Vietnam War was or could have been like World War II. Profesor Weigley deals overtly with respects in which the two wars were *unlike*. With regard to the events being compared, the two authors are not so much disputing with one another as, like the blind man in the fable, calling attention to different parts of the elephant.

. . .While Summers and Professor Weigley state very different theses, they share a common premise, namely, that the war in Vietnam could have been won. They differ as to *how* it could have been won. Comparisons with the War of the American Revolution and the 1862–67 French Intervention in Mexico provoke doubts about their premise. While it is certainly imaginable that Burgoyne and Howe might have severed New England from the rest of the United States or that Washington's army could have been overrun or that Yorktown could have been averted, perhaps even that the Americans might have returned to the British Empire, it is scarcely plausible that the British could have *won* the war in the sense of having the Americans reconcile themselves to an inferior status among subjects of an English king. Nor is it conceivable that France could, over any long period of time, have achieved its aims in Mexico, even if the French had won on the *Cinco de Mayo* and Juarez had thus been denied *his* Dien Bien Phu.

Going back to the 1965 decisions in Washington, in an otherwise faultless general appraisal, Richard Betts makes an assertion which, though not necessarily unfair, may be slightly inaccurate, when he says that McGeorge Bundy never "seriously questioned the imperative of carrying on the struggle." In research for his *Planning a Tragedy*, Larry Berman obtained release of several previously classified memoranda signed by Bundy in the early summer of 1965, when Johnson was deciding to order a large increase in the American ground force commitment. One, seemingly not at all at odds with Betts's generalization, compares in detail the French position in Vietnam in 1954 with that of the United States in 1965.[1]

I say "seemingly" because it is a curious document. Though signed by a man acknowledged to have one of the most incisive minds on the planet, the document is ridden with logical flaws apparent to any 15-year-old. Most obviously, it set a France sapped by eight years of bloody, costly, and divisive fighting alongside a United States just on the verge of sending soldiers into battle, yet its key point is that the French effort in Vietnam lacked public support while that of the United States, as of January 1965, commanded majority approval in public opinion polls.

Slippery Slope

One assumes that Bundy wrote the memorandum on and to an order from Johnson, who wanted something with which to answer George Ball. A quarter-suspicion rises that Bundy knew he was giving the President a brief which Ball could demolish. This becomes a half-suspicion when one reads a second document signed by Bundy on the same day — June 30, 1965 — this the one which could be cited to dispute Betts's assertion. Commenting on a Defense memorandum recommending, among other things, that the American troop level in Vietnam be increased to 200,000, Bundy wrote to McNamara (*not* to Johnson):

It proposes this new land commitment at a time when our troops are entirely untested in the kind of warfare projected. It proposes greatly extended air action when the value of the air action we have taken is sharply disputed. It proposes naval quarantine by mining at a time when nearly everyone agrees that the real question is not in Hanoi, but in South Vietnam. My first reaction is that this program is rash to the point of folly. . . .The apparent basis for doing this is simply the increasing weakness of Vietnamese forces. But this is a slippery slope toward total U.S. responsibility and corresponding fecklessness on the Vietnamese side.

The paper also omits examination of the upper limit of U.S. liability. If we need 200 thousand men now for these quite limited missions, may we not need 400 thousand later? Is this a rational course of action? Is there any real prospect that U.S. regular forces can conduct the anti-guerrilla operations which would probably remain the central problem in South Vietnam?

After listing a number of questions that had gone unanalyzed, ranging all the way to whether North Vietnam might bend, as North Korea supposedly had in 1953, under a threat of nuclear attack, Bundy concluded:

Any expanded program needs to have a clear sense of its own internal momentum. The paper does not face this problem. If U.S. casualties go up sharply, what further actions do we propose to take or not to take? More broadly still, what is the real object of the exercise? If it is to get to the conference table, what results do we seek there? Still more brutally, do we want to invest 200 thousand men to cover an eventual retreat? Can we not do that just as well where we are?[2]

When forwarding McNamara's recommendations to Johnson, Bundy did not voice the same reservations. On the contrary, he seemed to give the recommendation almost unqualified endorsement.[3]

Even more than the now famous memoranda by Ball, the Bundy memorandum to McNamara questioned not only whether the United States could achieve victory in Vietnam but indeed whether it could even define what "victory" might mean. Vice President Hubert Humphrey did likewise in a private letter to Johnson — one which, according to Humphrey, earned him exile from Johnson's inner circle. Humphrey wrote:

American wars have to be politically understandable by the American public. There has to be a cogent, convincing case if we are to enjoy sustained public support. In World War I and II we had this. In Korea we were moving under United Nations auspices to defend South Korea against dramatic, across-the-border conventional aggression. Yet even with those advantages we could not sustain American political support for fighting Chinese in Korea in 1952.
Today in Vietnam we lack the very advantages we had in Korea. The public is worried and confused. Our rationale for action has shifted away now even from the notion that we are there as advisers on request of a free government, to the simple and politically barren argument of our "national interest." We have not succeeded in making this national interest interesting enough at home or abroad to generate support. The arguments in fact are probably too complicated (or too weak) to be politically useful or effective.[4]

Retrospect surely bears out the wisdom of Ball, Bundy, and Humphrey. Both Colonel Summers *and* Professor Weigley could, to be sure, be partially right. A more urgent military effort concentrated against main force North Vietnamese units might have brought about immediate military results more satisfying to our army than were the actual ones. Equally, an effort limited to counter-guerrilla operations might have cost less, generated adverse domestic opinion more slowly, and similarly have altered somewhat the events between 1968 and 1975. It is not easy, however, to conjure up *any* plausible sequence of events which would have led to Vietnam's being by now a peacefully divided country on the model, say, of Korea. On the contrary, what can be imagined is Colonel Summers's military victory culminating in a prolonged occupation, comparable both in character and result to that of the French; or Professor Weigley's counter-revolutionary war proceeding at best in the pattern of British engagements in Ireland prior to 1923.

In one of O'Henry's stories, a young French poet stands at a crossroads. He takes one fork, has adventures, and ends up being killed by a certain Marquis de Beaupertuys. He is then described taking each of the other forks, having in each case a different set of adventures, but eventually dying at the hand of the same nobleman. Looking back from the 1980s, one can see that story serving as a parable for the

United States in Vietnam. There were many possible paths. The Americans were, however, aliens trying to control the outcome of another people's civil war. Given their fervor and determination, the North Vietnamese were bound to prevail. Short of treating all Vietnam as the Romans treated Carthage, the Americans had no more chance in the long run against communist nationalism than the British and the French had had against liberal nationalism in the United States and Mexico.

Why was the American government so slow to acknowledge and so much slower still to acquiesce in the hopelessness of its endeavor? For the same reason that it could not in practice have followed the courses recommended by either Colonel Summers or Professor Weigley: Americans are a ruthful people. Presidents have to provide them a moral, not merely an economic or cost-benefit justification for what they are asked to do, and Lyndon Johnson could make such a justification only for a policy of doing the utmost to induce a live-and-let-live compromise. The flaw in Hubert Humphrey's letter was that it established no "politically understandable" rationale for abandoning Vietnam. Humphrey could only say weakly:

> It is always hard to cut losses. But the Johnson Administration is in a stronger position to do so now than any Administration in the century. 1965 is the year of minimum political risk for the Johnson Administration. Indeed it is the first year when we can face the Vietnam problem without being preoccupied with the political repercussions from the Republican right.

Humphrey urged Johnson to capitalize on his reputation for "political ingenuity." But Johnson evidently felt unable to do so.

The paradox is that the Vietnam War, so often condemned by its opponents as hideously immoral, may well have been the most moral or at least the most selfless war in all of American history. For the impulse guiding it was not to defeat an enemy or even to serve a national interest; it was simply not to abandon friends.

NOTES

[1] Larry Berman, *Planning a Tragedy* (New York: Norton, 1982), p. 149.

[2] *Ibid.*, pp. 187–89.

[3] *Ibid.*, pp. 190–191.

[4] Hubert Humphrey, *The Education of a Public Man* (Garden City, N.Y.: Doubleday, 1976), pp. 318–28.

VIETNAM: IMPLICATIONS AND IMPACT

by Robert E. Osgood

What should we have learned from the Vietnam War that is relevant to American foreign and military policies? What do we think we have learned? How have the real and imagined lessons of Vietnam affected American foreign and military policies?

The answers to these three questions would tell us a great deal about the nature of the problem the United States faces in continuing to contain any armed expansion of Soviet influence and control outside Western Europe and Japan by means of limited war.

I shall deal with these questions by examining the reasons for the failure of the Vietnam intervention, the relevance of these reasons (that is, the lessons) for current U.S. foreign and military policies, and the effects of the Vietnam experience on U.S. policies and capabilities of military containment in the Third World.

I examine the reasons for failure and the lessons that should be and have been derived in relation to three kinds of decisions or policy choices: (1) whether or not to intervene with American armed forces in a local armed conflict; (2) how to fight a limited war successfully if we do not intervene; and (3) how to get out of a limited war if we are losing.

The decision of whether to intervene should depend, logically, on whether American security interests and the threat to them are sufficiently great to justify the costs of trying to protect them, and on the risk and consequent costs of failing. But these variables are highly subjective and subject to changing estimates, especially when they interact with each other under the stress of war.

During the years of French military involvement in Indochina the United States government developed a clear view of the great strategic importance of Indochina.[1] Numerous National Security Council and Joint Chiefs of Staff documents described Southeast Asia as an area of vital resources (especially food and raw materials and critical markets), athwart strategic lines of communication from India to Northeast Asia and Japan; and they depicted Indochina as the gateway to the conquest of Southeast Asia.

American security, and, more directly, the security and self-sustaining economic health of Japan, required preventing the Soviet Union from denying Japan and the West access to this area by fostering and supporting radical movements (like the Viet Minh) that exploited indigenous nationalism. Moreover, a Viet Minh defeat of France, according to the American view as early as the summer of 1949, would so weaken France, economically and politically, as to undermine its indispensable contribution to West European security.

China's intervention in the Korean War convinced the U.S. government that Chinese aggression in Asia had become the most serious and active threat to American global security.

In the face of this threat, Indochina became the potential domino whose fall would lead to the communization of all of Southeast Asia, the U.S. East Asian defensive perimeter, and Japan. So important was the containment of China that military plans, in the event of direct Chinese intervention in Indochina, called for a general U.S. war against China itself, complete with a naval blockade, interdiction of communication lines on the mainland, and extensive air operations against Chinese military targets, including the use of nuclear weapons where "advantageous."[2]

In view of the great security interest ascribed to preventing communist control of Indochina, it is no wonder that the United States intervened against North Vietnam's subversion of the South when it inherited France's war after the Geneva settlement of 1954.

Another Munich

Yet the more intensive American intervention became, the more general and intangible became the official and non-official justifications for the war, since those justifications were better suited to engaging public support of direct American involvement in another remote Asian war.

Both Presidents Eisenhower and Kennedy publicly proclaimed the geopolitical argument for containing the Communists in Vietnam in terms of preventing falling dominoes, but this argument was progressively superseded by more general propositions, such as those enunciated in the Truman Doctrine, about the necessity of saving international order and preventing World War III by avoiding a repetition [another "Munich"] of the kind of piecemeal totalitarian aggression that had led to World War II.

There was no significant opposition to this view of American interests until the nation's political elite, along with most of the civilian officials engaged in conducting the war, became convinced, after the Tet Offensive of 1968, that additional increments of military investment in the war would be so costly and so unlikely to prevent the North Vietnamese from eventually conquering South Vietnam that American interests required withdrawing with as much honor as possible.

But before this, as the human and political costs of the war increased, the more abstract justifications of national prestige, fidelity to commitments, and demonstration of national will came to dominate official and non-official arguments for resisting Communist aggression. Indeed, so prominent were these intangible justifications that in the eyes of some policy-makers and Congressmen they eventually became an argument for abandoning the war effort, on the grounds that the country had made its point so well that it could afford to withdraw with honor.

After Tet, when victory no longer seemed feasible or worth the cost, and after withdrawal in 1973, when American intervention was widely seen as a costly failure, significant doubts were raised about the wisdom of intervention on the grounds that neither U.S. security interests, the communist threat to them, nor the feasibility of winning justified the costs. These doubts, however, did not so much challenge the general rationale for containment as its application to Vietnam. And even there they did not really address the alternative — that is, the comparative costs of permitting a North Vietnamese military and political conquest of an independent non-communist country without even trying to defend it.

Nor did they signify that even massive intervention would not have been worth the cost if victory had been feasible.

The limited grounds on which judgments have been made about the wisdom of intervention in the Vietnam war — whether they are right or wrong — makes these judgments an inadequate standard for deciding whether to intervene in a broad range of possible contingencies throughout the so-called Third World.

Vietnam and the Persian Gulf

This reality is seemingly confirmed by the rediscovery of the threat of Soviet expansion and the necessity to contain it with limited-war conventional capabilities during the later years of the Carter administration. For this rediscovery, despite the widespread depreciation of military containment in the Third World which Carter himself articulated, culminated in the pronouncement of the Carter Doctrine and, to support it, the launching of the Rapid Deployment Force. Indeed, this force was assigned a military mission — countering a Soviet effort to gain control of Persian Gulf oil — that far surpassed in scope and risk anything anticipated during the Kennedy administration. (Whether the RDF will ever be capable of supporting its ultimate mission, and whether the U.S. government would, in any event, actually use it are different questions, to which I shall address some general observations at the end.)

The lessons of Vietnam for future American intervention are, therefore, quite inconclusive.

Surely, Vietnam stands as a warning against the inflation and overgeneralization of national interests in a limited war for limited stakes, especially against an adversary with truly unlimited stakes. The conventional wisdom that military containment must be applied more selectively (only after due consideration of specific interests, the various costs of intervening as compared to not intervening, the efficacy of American force, etc.) rather than as a conditioned reflex, is no less important because it is imprecise and, in practice, difficult to implement as an organized policy choice. But the number and ambiguity of the variables entailed in following this wisdom make it of little use as a guide to grand strategy and military planning.

I would guess that, partly (but only partly) because of the Vietnam experience, the American government and people have greatly downgraded the value of intervening with U.S. forces in revolutionary and other kinds of internal wars, principally because of the local political obstacles to effective intervention, and a growing appreciation of the constraints against the Soviet Union's intervening in such a way as to threaten vital tangible American interests in a lasting way.

But this leaves a broad range of other contingencies in which containment by limited wars of various kinds and dimensions is as open-ended a policy as ever.

With respect to these contingencies the most substantial constraints on American intervention will arise, indeed are already arising, not from any explicit reformulation of national interests — a difficult and possibly dangerous task for any government to undertake — but from an awareness of the economic and material limitations on effective and available American military resources.

How to Fight

Many critics of American intervention during the war, and increasingly afterward, have seen the decisive source of failure in the way we fought the war.

One criticism is leveled against the search-and-destroy strategy, intended to destroy the enemy forces, as opposed to the seize-and-hold strategy, designed to protect the people. There is considerable merit to this criticism, given the element of unconventional conflict and revolutionary warfare in the countryside. But the peculiar problem of fighting in Vietnam was that the war was a strange combination of conventional and unconventional war, for which a combination of these strategies was needed. Indeed, after Tet 1968, these combined strategies, coupled with more effective and intensive "pacification" efforts, did succeed in both devastating the Viet Cong and inflicting defeats on North Vietnamese regular battle formations.

Often associated with this strategic criticism is an institutional one: that the U.S. Army was incapable of fighting a combined regular and insurgent war, because, by national tradition and priorities, training, experience, organizational inertia, inter-service competition, and ingrained criteria of professional competence and advancement, it was prepared only to fight a version of World War II on the plains of Europe. This charge, also, is largely correct, particularly as it applies to professional resistance to translating fashionable and presidentially endorsed ideas of counter-guerilla war into operational reality. Indeed, the charge still applies. Yet, under General Creighton Abrams, the Army in Vietnam did partially adjust to the necessities of the strange human and physical environment of the war; and, by virtue of the adjustment, it won a substantial measure of military victory by 1972.

Proponents of the 1967–72 pacification effort are probably right that we would have suppressed the Viet Cong earlier if we had given this effort more support before Tet 1968. But because the war was not only an unconventional operation, it does not follow, as one school of military advocacy maintains, that the war could have been won by a low-level or, for that matter, a high-level guerrilla war, even if we had been willing to extend it over many more years.

In any case, the contemporary relevance of these lessons is doubtful, since we have — perhaps wisely — virtually ruled out intervention with American combat troops in a revolutionary war which, given anything like North Vietnam's determination and military capabilities, might reach such a large scale of combat. Perhaps unwisely, we may also have ruled out small-scale guerrilla operations under more favorable political circumstances, while failing to face up to a variety of possible circumstances in which small-scale conventional intervention in revolutionary wars might be imperative (for example, to thwart a Soviet proxy's intervention).

There is more agreement among the military re-assessors about the disadvantages of incremental intervention, in terms of both its debilitating domestic repercussions and its concession of military and diplomatic advantages to the adversary. But the relevance of this insight to future plans and operations is obscure. Whether or not "the system worked," as Leslie Gelb maintains,[3] it is hard to imagine the American political and bureaucratic system working any way other than in support of incremental intervention in a quasi-revolutionary war in which the strengths of attacking and resisting forces are obscure.

Even in the case of a concentrated conventional invasion the clarifying effects of direct military aggression by a well-armed Soviet proxy might be offset by a heightened fear of Soviet intervention, which would inhibit the pace and scope of U.S. escalation.

Intervening Forcefully

The preference of the U.S. armed services for quick and massive escalation against the base and forefront of an adversary's military operations presupposes an advance knowledge of the potential scale and effectiveness of the besieging forces and an assurance of civilian, executive, and congressional deference to military advice and requests, not to mention an insensitivity to foreign reactions, that is quite unrealistic.

It is equally unrealistic to expect the civilian leadership absolutely to eschew intervention unless it can foresee and guarantee a quick victory resulting from a military effort toward the top of the hypothetical scale of escalation. No U.S. administration can exercise that kind of foresight or back it unconditionally. Yet none can categorically exclude the option of giving direct military help to a friendly country trying to resist a conquest by hostile forces assisted by a communist country, despite the unpredictability of success or failure.

There is even more widespread agreement among critics of the military operations in Vietnam that one particular kind of incrementalism must be avoided. This is the kind of effort epitomized in the "Rolling Thunder" bombing campaign of 1965–67: to persuade Hanoi to negotiate a favorable settlement by inflicting escalating costs through air strikes. This effort suffered from the ambiguity of the "signals" that resulted from the several purposes the campaign was supposed to serve, and from the inadequate material effects upon Hanoi's fighting capabilities that resulted from the restraints against striking certain kinds of targets. But, essentially, it failed because of Hanoi's determination to win a total victory rather than bargain for a compromised settlement.

What failed, however, was not — as a common caricature by military critics portrays — a carefully calibrated exercise in the psychological and political exploitation of violence, following the imaginative bargaining notions of civilian strategists ignorant of military realities. What failed was a compromise between the Johnson administration's compulsion to do something to show the South Vietnamese that it was hurting the enemy, accentuated by the parochial perspectives and salesmanship of the land- and sea-based air forces, and its reluctance to do too much, partly out of fear of Chinese intervention and partly because of the hopes of civilian defense and intelligence officials, who were properly skeptical of air force claims that the bombing might have a marginal effect on the ability and willingness of Hanoi to continue the war before additional increments of American manpower had to be invested.[4] Before the U.S. bombing was terminated in 1968, the military had substantially succeeded in expanding the target list. The bombing still failed to achieve its military objectives.

Rolling Thunder

The failure of "Rolling Thunder" suggests the limits to useful civilian operational supervision, but is not an argument that bombing operations should be unrestrained by political considerations, or that unrestrained bombing would have confirmed air force claims. If it is true that "Linebacker II", the more comprehensive and intensive bombing campaign of December 1972 against the Hanoi-Haiphong area, contributed to Hanoi's resumption of serious negotiations under the altered political and military circumstances of the time, this confirms the unexceptionable proposition that bombing that exerts a significant material effect on military capabilities can affect the enemy's will. It does not argue that politically unrestrained air escalation is proper, safe, or decisive. It does not tell us much about the political efficacy of bombing under a great variety of military and political conditions in which it is only one factor among many.

More to the point is the criticism that President Johnson's unwillingness to mobilize the reserves and in other ways put the country on a war footing — his failure clearly to subordinate domestic economic and social programs to the war effort — doomed the United States to defeat.

The obverse side of this criticism is the superficially plausible assumption that the United States did not lack the physical potential to overwhelm North Vietnam but only the will to use it. But even if this were true and one discounts the risk of augmented Chinese or Soviet intervention — and perhaps the Korean example led the government to exaggerate this risk — the advocates of a full-scale war effort miss the point that Johnson's limitations on the effort reflected not just his but the widespread public realization that after all, we had only limited, if nonetheless important, interests at stake, whereas North Vietnam was engaged in a total war for complete victory. It will always be characteristic of the United States' limited wars that they impinge upon relatively limited interests, which, in turn, limit the costs and sacrifices the country will be willing to incur.

Nevertheless, every limited war need not be as unpopular as this one was because of the repulsive nature of insurgency and the inefficacy of the government we were defending. And some wars — consider the possible contingencies in the Middle East and Central America — may impinge on far more substantial interests than others. These and many other factors will affect the scope and pace of American involvement in future limited wars, no matter what military advice the civilian leaders receive.

In the final analysis, all of the controversies over how the Vietnam War should have been fought are less significant in explaining defeat or the prospect of victory than the likelihood that no military success could have enabled the government of South Vietnam to maintain independence by its own efforts, or perhaps even with the continued presence of American forces. It was primarily the popular and official perception of this fact that led to the U.S. government's decision to get out as gracefully as it could.

Might the Nixon administration, as Kissinger argues, have established a self-sustaining South Vietnam had it not been constrained, by public and congressional opposition and the loss of presidential authority inflicted by Watergate, from fully carrying out its assurances to President Thieu that in the event of massive North Vietnamese violations of the peace treaty of January 1973, the United States would respond with "swift and severe retaliatory action" and "full force" (the words used in private messages to Thieu in order to obtain his consent to the treaty)? I doubt it. Never mind the constitutional implications and political repercussions of resuming the war after 1973 without Congressional approval. There is no reason to think that the President's direction of retaliatory air strikes would have saved South Vietnam from eventual defeat by a country so determined to conquer it, especially since the peace treaty permitted the enemy to keep its forces in the South.

How to Get Out

Unless one assumes — as I do not — that the political and psychological impact of Vietnam and the material constraints on U.S. limited-war capabilities preclude the United States from becoming involved again in a limited war that cannot be won, the failure in Vietnam poses the question of how the nation can extricate itself from a losing war (or a war that becomes more costly than the effort to win it warrants) with the least damage to national values.

In some respects, the Nixon-Kissinger extrication from the Vietnam War was a remarkable success. A combination of national exhaustion, Vietnamization, and the compensatory diplomacy of rapprochement with China and détente with the Soviet Union enabled the administration to limit the international, and blunt the internal, damage of defeat.

So successful was this extrication that it substantially delayed the most adverse domestic reactions until the Carter administration. Despite the rash of congressional constraints on military and foreign policy and despite the onset of disillusionment with détente that took place in the Nixon-Ford administration, these policy-makers might have substantially restored the fabric of a chastened containment policy within the framework of a more lasting *modus vivendi* with the USSR but for Watergate. In any event, it fell to the Carter administration to undertake the full, enervating task of national expiation and retrenchment, substituting moral redemption for the crippled consensus of containment — only to reverse its course and begin the real process of overcoming the traumas of Vietnam in response to the Middle East "arc of crisis" and the undiminished Soviet military build-up.

The impact of defeat in Vietnam illustrates the fact that the greater the nation's investment of time, manpower, and money in a losing limited war, the more difficult and disadvantageous extrication becomes. Were there earlier occasions in the Vietnam War when the U.S. could have withdrawn with less internal and international damage? If so, they almost surely preceded the introduction of regular Army divisions.

Perhaps there is a lesson here, but it is a lesson that will be extremely difficult to follow in practice. If the basic cause of defeat in Vietnam was the weakness of the South Vietnamese government, how can one discover such a fatal weakness soon enough to withdraw support without U.S. humiliation? Should we conclude that if a government cannot protect the security of a besieged country with military and economic assistance short of American combat forces, it is too weak to warrant the risk of trying to save it with American combat forces? Or is this generalization, too, a misleading extrapolation from particular and perhaps unique circumstances?

Implications and Impact

It may help to understand the implications and impact of the Vietnam War with respect to the role of limited war in American foreign policy if we compare this experience with that of America's other limited war, in Korea.

For Americans, limited warfare — that is, war fought under self-imposed restrictions on military operations — that involves large numbers of American forces and imposes large casualties for a number of years is bound to be profoundly frustrating. It means incurring human, material, and political costs in a place of the enemy's choosing that is probably of too little intrinsic and tangible importance to seem to justify these costs. It probably entails fighting for a country whose government falls far short of American standards of political respectability. More than likely, such a war will lack the wholehearted approval or cooperation of allies. Certainly, it will restrain the United States from using its full military potential against the immediate adversary, while this adversary is permitted sanctuaries and external support from the *real* adversary.

Both the Korean and Vietnam wars demonstrate this reality. But with all its frustrations, the impact of the Korean War was far less traumatic. The Korean War became almost as unpopular as the Vietnam War before we began to win it; but although the achievement of merely the *status quo ante* deprived the war of the gratifications Americans had come to expect from the experience of World War II, it did prevent the war from seeming like a costly failure. The significant political opposition to the conduct of the war was directed against the self-imposed limits rather than against the war itself or on behalf of greater limits and withdrawal. The frustrations with the war did not foster doubts about the validity of intervention or challenge the containment consensus. On the contrary, they gave the Eisenhower administration, which earned the privilege of ending the war, a mandate to implement containment more forcefully as well as more safely and cheaply, while extending American commitments in behalf of containment into new areas of the Third World.

Nor did the Korean War raise questions about the soundness of military traditions, training, and tactics. Notwithstanding its novel limitations, this was the kind of war — a kind of truncated World War II — that the nation and the military were prepared to fight. Accordingly, it was managed in the World War II tradition of placing guns over butter — mobilizing the reserves and subordinating domestic social and economic programs to the military effort.

Underlying these contrasts to the Vietnam war were not only the fact that within a tolerable number of years [three] we won this one (or, at least did not lose it) and left a country that could defend itself with only modest American protection, but also several other circumstances that made it more acceptable to Americans: U.N. and allied support for the American effort, aggression by a sudden massive attack across a national boundary, attack by an unambiguous Soviet proxy, the assumption in the United States and Western Europe that this attack might foreshadow aggression against NATO, intervention by a major communist country (China) allied to the Soviet Union, defense of a government and people determined to protect their country, a strategic location of recognizable importance by virtue of proximity to Japan, and an American economy with a surge capacity capable of quickly quadrupling defense expenditures without adverse economic consequences.

No More Koreas or Vietnams

The contrast with the Vietnam War suggests that generalizations drawn from the Vietnam experience about the absolute unacceptability of American participation in a large-scale limited war may be misleading because they fail to take into account the many variables that can affect American decisions about intervening, fighting, and terminating such a war. The military and political conditions affecting U.S. participation in possible major limited wars in the Gulf, southern Africa, Southeast Asia, or Central America and the Caribbean would be significantly different from those in either Korea or Vietnam. As for the more likely shorter-term, lower-intensity conflicts in the Third World, generalizations drawn from either Korea or Vietnam provide us with even less guidance.

Moreover, it is notable that even though both of America's limited wars were sufficiently frustrating and unpopular to generate a powerful national resolve against participating in such wars again, the role of conventional limited war as an instrument of containment survived them both and has, indeed, been enhanced. The reason is that the core of the containment consensus survives and that Americans prefer to implement it, if necessary, with conventional limited war rather than run the risks of nuclear war or suffer the penalties of acquiescence to armed communist or communist-supported aggression.

Yet the enhanced role of conventional limited war does not necessarily lead to enhanced capabilities or enhanced national will to fight such wars. Indeed, not only the chastening memory of these two wars, but also the steadily growing economic, material, and international as well as domestic political constraints against direct armed intervention in local wars, have severely restricted American will and capabilities. Consequently, the gap between America's ever-expanding security interests in the Third World and the military power available to support them has never been greater since the first phase of the Cold War, before the North Korean invasion.

The Eisenhower and Nixon regimes tried to close this chronic gap within a strategy of military retrenchment — Eisenhower, by increasing reliance upon nuclear weapons and clarifying deterrence through alliances; Nixon, by engineering rapprochement with one major communist adversary (in Peking) and weaving a network of accommodations with the other (in Moscow). These methods are no longer available. Yet, it is clearer every day that the Reagan administration's effort to close the gap by unilateral augmentation of military power will be impeded by constraints that were never envisioned at the onset of America's wars in Korea and Vietnam.

NOTES

[1] *The History of the Joint Chiefs of Staff: The Joint Chiefs of Staff and the War in Indochina: History of the Indochina Incident, 1940–1954* (Historical Division, Joint Secretariat, JCS; August 20, 1971), chap. vii.

[2] *Ibid.*, pp. 429–430.

[3] Gelb first used this phrase as an antidote to the assertion of Arthur Schlesinger, Jr., and others that American Presidents had slipped inadvertently into the Vietnam "quagmire" because of repeated overestimations of the prospect of winning: Leslie H. Gelb, "Vietnam: The System Worked," *Foreign Policy*, No. 3 (Summer 1971), pp. 140–67. He later incorporated it in the title of the book he completed with Richard K. Betts, *The Irony of Vietnam: The System Worked* (Washington, D.C.: Brookings Institution, 1979). The best critique of the thesis that the system produced rational decisions is Robert Gallucci's *Neither Peace Nor Honor: The Politics of American Military Policy in Vietnam* (Baltimore: The Johns Hopkins Press, 1975), which points out the bureaucratic and political friction, and the resulting failures of logical, coherent policy-making, in the conduct of the war.

[4] On the interplay of the various organizations and individuals affecting the bombing of the North during 1965–67, see Gallucci, *op cit.*, chap. iv.

DISCUSSION

MAY: If you look at the evidence that we have now, my feeling is that the issue between Colonel Summers and Professor Weigley is to some extent a moot issue. But that's an uncertain call and may reflect an historian's bias toward feeling that whatever happened was inevitable. And so you explain why it happened rather than considering alternatives.

I'm not sure that you get very far in trying to say what could have been done in Vietnam that might have made the outcome different.

The interesting question and the one that Bob Osgood was focusing on is why it was that there weren't really any alternatives [in 1964–65] — why it seemed to very intelligent people, with records not marked by uniform good judgment but with good judgment not entirely absent from that record, that the options they chose were the best available.

There's a common lament which runs through criticism on both sides about the inability of the United States to act realistically in Vietnam. And in different ways that is what appears in Colonel Summers's and Professor Weigley's papers; it was eloquently stated last night by Colonel Gropman; it appears in the Schandler argument that the right strategy was the enclave strategy; it is the theme that runs through Kissinger's memoirs.

Why? It seems to me that you have to see the answer in the fact that American policy, American actions, whether in the diplomatic or military sphere, immediate actions, not necessarily the long-term actions, are primarily responsive to the perceptions at the center of the government of American public opinion.

That was what Johnson understood and what Nixon and Kissinger learned. American public opinion as perceived from the White House is essentially sentimental and I mean that in a literal sense, not in a pejorative sense; it is governed more by sentiment than it is by pragmatic calculation.

Johnson's problem was to find a choice that satisfied public sentiment. We talk in terms of "hawks" and "doves" and that language was carried over from the 1962 Cuban missile crisis. That's not the right way to think of the problem that confronted Johnson. What he wound up doing was choosing the option least precluded by the public sentiments that he could perceive. And that's so often the way of real choices; they're not the preferred course.

I don't think anyone denies Larry Berman's evidence that LBJ applied himself to trying to make the least unpreferable course seem a matter of consensus, to minimize to the extent possible the number of people who could go out [to the public] and say they had given him contrary advice or he hadn't listened to them. This was, after all, the man whose well-known motto was "I never trust a man unless I've got his pecker in my pocket."

If you look at 1965 and at the choices recommended, and you try to write the speech that he would have given saying that, because Westmoreland said there were three or four, maybe five, battalions representing a vanguard of North Vietnamese, we were going to go to war with North Vietnam. Make that speech to the sentimental American public!

Or make the speech that Vice President Hubert Humphrey recommended: "We're going to get out, we're going to cut our losses." With the image [in his mind] of what would happen in the Roman Catholic hierarchy in the United States and the probability as LBJ saw it that Robert Kennedy would be leading them in charging [that LBJ had ordered] the abandonment of South Vietnamese, the speech doesn't write itself.

How could the President have made another choice faced with these sentiments? That was Nixon's problem, and Kissinger's problem [in 1969]. They wanted to get out of Vietnam, and then they faced this problem of the sentimental disinclination on the part of the public to abandon a friendly government. The issue disappeared [in 1975] because that friendly government disappeared.

There's also a pragmatic element. People were also not willing to go over the brink.

In short, when you look back, you see all the points that have been made in the last several days — a failure to understand, not just the enemy or the ally, but also the domestic situation, the failure to understand ourselves.

It was not really a military failure, not even a political failure, it was worse: It was an intellectual failure.

WELLS: We've had the level of analysis raised quite a bit. Let's think about where Osgood and May have left us, which is something on the order of: In a limited military sense, the war probably could have been won.

There were, however, tremendous long-term difficulties in sustaining a government of free choice and moderate democratic tendencies in South Vietnam. Could the United States have stayed there for a longer period of time? The answer they both seem to imply is probably not.

So then you go back to earlier questions: Why intervene? The answer Ernest May is advancing is that there really was no better alternative because there otherwise would have been tremendous cost.

Let's think about the question: If one had a reasonably clear crystal ball and was sitting in the White House in 1964–65 and you could see the thing unfolding, do you see other alternatives to intervening that would have provided an American politician, even without all the qualities of LBJ, but just a slightly more modulated politician, could you reasonably make a case that such a person would have, or should have, acted differently?

SCHANDLER: Lyndon Johnson said, "I am not a President willing to see Southeast Asia go the way of Communist China." It appeared that this was a distinct possibility then, and in my opinion, there was no other alternative but to do something to stop this from happening.

WELLS: Events of the last five or six years have breathed new life into that general theory.

SCHANDLER: One of the questions asked yesterday was whether or not this effort was worthwhile, and the answer was no. I think the effort was worthwhile to the extent that we stopped that. We failed in Indochina, using a lot of bad policies at great cost, but in the rest of Southeast Asia, as we look at it today, partly because of the change in Chinese Communist party leadership and policy, but largely because our intervention gave many of these other governments time to get their economics and their politics straightened out, the West has a fairly strong group of allies and friends in that part of the world. This is perhaps the most favorable outcome of our intervention.

RAVENAL: Even if we had done every one of the intelligent things that in retrospect seem to have been necessary to bring about the end of the Vietnam War, would that have all added up to success?

I think that probably the conclusion is No. In fact, a radical statement of that conclusion would be that we might even have won the war, but we couldn't terminate it.

In this particular war, there was such a thing as winning the war without being able to end it. Therefore, what seems to emerge from this is the question of why it is that this country could not muster a collection of actions that would have been sufficient to terminate that war rather than just simply backing out of it or being defeated.

Should we have done it?

The elite judgment, that is the judgment of people like Nixon and Kissinger, although very intelligent, diverged considerably from popular judgment. Nixon and Kissinger, had they been able to stay the course [after 1973] with the level of U.S. materiel assistance to Saigon, plus the threat of punitive air strikes, could have continued that war indefinitely. This could not have mustered a set of conditions sufficient to end it, but they could have achieved what it seems to me was their objective: not a "decent interval" in which to get out, but a kind of low level of intervention that could have been maintained and tolerated almost indefinitely.

The problem is that their perception of what was necessary to do was not acceptable to the American public and to Congress. So as a last resort, it was a divergence of values between American leadership and the American public which turns out to be the thing that was very ill-understood by people like Kissinger; not only that he didn't understand battles, though I think he understood everything else, but that he despised the [American political] system that was generating those antithetical values. It was that [failure] that did in the American effort.

OBERDORFER: I just don't believe there were no choices [in 1964–65]. While I can see the [Central America] situation is very different, we had a rather interesting case in point just within the last few months. We're not going to have another Vietnam now because we've already had Vietnam. One of the things that came up was El Salvador. [Secretary of State Alexander] Haig was gung-ho to go down there and put a big blockade on Cuba and do all the rest, and that interfered with the American public stance which is different.

But it also interfered with the administration's other priorities. And they just shut him off, just like "Boom! you shut up."

WELLS: I would add one thing to what Ernest May was saying. It seemed inconceivable to LBJ at that time that there was any other alternative to intervention, in keeping with the image of the U.S. role in the world. We had through the early years of the Cold War talked ourselves into what I call a mindset so that we couldn't conceive of ourselves saying "We're going to take minimal losses in South Vietnam and simply not intervene there, but we will protect allies who are better situated in other places."

PIKE: One of the few conclusions I've come to about the Vietnam War has to do with the notion of effective conflict. In the past, generals tried to win wars as fast as they could, and Hanoi's notion that you deliberately dragged the thing out is one of the characteristics that made the Vietnam War different from any other. The conclusion I would come to is that probably the United States can fight a short, dirty war, but they will not fight a long, protracted conflict unless the enemy is landing in San Diego.

GROPMAN: I want to build on something that Oberdorfer just said that I think is very important. The most significant political action of 1965 for the United States of America was not the decision to bomb North Vietnam or the decision to build up the U.S. troop strength. It was the 1965 Voting Rights Act. With that blossomed Johnson's Great Society. So building on things that Betts and Schandler have written, we can't discuss that fundamental Vietnam decision without looking at what to LBJ was a much higher priority: the Great Society, in which the Voting Rights Act was the most important piece of legislation in 1965. What was the relationship between standing tough in Vietnam and getting his Voting Rights Act through the Congress?

MUELLER: I'd like to add a couple of points. One is the fact of North Vietnam's incredible resiliency. Even if they were willing to fight virtually forever, conceivably the war would have been brought down to the level at which it could have been policed in some sense, but it seems that we were up against the best enemy we ever faced in our history.

   If that's the case, if they were nowhere near the point at which they were really ready to stand down, if the North Vietnamese really believed that they would fight for 40 or 50 or 80 years, as they are still fighting in Southeast Asia against new enemies, it may be that almost anything we would have done would have just continued the war. If we'd invaded the North, if we'd invaded Laos, we would have just had a much bigger Indochina war, much like the one the French lost in 1954.

BETTS: It depends a lot on whether you assume there is some kind of cyclical pattern in foreign policy reaction or not, how much you make of the alternative possibilities.

   You asked if someone had seen in a crystal ball in 1964–65 what the results of military intervention in Vietnam would be, would they have acted differently? I suspect the answer is probably yes. But as long as it was a risk, the alternative seemed so bad that the risk had to be taken. The argument that we did prevent some of the dominoes from falling, that maybe after all the carnage and everything, it wasn't so bad given the alternatives, to a certain extent may be true. But what would be the situation in Cambodia now? I'm not so sure Sihanouk wouldn't still be in power if we had gotten out in 1965 and let North Vietnam have the other half of Indochina. But in 1965 there are all sorts of subjective influences supporting risk-taking. We'd had the May 1965 intervention in the Dominican Republic — a very messy sort of revolutionary situation. Sending in troops worked fairly well in Santo Domingo so maybe that, in some indirect sense, made the White House think things might work by sending troops into Vietnam.

   You can't attribute Ronald Reagan to Vietnam, but the dissipation of the Vietnam hangover compared to what happened in Iran, American decline in self-esteem, etc. — what were the Democrats worried about in 1965 if it wasn't the equivalent of Ronald Reagan?

It brings us back to the question we have to keep dancing around, and I don't see any answer other than that it's a dilemma, and that is the interrelationship between military and political factors. This goes back to the early 1960s when there were raging debates in the U.S. bureaucracy about whether Vietnam was a military or political war.

On the question: Could we have won? It's almost a divergence unless you define winning in a much more subtle sense than in classical terms. Probably we could have made a [satisfactory] peace. The question is at what price? The majority of commentaries have suggested that such a victory could not have been won at an acceptable price.

The final question I have is to what extent you can clearly balance off military and political options against each other, depending on the circumstances. Had Vietnam been an island or a peninsula, maybe we wouldn't have had to worry about how feeble the political situation in the South was. You could have just killed or expelled everybody who was causing the problem; you couldn't do that with all the sanctuaries [in Laos, Cambodia, and North Vietnm].

By the same token, if the political situation in the South had been better, we might not have had to do so much militarily. Because we're richer than North Vietnam's [Soviet and Chinese] allies were, we could have given more support to the South and if they had been as politically capable as the North, maybe there would have been no problem.

But can these calculations really be made in other situations? Is the Central American problem both so subjective and the other political restraints so overwhelming that we can't really hope to calculate in that pragmatic way?

WELLS: Your point about the large range of things that always remain unknown and unquantifiable or unable to be matched up [with precedents] is a very good one.

DESTLER: Was there a domestically plausible different choice in 1965? I'm not sure that there was, but one plausible choice stems from one of the many contradictory Kennedy quotations: "In the end, they have to win it — the people of Vietnam." We needed in early 1965 to define the issue not in terms of "Will the free world prevail against communism?" but "Will the South Vietnamese be given not a decent interval but a decent and fair opportunity and reasonable support in fighting what is in the end their war?"

It's conceivable that a policy decision might have been made by the American President (in 1965) that could have brought some variant of an "enclave strategy" with U.S. assistance out there. Now maybe we were already losing and [the enclaves] might well have brought a military failure, but it might have been a military failure which could have been defined in a different way, a way that would have responded to the sentiments of the American people: "It wasn't our fault, we weren't losing the war."

KOHN: We are so mired in the issues of the war itself. We're still always asking the question "what if." Those questions are essentially unanswerable because they're ahistorical. The Vietnam War is history now. We have to ask: What happened and why did it happen and what does it mean?

BERMAN: I'm struck by "The Lessons of Vietnam" — it seems really that most of us have changed our dialogue.

Take the argument of strategy, for example. I haven't heard in two days anyone say about Vietnam that it was a morally wrong war. By the time Lyndon Johnson looked around in 1965, some really fundamental questions might have been asked: What right do we have in 1965 to discuss sending B-52s to bomb the crap out of North Vietnam? Would that serve American interests? Would it be right? What is really the lesson there?

I think we should think about that. Not whether we could have won that war, but whether it should have been fought in the first place.

I've said that LBJ should have had the political guts — after having been given scenarios by George Ball and Bill Moyers privately, being urged in some of the declassified documents I've just read on my last trip to Austin — to plan the politics of getting out in July 1965, to accept the backlash, to recognize it was going to happen. Great political leaders at times have risen to those occasions, and the American public can be lead or educated in this regard.

The fundamental lesson of Vietnam was that American political leaders in Washington, either civilian or military, misread the importance of South Vietnam, and losing South Vietnam took on a significance it never should have had and therefore some of the lessons we're talking about are inappropriate.

SPECTOR: Why did we not intervene in 1954? The situation in some ways was very similar to 1965. The difference was that the U.S. military leadership in 1954 strongly objected to fighting in Indochina.

WELLS: Another difference between 1954 and 1965 was the proximity of the 1950–53 Korean War experience in the minds of American leaders in 1954.

HERRING: We also wished to dissociate ourselves from French colonialism in 1954. The more important decision by Washington was that of September—October 1954 to support a South Vietnamese government.

GIFFORD: What has always fascinated me is why we accepted the French arguments on Indochina. In 1956, we didn't accept the French arguments on Suez, in 1954–62 we didn't accept the French arguments on Algeria. Why did we accept the French arguments on Indochina?

MURRAY: My question is: How obvious does a thing have to be before it becomes obvious?

If you want to know about Vietnam, you have to know about war; if you want to know about war, you have to know a little bit about arithmetic. At the height of American power over there, we had 433 U.S. and allied combat battalions; the enemy had 60 (larger) combat regiments. In 1974 when we had pulled out, the ARVN had 189 battalions, and the enemy had built up to 110 regiments. There was a 40% decrease in allied ground firepower. Take away the B-52s, take away the F-4s, and take away U.S. naval gunfire —take all that away. Then we started to support the South Vietnamese with two percent of the money that we had used to support our own U.S. force in Vietnam against a lesser enemy. You know what Napoleon said: "God is on the side of the biggest battalions. . . ." And right about then, God was on the side of the Communists; they were bigger, they were stronger. That's why we lost the war.

Regarding our having choices, of course we had a lot of choices. I think the best choice was that of Ambassador Maxwell Taylor. He believed in 1965 that we should not support the Vietnamese except logistically. That's all they needed. The biggest secret about that war is this: We had half a million men over there, the Army alone had 100,000 contractor [personnel]; we had 5,000 helicopters and we had 5,000 contractors [civilian technicians] turning the wrenches to keep that war going. When we pulled out, the disastrous thing we did was not pulling our troops out — but pulling out the technicians.

The next war we fight, we ought to do it like the Mafia: Contract it out.

WEBB: Our reasons for going into Vietnam had nothing to do with colonialism. As a result there was a distinction that we could have drawn very clearly when we, as an outside power, went in to help the South Vietnamese. We arguably had the angels on our side. For all the frustrations with the different Saigon governments, consider the alternative which is there now: It's a totalitarian state. What we were doing was pretty clearly a moral attempt. I will always view the war as one of good intentions.

With respect to what options Lyndon Johnson might have had in 1965, you see him proceeding on the premise that we are a nation of principle. We don't turn our backs on principles. This is a different way of operating than that used by a lot of totalitarian states, which use whatever works. In contrast to what is going on in El Salvador, we had a many-year involvement with pledges made to the South Vietnamese. For that reason, coming to their aid was inarguable, but the method we used was something that was debatable.

WEIGLEY: Perhaps it would be best to compare World War I with Vietnam. In 1914, Wilson quickly won congressional assent to a declaration of war, stopped public debate, and mobilized the country to fight the war. In that way, the Executive was not stuck with assuming total responsibility for the war.

KARNOW: We start off on the proposition that we were propelled into Vietnam by notions of containment, domino theory, manifest destiny. By 1961, we're seeing the light of stars that have died. The Soviet Union and China are beginning their dispute. Even earlier the Chinese sold out the Viet Minh. Our policy-makers are making policy as if we are containing China, that there is a unity between China and North Vietnam. The question therefore is when do the facts of the situation begin to catch up with policy-making?

One point that's never been made is one that I think Hans Morgenthau would make: Clausewitz ought to be thrown out the window in the nuclear age. Dean Rusk had told us that one of the reasons he kept advising against publicity when we began to get into Vietnam in 1965, especially the July 28 decision to build up to 44 battalions, was not to scare the Russians. It was always this concern in the Johnson administration that led to the incrementalism and gradualism, a terrible concern that somehow this thing could get out of hand and explode the world. How do you deal with a limited situation in a nuclear age?

CAMERON: Let me say that a lot of the consequences of the problems we're addressing are still with us, including the role of the professional military as policy advisers. A current issue is a proposal before Congress to reorganize the Joint Chiefs of Staff. A major thrust of that reorganization is to make the Joint Chiefs more effective policy advisors to the President and to the Secretary of Defense — to get more military advice, not less. The corollary of the proposal is to unitize the Joint Chiefs so that you do not get the kind of "my Service" interest and dissent that was commented on yesterday.

DIEM: For us South Vietnamese, it was not a problem of choice for Washington to intervene or not to intervene by massive military intervention in 1965. At that time there was never a conversation between Vietnamese and Americans about how to help the South Vietnamese. The Americans should have asked us at that time, "How can we help you? Is it necessary to bring in all the troops into this country? Is there any other way to help you in South Vietnam?" But once you have made your decision, we would think, please go ahead with it, all the way, accept the consequences of such a choice.

Later on in 1974 when I came back to Saigon, I was supposed to be a man who understands a little bit about the American "system." The man in the street in Saigon would ask me "whether it was for the containment policy or for the domino theory, we knew about it. But anyway, the Americans forced their way into South Vietnam. They put our house in shambles. They cannot simply call it quits and say that they made an error. It is not possible for a big nation to behave such a way with a small nation like South Vietnam."

Another lesson for small nations from the war: "Look carefully at the United States. You have to expect changing circumstances in the public opinion, in the mood of the Congress, and in the mood of the leaders of the United States, too. You have to be careful. We end up losing higher stakes than the United States, because for the Americans, [they] can turn the page and say it is an unhappy chapter of U.S. history, but that is not the same for the South Vietnamese."

OSGOOD: We must operate on the assumption that there are alternatives; there are choices to be made, and they can and should be made on the basis of analysis. In fact, even given a mindset and all the other circumstances of the time, we had a choice from the 1950s and '60s through the '70s. Some of the choices we could have made then and we may have to make in the future.

First, we cannot anymore afford to intervene any place on a kind of abstract political basis that prevailed and led to an almost automatic intervention with American forces in Vietnam. We exaggerated the Chinese threat and analysis could have told us more about the actual Chinese strength; we were right about dominoes up to a point, but we exaggerated the dominoes. That was accessible to analysis and some CIA and other analyses did get it right. We shouldn't intervene just on the grounds of prestige if these other factors are not present. If our interests are such that a communist victory would affect the larger balance of power with the Soviet Union or another major adversary, that's one thing. But I don't think that was the case in Vietnam. So we should not have intervened.

We should not intervene in a revolutionary situation in any case unless, as Dean Acheson put it, we are the missing component. How do you determine whether you are the missing component? That's very difficult. I don't know whether we could have foreseen how difficult, if not impossible, it would be to establish in South Vietnam a government that could sustain itself after we helped them. But I believe that in other cases we can make that kind of estimate. We should be much more cautious.

If it is not a revolutionary situation, as in Korea in 1950, and we are the missing component and it would affect a strategic balance in the global setting, then we should intervene. And if we intervene, we shouldn't intervene as incrementally as we did in Vietnam. If it is a revolutionary situation, we can still intervene with aid; that doesn't automatically mean that we're going to have combat forces involved — which was one of the false lessons drawn from Vietnam. If combat forces are involved, that doesn't mean inevitably that we can't cut off our involvement, if it's a losing or too costly proposition, before there's a massive involvement.

We've talked a lot about circumstances in which we ought not to intervene again, because we're talking about a failure. This shouldn't conceal from us the fact that there may be situations in the future in which we should intervene when we won't.

And one of the reasons will be the great caution of the U.S. military. They will advise that unless we can have absolute assurance of no sanctuaries, plenty of support, all these other desirable circumstances, there should be no intervention. That is not necessarily wise advice.

Where we are now in terms of U.S. policy is a revival of containment and the limited war doctrines that go with it, but a mindset against preparing for it adequately.

MAY: I did not intend to say that there was no alternative in 1965; I was saying that I think it is not very fruitful to explore the question of what would have happened if one or another of those alternatives had been chosen. The interesting and possibly answerable question is why, in the circumstances of the time, people who made the choices saw the ones they did choose as the preferable ones.

It is a chronic tendency [among Americans] not to stop and ask what the problem is, but to think what we can do and then define the problems in terms of what we're able to do. We need to stop and ask: What is the problem and whose problem is it, recognizing that the problems of the United States and the problems of the incumbent President are not necessarily the same. We have to apply our brains.

WEIGLEY: In 1965, we did not have a George C. Marshall who, even in connection with World War II, worried that a democracy cannot fight a Seven Years' War. What we did still have in 1965, even without Marshall, was the aura of omnipotence surrounding the image of the United States, and the Americans' own image of their country that had come out of World War II. We haven't stressed that aura enough in these discussions.

The image of American power frightened the North Vietnamese, according to Pike; but we also retained that image, and Korea hadn't really deflated us all that much. We were still very self-confident in 1965; we're no longer so self-confident.

One lesson Vietnam has taught us is the lesson of our limitations. As usual we've probably learned that lesson too well. The Army now knows its lessons from Vietnam so well that its reaction is not to think about such wars. We think about World War II instead, or the big war fought in the NATO area. We now give most of our attention to the kind of war that is least likely to be fought precisely because Vietnam has frightened us off.

The most difficult thing of all for American strategists and policy-makers to do is to come out with some kind of balance in which we have learned the lesson of our limitations, but not been so impressed with our limitations that we're paralyzed.

SUMMERS: If Vietnam proved nothing else, it proved that the equivalent of a declaration of war — that is, the fixing of public will and the sharing of the responsibility for the war among the American people and the Congress and the Executive — is absolutely vital for any future war of the United States.

If you see war as a continuation of politics, then those kinds of constraints (imposed by LBJ in 1965) are a legitimate part of war and a legitimate thing that must be considered. The way that you limit the war is to limit the political objectives. One of the fallacies of Vietnam was that we looked at limited war in terms of limited means, rather than in terms of limited ends. That's a critical distinction.

I'm not really concerned whether General Westmoreland did or did not read Clausewitz, but it sure would have been nice if Earle Wheeler and Maxwell Taylor and Harold K. Johnson had read Clausewitz, because they were [in Washington] where that kind of advice was absolutely crucial.

SPECIAL PAPERS

REFLECTIONS ON THE VIETNAM ANTIWAR MOVEMENT AND ON THE CURIOUS CALM AT THE WAR'S END[1]

by John Mueller

One of the most memorable aspects of the Vietnam War was the rise within the United States of a large, vocal movement in opposition to the war, or to American participation in it. The movement collected enormous press attention during its years of existence and has inspired something of a folklore since.

This paper presents some disconnected speculations about the effect of the Vietnam antiwar movement on public opinion, political elections, American Vietnam policy, and North Vietnamese strategy. It concludes with some observations about the unexpected calm with which the American public accepted the ending of the tumultuous war in 1975.

Some years ago I did a study comparing public opinion on the war in Vietnam with public opinion on the Korean War. Using various tests I found that, although television supposedly made Vietnam somehow unique, the wars actually affected public opinion quite similarly. Both wars were supported by the same demographic groups: the young and the well-educated, in particular. Sentiment for withdrawal and escalation was about the same and mostly came from the same groups. Moreover, the wars were about equally popular during the periods in which they were comparable; that is, while the war in Vietnam eventually became more unpopular than the Korean War, it became so only after American casualties there had substantially surpassed those of the earlier war. Trends in support for the wars followed the same course: basic support declined as U.S. casualties increased, and it did so according to the same mathematical relationship.[2]

This similarity seems surprising because, while the two wars had many things in common, the Korean War inspired no organized public protest remotely comparable to the one generated during the Vietnam War. If one paid attention to vocal protest and to media reports about that protest during the two wars, it would certainly *seem* the later war was far more unpopular.

It seems to me these findings suggest two cautions about assessing vocal protest. The first is fairly obvious: One should be careful about assuming vocal agitators necessarily represent the masses they purport to speak for. Labor union leaders may not speak for workers, active feminists may not accurately represent women, and the Moral Majority may, as the bumper sticker suggests, be neither.

Second, and perhaps more interestingly, it may be that the Vietnam protest movement, at least through 1968, actually was somewhat counter-productive in its efforts to influence public opinion — that is, the war might have been somewhat more unpopular had the protest not existed.

The reasoning behind this latter suggestion is developed from a well-known public opinion phenomenon. Many people, in making up their minds on an issue, are not influenced so much by its substance as by its endorsers. If an issue comes up and if Franklin Roosevelt is for it and if, in general, I find myself in agreement with Roosevelt and trust him, it is reasonable for me to adopt his view as my own, at least as a first approximation.

This endorsement procedure, with its obvious efficiencies, can work both ways. An endorser with negative vibrations can decrease the acceptance of an issue. For example, in 1940, if the name of the then-controversial Charles Lindbergh was associated with a proposal to be nice to the Germans, support for the proposal dropped considerably.[3]

Now, as it happened, the Vietnam protest movement generated negative feelings among the American public to an all but unprecedented degree. In a poll conducted by the University of Michigan in 1968, the public was asked to place various groups and personalities on a 100-point scale. Fully one-third of the respondents gave Vietnam War protesters a zero, the lowest possible rating, while only 16 percent put them anywhere in the upper half of the scale. Other studies suggest that popular reaction to the disturbances surrounding the Democratic convention of 1968 was overwhelmingly favorable to the Chicago police and unfavorable to the demonstrators, despite press coverage that was heavily biased in the demonstrators' favor.[4] Opposition to the war came to be associated with violent disruption, stink bombs, desecration of the flag, profanity, and contempt for American values. Not only would these associations tend to affect public opinion in a negative way, they also would tend to frighten away more "respectable" would-be war opponents from joining the cause.

The Antiwar Movement and Political Elections

In addition to its efforts to influence public opinion on the war, the Vietnam protest movement was concerned with electing candidates it approved. Although friendly candidates did do well here and there, particularly in some primaries, and, although some local antiwar referendums were passed, it does not appear the movement was very successful in this effort. Even the massive efforts to influence the congressional elections of 1970 in the wake of the Cambodian invasion do not appear to have shifted many seats.

In presidential elections, however, the protest movement may have had some impact: It may have been instrumental in electing Richard Nixon. Twice.

In 1968, the alternative to Nixon was Hubert Humphrey. In rage over the fate of antiwar candidates such as Eugene McCarthy during the Democratic primaries and convention, the protest movement — or at least its most vocal elements — concentrated on assuring the defeat of Humphrey, the man it saw as the legatee of Lyndon Johnson's policies and as an important co-author of the Vietnam War.

This is an understandable point of view and, while Humphrey later sought to demonstrate his many misgivings about Johnson's policies in Vietnam, it would have been difficult for the protesters to have known that in 1968. However, even granting that point, the alternative in the election was Nixon, a man who had rigidly supported the war effort and had a long record in favor of escalation and militant anti-communism. Humphrey, on the other hand, had long supported international negotiation, arms control, conciliation. Their verbal policies in 1968 may not have differed much (Humphrey obviously could not afford to alienate the Johnson wing of the party during the election), but their instincts about issues of war and peace were clearly on the public record.

The protest movement not only chose to ignore these well-documented differences, but also actively sought to humiliate and defeat Humphrey. When the Vice President campaigned in Chicago he was greeted by "Dump-the-Hump" clamor and chaos; when Nixon ventured there he came as the prince of peace and could draw the lesson that his election would return tranquility to the streets of America.

Amazingly, despite all his problems, Humphrey almost won the election. Many war opponents in the party joined up at the end, but their support was grudging, belittling, and too late. Others sat on their hands. The margin was enough to send Nixon to the White House.

Four years later the machinery of the Democratic party was largely in the hands of the antiwar element. It changed the rules to avoid the debacle of 1968 and committed another one: the nomination of George McGovern, the worst presidential candidate any party has put forward in modern times. McGovern managed to do the seemingly impossible: He gained a lower percentage of the popular vote than Barry Goldwater had in 1964, even though McGovern represented the majority party and even though he was up against a candidate who, though difficult to defeat, was far less popular and far more vulnerable than Goldwater's opponent, Lyndon Johnson, had been in 1964.

The Antiwar Movement and Vietnam Policy

The impact of the antiwar movement on American policy and policy-makers seems to be fairly limited, especially through 1968. Perhaps Lyndon Johnson's efforts at negotiations were increased by the rancor at home, but, since these efforts led to little until 1968, that is not much of an achievement.

There probably was some atmospheric impact of the peace movement on the various changes in American policy that took place in the post-Tet spring of 1968. But the accounts of major participants like Johnson and Clark Clifford, as well as the general histories of the period such as Herbert Schandler's, tend to suggest these changes — perhaps even Johnson's decision not to run again — were fairly likely to have come about for reasons that have little to do with the protest at home.[5]

The antiwar movement probably had a greater impact later, in the Nixon era. Of all the major party presidential possibilities of 1968 (including even Johnson), Nixon was probably the one most reluctant to relax the military presence in Vietnam, to withdraw U.S. troops, to make central concessions in negotiations, to want to see the nation "accept the first defeat in its history." The antiwar movement may have been influential in getting Nixon to speed up troop withdrawals somewhat and in causing him to pull back from the Cambodian incursion a bit earlier than planned. Certainly memoirs by Nixon and by foreign policy adviser Henry Kissinger suggest a considerable preoccupation with the opposition movement. It seems of interest that when Nixon felt he had to do some punishment bombing of North Vietnam in 1971, he chose to do it at the only time of the year when he could guarantee American colleges would be deserted: between Christmas and New Year's.

But it should also be kept in mind that the antiwar movement became considerably broader after Nixon's election. In particular, many liberal Democrats who had supported the war out of loyalty to the Johnson administration were released by the election from this commitment and could move toward opposition to what quickly began to become "Nixon's war." Moreover, twin developments — the increasing costs of the war and the declining importance of South Vietnam in containment theory (due to threat-moderating changes in Indonesia and China in the late 1960s) — caused disillusion with the war.[6] Thus, while elements remained from its earlier, more romantic past, the antiwar movement came to be dominated by more respectable types — including even Hubert Humphrey, in fact. It was quite a different animal in that era and its demands were more likely to be effective. The most consequential antiwar measures, the war powers restraints enacted by Congress in 1973, were adopted long after the antiwar movement had ceased to exist as a street phenomenon.

Ending the War

Some of the movement's ineffectiveness, particularly in the 1965–1968 period, may have been due to the way it dealt with the issues. Most of the protest seemed to be directed toward getting negotiations going, and a prerequisite for that, according to North Vietnam, was that all bombing of its territory be halted unconditionally. For the most part the issue between the administration and the war protesters was never met, because the antiwar movement kept asking for a bombing halt to "get negotiations going" and simply ignored the Communists' demand that the halt must be unconditional.

In some respects, in fact, the antiwar movement may have inadvertently played into the hands of those within the administration who favored bombing. By constantly stressing that the bombing was doing tremendous damage and killing "innocent civilians," the protesters suggested the bombing was militarily potent. Proponents of bombing were thus bolstered in their contention that the enemy was "hurting" because of the bombing, and to counter the argument about "innocent civilians," could say that efforts would be made to reduce "collateral damage." In addition some may have argued internally that no civilian in a totally mobilized country like North Vietnam was innocent anyway and therefore that civilian casualties were all to the good.

An argument likely to have been far more effective with members of the administration would have been to stress the costs of the bombing in *American* lives and dollars. When disillusionment with the bombing occurred inside the establishment, it mostly came from the realization that the bombing was ineffective militarily — that meaningful targets were few in number, very difficult to destroy with bombs, and easily repaired or compensated for when damaged. Thus the bombing was not having enough effect on the Communist war effort, particularly in the North, to justify the cost in planes and pilots.[7] Robert McNamara and other defense planners were among those most impressed by this dawning realization, but this potent argument was only occasionally emphasized by the antiwar movement, caught up as it was in rhetoric about the murderousness of American pilots and the innocence of the enemy.

The Antiwar Movement and North Vietnam's Strategy

It is often maintained by supporters of the Vietnam War that the antiwar movement strengthened the will of the Communists to continue the war, and thus that the war protest had the effect of prolonging the war.[8]

The war, as General William Westmoreland often observed, was a war of attrition, a "war of will" in which each side would punish the other until one finally caved in. (His analysis seems to have been generally correct, though the war didn't come out the way he intended.) Thus the ability to maintain morale was especially important in this war.

It seems likely the war protest in the United States was encouraging to Hanoi, even as the absence of signs of war opposition in North Vietnam was discouraging to Washington. At least one Communist leader in Vietnam has, in fact, admitted this in a postwar interview shown on public television.[9]

The crucial consideration, however, is not whether the war protest was encouraging to the Communists but whether that encouragement was important to their ability to continue their war effort. All the evidence on this issue is not in, but it seems likely the North Vietnamese were prepared to continue the war for as long as necessary regardless of how much encouraging opposition there was in the United States.

The mechanisms used to build and maintain morale both in the North and, more importantly, on the battlefield in the South, relied on organizational and political skills that had little to do with news from foreign locales. In the course of the war the Communists probably suffered more battle deaths as a percentage of population than virtually any country in the last 160 years, and they seem to have been psychologically committed to continuing that conflict for a long time — even decades.[10] Indeed, today, more than eight years after their victory in the South, they continue to fight without let-up against new enemies in Indochina. A commitment to prolonged war seems to have been an essential part of their psychological make-up well before the antiwar movement came into being.

The antiwar movement faded as American troops were withdrawn from Vietnam and it was scarcely an element on the political scene in 1975 when American foreign policy in Indochina ended in debacle as U.S.-supported governments collapsed ignominiously under Communist attacks. During the war many supporters of the war had warned that a Communist takeover in the area would, among other things, cause widespread political ramifications within the United States — the rise of a new McCarthyism, for example, since the old McCarthyism often seemed to have been impelled by the "fall" of China to Communism in 1949.[11]

Contrary to such dire predictions, the collapse in Southeast Asia was greeted with remarkable equanimity by the American public and there was very little debate over "who lost Vietnam." Most amazingly, the man who presided over the debacle, President Gerald Ford, actually used the events in Indochina as a point in his *favor* when running for re-election in 1976: "When I came into office in 1974," he repeatedly argued, "we were still involved in a war in Southeast Asia; now we are blissfully at peace." His challenger, Jimmy Carter, seems to have concluded it was disadvantageous to point out the essential absurdity of Ford's argument.

I would like to suggest there were at least three reasons why the public found it so easy to accept the collapse of 1975.

First, to a considerable degree the war had become decoupled from American sensibilities by the settlement of January 1973; that is, there had been a "decent interval" of two years during which the war had seemingly been given back to the Indochinese.

Crucial to this development was the return of the American prisoners of war in early 1973. It is often suggested that Vietnam differed from other wars in that there was never a glorious homecoming for the returning soldier-heroes. But for this small group of men there *was* an emotional and well-publicized homecoming, and their return constituted a highly visible end to the war for the public.[12] The importance of the prisoner-of-war issue to American identification with the war should not be underestimated. In May 1971, a public opinion poll asked if American troops should be withdrawn from Vietnam by the end of the year; 68 percent agreed. When asked if they would still favor withdrawal if such an action would mean "a Communist takeover of South Vietnam," only 29 percent of the respondents agreed. When asked if they approved withdrawal "even if it threatened [not *cost*] the lives or safety of United States POWs held by North Vietnam," support evaporated: only 11 percent agreed.[13]

The Acceptance of Defeat

This visceral public attitude was generally well appreciated by politicians (except, perhaps, by George McGovern), and the political necessity of winning release for the POWs helped keep the peace talks — and American participation in the war — dragging on for years. Rationally, one might question a policy of spending thousands of lives to save hundreds of prisoners, but to a considerable degree, there was no choice.[14] However, once the prisoners returned and this issue was disposed of, the war could quickly be forgotten.[15]

Second, since the Cold War importance of South Vietnam diminished greatly after 1965, as suggested above, the chief reason to reinsert U.S. troops into the war in 1957 was to save or to defend the South Vietnamese. But poll evidence demonstrates that the American public viewed the South Vietnamese with considerable disrespect, even contempt, and the public had long been prepared to abandon them if they could not effectively fight for themselves. This could be seen as early as 1966. At that time some 15 to 35 percent of the public favored withdrawal from Vietnam; but this percentage jumped to 54 percent when the poll question was phrased to include the condition "suppose the South Vietnamese start fighting among themselves," and to 72 percent when it included the phrase, "if the South Vietnamese government decides to stop fighting." Other polls suggest the commitment to the South Vietnamese and fear of a postwar blood bath in Vietnam were relatively minor elements in popular support for the war.

Third, the collapse in Indochina was probably made easier to accept by an ancillary, if essentially insignificant, event: the capture in 1975 of the American ship *Mayaguez* by Cambodian Communists and its subsequent daring recapture by American troops. Although it cost about as many lives to rescue the ship as there were sailors aboard, the drama and macho derring-do of the venture probably served to mollify American anguish. It was possible to believe that, while the Communists could defeat our erstwhile allies in Southeast Asia, they were impotent against true American might.

NOTES

[1] Copyright© 1984 by John Mueller.

[2] John Mueller, *War, Presidents and Public Opinion* (New York: Wiley, 1973), chs. 2–6. See also "Public Opinion and the War in Vietnam" elsewhere in this volume.

[3] Hadley Cantril, *Gauging Public Opinion* (Princeton, NJ: Princeton University Press, 1947), p. 41.

[4] John P. Robinson, "Public Reaction to Political Protest: Chicago 1968," *Public Opinion Quarterly*, Spring 1970, pp. 1–9.

[5] Lyndon B. Johnson, *The Vantage Point* (New York: Holt, 1971), Clark Clifford, "A Viet Nam Reappraisal," *Foreign Affairs*, July 1969, Herbert Y. Schandler, *The Unmaking of a President* (Princeton, NJ: Princeton University Press, 1977).

[6] Leslie Gelb and Richard Betts argue in their important *The Irony of Vietnam* (Washington, DC: Brookings, 1979) that the postwar consensus on containing communism broke down between 1965 and 1968 through disillusionment over the *costs* of the war (see also Richard K. Betts, "Misadventure Revisited," *The Wilson Quarterly*, Summer 1983, p. 105). But it should be added that at the same time the threat of communism in Southeast Asia, and therefore the *value* of containing communism in Vietnam, had decreased dramatically; Indonesia no longer seemed on the brink of communism due to the coup of 1965–66, and China had turned inward on its self-destructive Cultural Revolution. On this "de-vitalization" of Vietnam, see John Mueller, "Vietnam Revised," *Armed Forces and Society*, December 1982.

[7] See Alain C. Enthoven and K. Wayne Smith, *How Much is Enough?* (New York: Harper, 1971), ch. 8.

[8] For example, Paul Nitze in William S. Thompson and D. D. Frizzell (eds.), *The Lessons of Vietnam* (New York: Crane, Russak, 1977), p. 6. See also Allan E. Goodman, *The Lost Peace* (Stanford, CA: Hoover Institution Press, 1978), p. 116.

[9] On the series, "Vietnam: The 10,000 Day War."

[10] The Communist battle death percentage in Vietnam was twice that of the Japanese in World War II. For a discussion of these issues, see John Mueller, "The Search for the 'Breaking Point' in Vietnam," *International Studies Quarterly*, December 1980, pp. 497–519. Commentators who suggest North Vietnam was desperate after the Christmas bombings of 1972 and on the verge of collapse need to supply convincing evidence not that the damage was extensive, but that the Communists' "breaking point" was reached — that they were no longer willing to recoup losses as they had after costly ventures in the past, and that they were finally about to abandon their fanatical commitment to protracted warfare.

[11] An imperfect analogy. The reaction in the early 1950s was not simply to the Communist success in China in 1949, but to the fact that a year later the United States found itself at war with Communist China in Korea.

[12] As an example of the thoroughness with which this decoupling has been accepted, Harrison Salisbury opened a conference on Vietnam in 1983 by declaring, "It's 10 years down the line since the war came to its halting end." ("On Reopening a Chapter," *The Journalist*, May 1983, p. 6).

[13] Opinion Research Corporation release, May 8, 1971.

[14] The utter necessity of getting the prisoners back is suggested by Henry Kissinger in his review of the options in the Vietnam negotiations. "Unilateral withdrawal. . .would not do the trick; it would leave our prisoners in Hanoi's hands"; and "Vietnamization pursued to the end would not return our prisoners" (*White House Years*, Boston: Little, Brown, 1979, pp. 1011, 1039). The option of ending the war without the return of the prisoners seems not to have been even a theoretical consideration.

[15] The emotional attachment to prisoners of war has often been a dominant theme in American history. The issue was central to the lengthy peace talks in the Korean War, and outrage at the fate of American POWs on Bataan intensified hatred for the Japanese during World War II almost as much as the attack on Pearl Harbor. Another case in point is the almost total preoccupation by politicians and press with the Iranian hostage crisis of 1979–81, to the virtual exclusion of issues and events likely to be of far greater import historically.

COMMENTS ON THE INFLUENCE OF TELEVISION ON PUBLIC OPINION

by Lawrence W. Lichty

Many commentators claim that television coverage was influential in forming American public opinion of the Vietnam War; both the perceived antiwar bias of TV's analysis and the blood and gore it depicted are seen as helping to turn Americans against the war.

One commentator, General William Westmoreland, charges that "television's unique requirements contributed to a distorted view of the war" being brought into the American home. "The news had to be compressed and visually dramatic," and as a result, Westmoreland states, "the war that Americans saw was almost exclusively violent, miserable, or controversial."[1] Another commentator, Robert Elegant, focusses on the impact of the TV coverage, saying, "For the first time in modern history, the outcome of a war was determined not on the battlefield, but. . .on the television screen."[2]

But as a matter of fact, while about half of all the TV reports filed from Vietnam were about battles and military action, most showed very little actual fighting. From August 1965 to August 1970, only about three percent of all the evening news film reports from Vietnam showed "heavy battle" (defined as "heavy fighting, incoming, with dead or wounded seen"). That amounts to only 76 "heavy battle" stories, out of more than 2,300 on the air during those five years.

A sample of Vietnam-related evening news stories from 1968 to 1973 found that only about three percent of the stories contained combat footage, and only two percent showed any dead or wounded. Much of the coverage actually dealt with various "instruments," such as the newest American military hardware.

Perhaps the best summary of what actually did appear in American living rooms, then, is Michael Arlen's:

> . . .a nightly stylized, generally distanced overview of a disjointed conflict which was composed mainly of scenes of helicopters landing, tall grasses blowing in the helicopter wind, American soldiers fanning out across a hillside on foot, rifles at the ready, with now and then (on the soundtrack) a far-off ping or two, and now and then (as the visual grand finale) a column of dark, billowing smoke a half mile away, invariably described as a burning Viet Cong ammo dump.[3]

Far from being biased *against* the war, American TV coverage of the Vietnam War was generally positive from 1965 to mid-1967: The coverage implied that the United States could win the war in Vietnam, probably with a minimum of effort.

During that period, on documentaries and news interview programs, there were always more administrative spokesmen and supporters than critics, at least until 1970. Before 1966, "hawks" appearing on such programs outnumbered "doves" by about nine to one; between 1966 and 1970 about two-thirds of those discussing Vietnam policy on such programs were "hawks."

But by late 1966, and especially in the spring of 1967, the "direction" of the TV coverage began to change — toward an increasingly critical questioning of the ultimate success of the American effort. (Also in early 1967 there appeared in the print media Harrison Salisbury's report from Hanoi on the bombing and Jonathan Schell's *New Yorker* story on the village of Ben Suc, which sparked a debate on U.S. strategy and tactics.)

Just after the Communist Tet Offensive of 1968, all three of the national TV networks presented on their talk shows (e.g., NBC's "Meet the Press") about an equal number of supporters and critics of the war. But after 1970, until the end of the war, more than half of the guests interviewed on these shows were critical of Nixon administration policy. This opinion trend paralleled the trend in the publicly expressed opinions of many senators and congressmen, perhaps because senators and congressmen were so often those interviewed.

(It is interesting to note that in October 1967 a Gallup poll reported that 44 to 46 percent of Americans thought it was a mistake to send troops to Vietnam.)

No senator or congressman, or TV anchorman, can speak to the nation about foreign affairs with the authority of the President, however. American public opinion has almost always supported the President in matters of foreign policy, especially when he takes a hard line. Yet approval of the war declined steadily through 1971, from a peak in late 1965. During that period, public approval of President Johnson's handling of his job declined, as did public approval of President Nixon's handling of the war (at least until late 1970, when public approval began to increase slowly, particularly as more American troops were withdrawn from combat).

Still, an analysis of Gallup ratings following television speeches by both Presidents Johnson and Nixon shows that an appearance on TV to speak about the Vietnam War *improved* both Presidents' chances to rise in the polls. Conversely, if they did not appear on TV, it was much more likely that their rating would go down. For example, Johnson's rating rose more than two points on the question of "handling the Vietnam war" after TV appearances. Nixon's rating rose more than four points after his TV speeches devoted exclusively to Vietnam. We cannot, of course, separate the medium and the message, but it is clear that the President can, and has, used TV to effectively boost his image — especially when bringing "good news."

Finally, the evidence shows that those whose opinions of the U.S. involvement in Vietnam changed the most were those *least* reliant on TV. The gradual decline of support for the war occurred mostly among young, well-educated people who could be categorized as "managers," college graduates, and "strong" Republicans; people who were least likely to say that TV was their most important source for news. These were also the people who were the strongest supporters of the war from the beginning, and who, even by the end, were still less likely to think the war was a mistake than were those over 50 or those with only a grade-school education.

Notes

[1] Westmoreland, William. *A Soldier Reports* (Doubleday, 1976).

[2] Elegant, Robert. "How to Lose a War," *Encounter*, August 1981.

[3] Arlen, Michael. "The Falklands, Vietnam, and Our Collective Memory," *New Yorker*, August 16, 1982.

I would like to acknowledge the help of Tom Hoffer, George Bailey, Ray Carroll and Sandra Kautz Carruthers in preparing some of the research mentioned in this paper.

APPENDICES

A BRIEF CHRONOLOGY

1954–1975

1954

JUL 21   Geneva Accords end Indochina war between French and Viet Minh, dividing Vietnam into North and South.
SEP 8   Southeast Asia Treaty Organization created.
OCT 23   President Eisenhower offers aid to South Vietnamese government.

1955

FEB 12   U.S. advisors take over training of South Vietnamese army (ARVN) from French.
OCT 23   Ngo Dinh Diem becomes President of South Vietnam.

1958

Growth of Communist guerrilla war against Diem regime.

1959

Hanoi decides to unify Vietnam by force, sets up 559 Group to organize Ho Chi Minh Trail infiltration routes to South Vietnam.

1960

NOV 8   Kennedy elected President; South Vietnamese government charges North Vietnam is infiltrating troops into South Vietnam.
NOV 10   Revolt of South Vietnamese paratroopers against Diem fails.
DEC 20   Hanoi announces formation of southern National Liberation Front (Viet Cong).

1961

FALL   As Viet Cong pressure grows, decisions by Kennedy administration to increase military and economic aid to South Vietnam, and to raise number of military advisors from 685 to 16,000—by late 1963.

1962

Soviet-American agreement in Geneva provides for "neutral" Laos, but does not end Hanoi's use of Ho Chi Minh Trail or CIA counter-insurgency effort.

1963

OCT 2   Defense Secretary McNamara predicts most of 15,000 U.S. military advisors in South Vietnam can be withdrawn by the end of 1965.
NOV 1   Diem is ousted from office and killed by army, after suppressing Buddhist dissidents.
NOV 22   Kennedy assassinated; Johnson becomes President.
DEC 21   McNamara abandons plan to withdraw U.S. advisors by end of 1965, notes Viet Cong gains after anti-Diem coup.

1964

JAN 30   Another coup in South Vietnam.
MAR 17   United States pledges continued assistance to South Vietnam as long as required to defeat "Communist aggression;" issues warnings to Hanoi.
AUGUST   After clash between North Vietnamese PT boats and U.S. destroyers in Gulf of Tonkin, North Vietnamese PT boat bases are bombed; Congress passes Tonkin Gulf Resolution supporting U.S. efforts to "prevent further aggression."
OCTOBER   Hanoi begins dispatching regular army (PAVN) units to South Vietnam.
NOV 2   Johnson elected President in landslide victory over Barry Goldwater, as his Great Society gets under way. 23,000 advisors are in Vietnam.

1965

FEB 7   North Vietnam bombed by U.S. planes in retaliation for Viet Cong attack on U.S. bases in South Vietnam; U.S. "Rolling Thunder" bombing campaign against North Vietnam begins.
FEB 24   United States planes bomb Viet Cong targets in South Vietnam for first time. Viet Cong continue to batter ARVN units in pitched battles.
FEB 27   State Department White Paper on North Vietnamese aggression.
MAR 8   Marines land at Da Nang to defend U.S. airbase.
MAR 21   Communist China says it will fight in Vietnam if United States invades the North or if aid is requested by the North Vietnamese.
APR 17   15,000 demonstrators in Washington protest bombings; teach-ins follow.
JUN 21   Nguyen Cao Ky becomes President of South Vietnam.
JUL 28   LBJ announces increased draft calls to allow build-up in Vietnam from current 75,000 to 125,000, but refuses to call up reserves.
SEP 23   Hanoi reaffirms earlier rejections of U.S. offers to negotiate.
DEC 24   Month-long bombing halt begins as LBJ sends out peace envoys.
YEAR END   U.S. TROOP TOTAL: 184,300
        ARVN TROOP TOTAL: 643,000

        U.S. BATTLE DEAD (TO DATE): 1,636
        ARVN BATTLE DEAD (TO DATE): 35,759

1966

JAN 2   Vice President Humphrey announces that South Korea will send more troops.
JAN 4   Foreign Secretary Ramos of Philippines backs dispatch of Filipino unit.
FEBRUARY   U.S. Senate hearings on Vietnam war policy.
SPRING   Many antiwar demonstrations.
MAY   In China: Rise of Lin Piao, beginnings of purges, Red Guard movement, Great Proletarian Cultural Revolution.
MAY 4   *New York Times* reports dispatch of more troops by Australians.
JUN 29   Extension of U.S. bombing raids to oil dumps near Hanoi.
DECEMBER   Reports from Hanoi by *New York Times's* Harrison Salisbury on civilian damage caused by U.S. air strikes.
   Hanoi secures secret permission from Prince Norodom Sihanouk of "neutral" Cambodia to use Sihanoukville (Kampong Som) as supply port. War of attrition grinds on in South Vietnam.
YEAR END   U.S. TROOP TOTAL: 385,300
                 ARVN TROOP TOTAL: 735,900
                 U.S. BATTLE DEAD (TO DATE): 6,644
                 ARVN BATTLE DEAD (TO DATE): 47,712

1967

FEBRUARY   Wilson-Kosygin probes for negotiations on war; North Vietnam continues to demand unconditional bombing halt before talks can begin.
MAR 20   Guam "summit" on Vietnam; Westmoreland tells LBJ more decisive strategy (i.e., cutting Ho Chi Minh Trail) is required to end war. No LBJ response.
APR 15   Mass antiwar rally of 100,000 in New York.
AUG 3   President Johnson announces he has raised U.S. troop ceiling in South Vietnam to 525,000 (200,000 below military request); calls for 10 percent surtax on individual and corporate income.
AUG 20   Associate Press survey reports U.S. Senate support for Johnson war policy has eroded sharply; of senators replying to survey, 44 generally support war policies, 40 disapprove.
AUG 25   Secretary of Defense McNamara tells Senate Preparedness Sub-committee the war cannot be won by bombing, gives pessimistic report on effects of bombing to date.
SEP 3   Elections of Thieu and Ky in South Vietnam.
OCT 21   Antiwar demonstrators storm Pentagon.
NOV 1   Defense Secretary McNamara privately urges end of U.S. bombing and limit on U.S. manpower in Vietnam.
NOV 2   Senior unofficial advisors—"Wise Men"—give broad approval of Johnson administration war policies in Washington meeting.
NOV 29   President Johnson announces Robert McNamara will step down as Secretary of Defense to become president of the World Bank in 1968.
DEC 20   Westmoreland warns Washington of impending major effort by enemy.

1968

JAN 1   LBJ imposes mandatory curbs on most direct U.S. investments abroad, and asks for restrictions on overseas travel of U.S. citizens, to cut growing balance-of-payments deficit and gold drain.

JAN 10   Westmoreland, after conference with Lt. General Fred Weyand, orders redeployment of U.S. forces to positions closer to Saigon.

JAN 15   Westmoreland at U.S. Mission Council in Saigon predicts attacks before or after Tet, echoing his public statements.

JAN 21   Siege of Khe Sanh by Giap's forces begins.

JAN 23   North Korea seizes U.S. Navy "spy ship" *Pueblo*.

JAN 30   Beginning of major offensive against cities by Communists during Tet cease-fire.

FEB 2   LBJ in White House news conference says Tet Offensive "complete failure" militarily, but promises more heavy fighting.

FEB 6   U.S. spokesman in Saigon says 21,330 enemy troops killed since Tet began. National Liberation Front guerrillas (Viet Cong) suffer grave losses.

FEB 13   Pentagon announces 10,500 additional men being airlifted to South Vietnam in response to Westmoreland request. No major reserve call-up.

FEB 17   All-time weekly high of U.S. casualties is set, Feb. 10–17: 543 killed in action, 2547 wounded in action.

FEB 24   Hue, last city held by Communists, cleared. Heavy damage.

FEB 28   Military requests 206,000 more men.

MAR 1   Clark Clifford sworn in as Secretary of Defense.

MAR 12   Sen. Eugene McCarthy, peace candidate, wins 42.4 percent of Democratic Party vote in New Hampshire presidential primary; LBJ receives 49.5 percent.

MAR 15   Former Secretary of State Dean Acheson, in private report to Johnson, says U.S. victory in Vietnam is not feasible within the limits of public tolerance; Acheson recommends liquidation of war.

MAR 16   Sen. Robert Kennedy announces candidacy for Democratic presidential nomination.

MAR 22   LBJ announces Westmoreland will leave as commander in Vietnam and be promoted to Chief of Staff of the Army (in July).

MAR 26   In White House meeting, most Wise Men say public has lost confidence in war and U.S. disengagement is necessary.

MAR 31   LBJ orders partial bombing halt, calls for talks, and announces he will not run for re-election.

APR 3   Hanoi agrees to preliminary peace talks in Paris.

APR 9   Defense Secretary Clifford fixed 549,500-man troop ceiling and gradual transfer of war burden to South Vietnamese.

SPRING   Many antiwar demonstrations.

MAY   Communist "mini-Tet" offensives against Saigon; preliminary peace talks begin in Paris with U.S. delegation headed by W. Averell Harriman.

AUG 8   Nixon nominated by Republicans.
AUG 29   Humphrey nominated by Democrats at tempestuous Chicago convention.
OCT 31   Full bombing halt agreed to, "productive discussions" to begin in Paris.
NOV 1   LBJ halts all bombing of North Vietnam.
NOV 6   Nixon elected president with 43.4% of popular vote.

YEAR END   U.S. TROOP TOTAL: 536,100
ARVN TROOP TOTAL: 820,000
U.S. BATTLE DEAD (TO DATE): 30,610
ARVN BATTLE DEAD (TO DATE): 88,343

1969

SPRING   Peak strength (543,400) U.S. troops reached. Gen. Creighton Abrams is U.S. commander.
APR 30   Communist "high-point" attacks.
SEP 3   President Ho Chi Minh of North Vietnam dies.
SEP 16   Nixon announces withdrawals of 35,000 more men as pace of war slackens.
OCTOBER   Nationwide protests against the war (Moratorium).
NOV 3   President Nixon first publicly uses term "Vietnamization" in an address to the nation.
NOV 13   40,000 march in Washington, D.C., in protest of war.
NOV 15   Mass antiwar march in Washington of 250,000 to 300,000.
NOV 16   Reports of "My Lai massacre" by U.S. troops in March 1968.
DEC 15   Nixon announces further withdrawal of 50,000 troops.

YEAR END   U.S. TROOP TOTAL: 475,200 (68,000 withdrawn over course of the year)
ARVN TROOP TOTAL: 897,000
U.S. BATTLE DEAD (TO DATE): 40,024
ARVN BATTLE DEAD (TO DATE): 110,176

1970

APR 20   Nixon pledges to withdraw 150,000 troops over the next year.
MAY 1   Joint U.S.-South Vietnamese invasion of Cambodia after Lon Nol coup ousts Sihanouk.
MAY 4   Four students at Kent State University in Ohio are slain and nine wounded by National Guardsmen during demonstration against incursion into Cambodia. Within week, students close 100 colleges in protest over Cambodia and Kent State.
SEP 7   U.S. troop strength falls below 400,000 for first time since early 1967. Pacification program scores major gains in countryside.
OCT 7   Nixon proposes a standstill cease-fire throughout Indochina.
NOV 16   Number of Americans killed in Indochina passes 44,000.

YEAR END   U.S. TROOP TOTAL: 334,600
ARVN TROOP TOTAL: 968,000
U.S. BATTLE DEAD (TO DATE): 44,245
ARVN BATTLE DEAD (TO DATE): 133,522

1971

FEBRUARY   South Vietnamese troops, with U.S. air support, invade southern Laos in raid on Ho Chi Minh Trail.
MAR 29   Lt. William Calley convicted of civilian mass murders at My Lai.
JUN 13   *New York Times* begins its controversial publication of the "Pentagon Papers."
SEP 21   Congress votes to end draft in 1973.
OCT 4   Re-election of Thieu.
OCT 21   Five G.I.s killed in Vietnam in previous week—lowest U.S. toll in six years.
NOV 1   U.S. troop strength in Vietnam drops to below 200,000.
DECEMBER   Series of bombing raids ("protective reaction strikes") on North Vietnam.

YEAR END   U.S. TROOP TOTAL: 156,800
ARVN TROOP TOTAL: 1,046,250
U.S. BATTLE DEAD (TO DATE): 45,626
ARVN BATTLE DEAD (TO DATE): 156,260

1972

U.S. election year.
JAN 13   President Nixon announces new troop withdrawals to bring U.S. ground forces in Vietnam to 69,000 by May 1.
FEB 21   Nixon in China, meets with Chou En Lai.
MAR 23   U.S. declares indefinite suspension of Paris peace talks.
APR 1   Equipped by Soviets, North Vietnamese launch massive tank-led Easter Offensive.
APR 16   U.S. resumes bombing North Vietnam.
MAY 8   President Nixon orders mining of North Vietnam's ports. South Vietnamese counterattack north of Hue.
MAY 22   Nixon is in Moscow for summit meeting.
JUN 17   Watergate break-in.
JUL 13   McGovern nominated by Democrats on antiwar platform. Paris peace talks resume; one battalion remains as the only U.S. combat unit in South Vietnam.
AUG 20   President Nixon announces cut of 12,000 in ground troops.
SEP 21   For first time since March 1965, a week passes without a U.S. combat death in Indochina.
OCT 26   Hanoi announces that secret talks in Paris have produced tentative agreement on a nine-point plan to end war; Henry Kissinger says "peace is at hand." But year ends with peace agreement unsigned.

NOV 7   Richard Nixon is elected President for a second term.

NOV 11   Long Binh base north of Saigon is turned over to South Vietnamese army, marking end of direct U.S. Army participation in war.

DEC 18   President orders all-out "Linebacker II" bombing of North Vietnam, including Hanoi-Haiphong area, in effort to force North Vietnamese back to Paris conference table.

DECEMBER   Year ends with continuing B-52 attacks.

YEAR END   U.S. TROOP TOTAL: 24,200
ARVN TROOP TOTAL: 1,048,000
U.S. BATTLE DEAD (TO DATE): 45,926
ARVN BATTLE DEAD (TO DATE): 195,847

1973

JAN 15   President Nixon orders halt to all U.S. offensive air operations in North Vietnam, privately assures Thieu that U.S. will react with force to any massive Communist "true violations."

JAN 23   President announces accord with Hanoi on ending war in Vietnam; cease-fire will begin Jan. 27, and all prisoners of war will be released within 60 days.

JAN 27   Secretary of State William P. Rogers and representatives of North and South Vietnam and the Viet Cong sign peace pact in Paris. Longest war in U.S. history (over 12 years) ends. North Vietnamese forces remain in Laos, Cambodia and South Vietnam.

MAY 10   U.S. House of Representatives agrees on date to stop bombing (Aug. 15).

AUG 15   U.S. bombing of Khmer Rouge insurgents in Cambodia, and thus all direct American military intervention in Indochina, ends in obedience to Congress's mandate.

SEP 21   Henry Kissinger is confirmed as Secretary of State.

NOV 7   Congress passes War Powers Act as Watergate disclosures engulf White House.

YEAR END   U.S. TROOP TOTAL: less than 250
U.S. BATTLE DEAD (TO DATE): 46,163
ARVN BATTLE DEAD (TO DATE): 223,748

1974

Both sides violate cease-fire agreement in South Vietnam.

JAN 6   Khmer Rouge reach outskirts of Phnom Penh.

MAY 6   U.S. Senate rejects Nixon administration request for $266 million in additional military aid to South Vietnam.

MAY 9   U.S. House of Representatives' Judiciary Committee formally begins inquiry into possible impeachment of President Nixon.

MAY 22   House turns down 100,000-man overall reduction in U.S. forces abroad; but approves $474-million cutback in military aid to South Vietnam.

AUG 9   Richard Nixon resigns as President as result of Watergate scandal, is succeeded by Gerald Ford. Ford announces Kissinger will remain as Secretary of State.

1975

JAN 1   In Cambodia, Khmer Rouge launch annual dry-season offensive against Lon Nol forces.

JAN 8   North Vietnamese seize Phuoc Long Province north of Saigon; U.S. does not intervene with airpower.

MAR 10   North Vietnamese army offensive against Ban Me Thuot, provincial capital in Central Highlands.

MAR 30   Da Nang falls to NVA.

APR 1   President Lon Nol and entourage leave Cambodia.

APR 10   President Ford requests $722 million in military assistance and $250 million in economic and humanitarian aid for Saigon from Congress, which rejects the request.

APR 16   Pol Pot's Khmer Rouge capture Phnom Penh and begin massacres across Cambodia.

APR 21   Thieu resigns.

APR 30   Saigon falls to North Vietnamese assault. Americans help 150,000 South Vietnamese escape.

AUG 22   Pro-Hanoi Pathet Lao forces occupy Vientiane, Laos's capital. Peace.

Prepared from:
   Department of Defense, "Selected Manpower Statistics" (May 1977).
   Department of Defense, "Southeast Asia Military Hostile Casualties" (March, 1975).
   Golenpaul, Dan (Ed.). *Information Please Almanac 1975* (Simon & Schuster, 1975).
   Golenpaul, Dan (Ed.). *Information Please Almanac* (Simon & Schuster, 1976).
   Mueller, John E. *War, Presidents and Public Opinion* (John Wiley & Sons, Inc., 1973).
   New York Times Index, 1960–75. (New York Times Co. 1960–75).
   Oberdorfer, Don. *Tet!* (Doubleday & Co., Inc., 1971).
   Shawcross, William. *Sideshow* (Simon & Schuster, 1979).
   Stanton, Shelby. *Vietnam Order of Battle* (U.S. News & World Report Books, 1980).
   Wilson Quarterly, "Vietnam as the Past," Summer 1983.
   Note: This chronology was originally prepared for the Wilson Center's Conference on the History of the Vietnam War (January 7–8, 1983), and revised for this book.

A SUMMARY OF PUBLIC OPINION AND THE VIETNAM WAR[1]

by John Mueller

In their important study of the politics of the Vietnam War, Leslie Gelb and Richard Betts observe,

> The war could be lost only if the American public turned sour on it. American public opinion was the essential domino. U.S. leaders knew it. Hanoi's leader's knew it. Each geared its strategy, both rhetorically and in the conduct of the war, to this overwhelming fact.[2]

This essay is a report on some of the evidence from the public opinion polls concerning this "essential domino."[3]

It is useful — essential, in fact — to keep in mind how public opinion data are generated. The numbers are derived from a fairly primitive stimulus-response situation in which a sample of Americans is peppered with a series of questions, most of them fairly simplistic, concerning issues to which few have ever given much thought.

The experience is often flattering for the respondents — few people are accustomed to having their pronouncements taken down carefully as some sort of divine writ (or at least as valued ephemera), and most rise nicely to the occasion, obligingly generating instant opinion founded upon the whim of the moment. In short, many respondents don't know what they are talking about much of the time, a fact which is continually being forgotten and then rediscovered. On July 1, 1983, for example, the *New York Times* deemed it front page news to report that its poll had found that, after months of public debate, 92 percent of the American public did not know whose side the United States was on in the ongoing conflicts in El Salvador and Nicaragua. Nonetheless, well over 80 percent of these people were entirely willing, when asked, to supply their unvarnished opinion about American policy in that area.

What this means, in particular, is that the responses are often highly sensitive to the nature of the stimulus — that is, to the precise wording of the question posed. When the question is changed slightly, response patterns can often change enormously.

Sometimes changing the mere tone of the question can alter the response: Studies have found the portion of the population in favor of "forbidding" speeches against democracy to be 15 to 25 percentage points lower than the portion in favor of "not allowing" them. More often, however, the difference is in response to changes of a more substantive sort. Thus in 1966, 60 percent favored bombing "industrial plants and factories" in North Vietnam, but only 28 percent favored bombing "big cities." In June 1969, 59 percent of the public favored "month by month" troop withdrawals from Vietnam, but only 29 percent favored "immediate" withdrawal.

Or one could change the response options. Another poll at the time added an option something like "withdraw gradually, but with gusto," and, when given that option, the percentage supporting "immediate" withdrawal dropped to 10 percent. Throwing the word "communist" into a question about Vietnam almost always altered the response, often by 20 percentage points or more.

The central lesson of all this, obviously, is that a lot of power resides with the stimulus-maker, the author of the question. It also means it is sheer nonsense to declare with any sort of precision that a percentage of the population is "in favor of" bombing or withdrawal or negotiation or abortion or gun control or free speech or cancer research. Yet very often that is all newspaper poll reports do.[4]

Despite this phenomenon, analysis of public opinion poll data can often yield useful information about attitudes. Mostly, this can be accomplished by keeping the question-wording bias constant through adopting a comparative approach. One can do trend analysis, for example — comparing reactions to the same question at different times. One is then in a position to say how measured response has changed over time. But one *cannot* make meaningful statements about when trends pass the "fifty percent mark," since the location of the trend at any point is a function of how the question is worded (any more than having the Dow-Jones average "break through the 1,000 point barrier" suggests anything substantively significant about the American economy — if a different collection of stocks had been averaged, the 1,000 point breakthrough would occur at a different time).

One can compare how subgroups — men and women, for example — react to the same question. Or one can compare differently worded questions about the same issue to see what words and symbols change response patterns.

The Korean Comparison

In the case of public opinion on the war in Vietnam, a special, highly useful comparison is possible: Attitudes can be compared to those which prevailed during the Korean War, another costly conflict on the fringes of Asia marked by frustration and popular confusion.

Popular support for the wars in Vietnam and Korea can most clearly be compared by looking at the results for a question asked repeatedly by Gallup during both wars. It is of the form: "Do you think the United States made a mistake in getting into the war?"[5]

In both wars, support declined, seemingly inexorably, as the wars wore on. At first glance the patterns of declining support seem to have followed different trajectories in the two wars: Both generated high levels of support when U.S. troops entered the fighting, but support for the Korean War dropped quickly and then held fairly steady, while support for the war in Vietnam was marked by a gradual, persistent decline.

These trends, however, reflect the different way U.S. casualties were suffered in the two wars: Losses were heavy during the first year of the Korean War, then lighter; in Vietnam, they were light at the beginning, then progressively greater as the fighting intensified. When one takes this difference into account, trends in support for the wars followed remarkably similar patterns. They were a function of the logarithm of U.S. casualties: Both started at about the same level and then dropped by some 15 percentage points whenever the cumulative U.S. casualties increased by a factor of ten — that is, when they rose from 100 to 1,000, from 1,000 to 10,000, from 10,000 to 100,000.

In general then, despite the fact that vocal opposition in the Vietnam War was far greater than in the Korean War, popular support for the two wars *by this measure* was the same for the period during which they were comparable. Support for the war in Vietnam did finally slump to levels lower than in Korea, but it did so only after U.S. casualties in Vietnam had substantially surpassed those of the earlier war.[6]

Trends in Support: Other Questions

This central conclusion generally holds when responses to other questions, questions about military options such as escalation or withdrawal, are analyzed. Precise comparison is very difficult because the polling agencies continually altered the wording of the questions they asked on these issues, but it seems that in both wars sentiment for withdrawal and for escalation was about the same and followed the same general trends during the period for which the wars were comparable. Then, in 1969, after U.S. casualties in Vietnam had far surpassed those of Korea, official U.S. policy shifted toward (very gradual) withdrawal and, partly in response, sentiment for withdrawal increased while approval of escalation diminished greatly.

One area in which attitudes toward military policy seems different between the wars concerns the use of nuclear weapons. There was more willingness to use these weapons in Korea than in Vietnam, perhaps in part because they were at that time smaller and far less numerous.

When one compares the wars to see what kinds of people supported and opposed them, it is found that the wars were quite similar in this respect as well.

Rather than classifying everyone as either a "hawk" or a "dove," it is useful to distinguish two kinds of people: Those who cue on the issue itself (Believers) and those who take their cue from prominent people, particularly the President (Followers). "Hawks" and "doves", for example, are Believers — they tend to support or oppose the war and the use of force regardless of what national policy is. Followers, on the other hand, will react like hawks if the President is pursuing a forceful or warlike policy, like doves if he is reducing war or seeking negotiation.

Followers

The Follower phenomenon can lead to major shifts in measured opinion when the President changes policy. In May 1966, for example, half the public advocated bombing Hanoi and Haiphong; when bombing in that area was instituted in June the proportion in favor surged to 85 percent. Then, in late 1967 and early 1968, between 48 and 70 percent (depending on how the question was phrased) favored continued bombing of North Vietnam; but when the President halted the bombing (and even before the Communists responded by agreeing to preliminary peace talks), that percentage dropped to 26 percent.[7]

Among the demographic groups easily separated out on polls, two were clearly inclined to be Followers. Contrary to accepted and constantly repeated lore, it was the well-educated and the young who were particularly inclined toward supporting the wars in general and prevailing presidential policy in particular. This does not mean they were hawks on the wars; rather they were supporters of whatever current policy was. For example, the polls often gave respondents a three-point policy option: withdraw completely, continue present policy, go all out and escalate. The well-educated and the young tended to endorse the middle opinion and to reject the two extreme positions.[8]

These correlations, which occur on literally hundreds of polls and have been observed by many researchers, continue to surprise people, at least for the Vietnam War, because the antiwar protest was continually depicted as a "youth movement" centered on the colleges, and a vast amount of ink was spilled over a largely nonexistent phenomenon known as the "generation gap." The most obvious members of any public political movement tend to be young and well-educated — the conservative Goldwater movement of 1964 was often seen to be a youth movement, for example. The protest movement represented an important point of view, but it represented neither youth nor the well-educated. It was centered primarily on a group of elite colleges in the Northeast, colleges which enrolled neither a substantial percentage of the youth of the country, nor even a substantial proportion of the country's college students.

In addition to those who rally around presidential policy, there are other sorts of Followers whose cue is the current position of their party's leadership whether it occupies the White House at the present moment or not. These people are segregated out when one looks at how people who call themselves Democrats, Independents, and Republicans relate to the war.

Since the basic war-support question asks if "we" made a "mistake," and since both wars were begun under Democratic administrations, Democrats tended to be more supportive of the wars on this measure than Republicans. This difference was small at the beginning of each war, reflecting consensus among party leadership, and then wider as the frustrating wars wore on. In Vietnam, polarities neatly reversed when Nixon entered the White House. Within a year it had become "Nixon's war": Democrats were now substantially more likely to find the war a mistake than were Republicans. Under Johnson, Democrats tended to be optimistic about the war's progress and about the prospects for resolution; under Nixon, Republicans became the optimists.

However, during the Korean War and under Johnson in the Vietnam War, there was very little difference between partisans over the relative merits of escalation and de-escalation; this reflected consensus at the top — the Republican leadership grumbled, but had no really tangible alternate policy to offer. Under Nixon, for the first time in either war, a considerable difference in policy preferences was evident at the party leadership level and substantial differences were accordingly measured among rank-and-file partisans by the polls. (With an almost gracious sense of propriety, those who labeled themselves "independents" fell neatly between the partisan groups on all questions.)

Believers

As noted, Believers are those whose cue is the war itself rather than the position of the leadership. Hawks consistently find the war worthwhile; they support escalation and reject withdrawal. Doves find the war a mistake, and support de-escalation, bombing halts, and efforts at negotiation.

Among the demographic groups easily sorted out on polls, it was sex which most clearly defined this dimension: In both wars (and on most issues of military policy, for that matter), women tended to be doves, men hawks, no matter what the current position of the President or party leadership happened to be. Race also proves to be relevant on this dimension. Whites tended to be hawks, blacks doves — a relationship which held for both wars and also, as far as data are available, for World War II.

Another area in which Believer reaction ought to be evident is self-interest: Those likely to be drafted, and their relatives, ought to be more dovelike than those unthreatened. Poll evidence is sketchy on this issue, but data from both wars, as well as from World War II, suggest no pattern exists. An inkling of this may perhaps be evident in the finding that non-draftable women are more dovish than men. But even controlling for age and sex, the draft-threatened seem no different from others in their view of war policy. Whatever self-interest may dictate, it is apparently undercut by other psychological forces and identifications.

Although the overwhelming conclusion from these analyses is that both the wars in Korea and Vietnam were supported by the same demographic groups, there is one group which clearly had a different perspective on the two wars. Jews strongly supported the Korean War, but opposed the Vietnam War, particularly after it was a year or two old. It is possible some of this reflects analogies with Israel: The Korean action may have been seen as relevant to U.S. Mideast policy while Vietnam may have seemed an enervating distraction from that area.

But more likely the Jewish shift is a reflection of the shift of another group, one not readily measurable on polls: the intellectual Left. To many in this group, Korea seemed a tragic necessity to contain the dynamism of Stalin's Soviet Union. The Cold War — particularly the one with the Soviet Union — had mellowed considerably by the mid-1960s and, where the Johnson administration saw Vietnam as vital to containing Communist China, many on the intellectual Left were doubtful; those doubts increased, and vocal war opposition grew, as the Communist threat in the area diminished with the anti-Communist purges in Indonesia in 1965–66 and with China's inward-directed and self-destructive Cultural Revolution.[9]

Some Concluding Comments

It has been found that popular support for the Vietnam War was remarkably similar to that for the Korean War during the period in which the wars were comparable. Levels of support were the same, trends were the same, and both wars were supported by much the same demographic groups.[10]

Of course Vietnam generated far more *vocal* opposition than did Korea, but this seems to reflect the vocalism of the intellectual Left far more than it represents a substantial change in opinion among the wider public. The impact of the Vietnam antiwar movement is discussed at greater length in a separate essay elsewhere in this volume.

The similarity of popular support for the two wars suggests that television, a rampant fact of life during Vietnam but a mere infant during Korea, may not have been as vital a force in shaping attitudes toward Vietnam as is often supposed. War, after all, is a singularly unsubtle phenomenon, and the assumption that people will know how they feel about it only if they see it regularly pictured on their television screens is essentially naive and patronizing.[11]

Notes

[1] © 1984 by John Mueller

[2] Leslie Gelb and Richard Betts, *The Irony of Vietnam: The System Worked* (Washington, D.C.: Brookings, 1979), p. 332.

[3] The discussion is principally developed from John Mueller, *War, Presidents and Public Opinion* (New York: Wiley, 1973), chs. 1–6. Material also comes from John Mueller, "Changes in American Public Attitudes Toward International Involvement," in Ellen P. Stern, *The Limits of Military Intervention* (Beverly Hills, CA: Sage, 1977), pp.323–44; from John Mueller, "Public Expectations of War During the Cold War," *American Journal of Political Science* May 1979, pp. 301–329; and from recent research and reflection.

[4] For further discussion of the question-wording issue, see Howard Schuman and Stanley Presser, *Questions and Answers in Attitude Surveys* (New York: Academic Press, 1981), and John P. Robinson and Robert Meadow, *Polls Apart* (Cabin John, MD: Seven Locks Press, 1982). The polls do better at estimating election results. But that is because in these cases they are dealing with *behavior*, not attitude. They are essentially asking what the respondent plans to *do* on election day, a concept far easier to deal with than something as ephemeral as abstract opinion. The polls' considerable, if not unrelieved, success at estimating what people will *do* in the voting booth has often led to the erroneous assumption that their measurement of attitude has the same tangible relation to what people *think*.

[5] Various forms of this question were asked during the Korean War. Measured support for the war was increased whenever the question added the words "to stop the Communists"; adding the words "to defend South Korea," however, made no difference. Finally, if it was recast to ask, simply, do you think the war "worth fighting," rather than did "we" make a mistake, measured support dropped substantially. These observations, found also in various questions for the Vietnam War, suggest the notion of stopping communism was an important element in support for the wars, as was the idea of carrying out a commitment; saving or defending the South Koreans or the South Vietnamese, however, was not.

[6] By and large, trends on the "mistake" question were not significantly perturbed by specific events. Thus even the supposedly traumatic Tet Offensive of 1968 did not seem to speed the support trend's downward progression noticeably. That event did affect other attitudes, however: The percentage feeling the U.S. was "losing ground" in Vietnam rose 15 percentage points and the number expecting the war to end in two years dropped 13 percentage points. Data are sparse, but the Tet Offensive seemed to have first increased a willingness to step up military action and then, a month or two later, there was a reaction toward favoring a reduction of military effort.

[7] While there was often a strong Follower, or rally-round-the-flag, effect during the wars, it should not be assumed that the Presidents were all-powerful manipulators of public opinion. Support for the wars eroded despite the Presidents' continual efforts to shape and increase public acceptance of their war policies. Thus it seems visionary to suggest President Johnson's Vietnam problem could have been mitigated, and the war's popularity maintained, if he had straightforwardly sought to "rally" or "mobilize" the "American people for war" (see Harry G. Summers, Jr., "Lessons: A Soldier's View," *The Wilson Quarterly*, Summer 1983, pp. 125–35).

[8] While young people disproportionately supported Vietnam policy throughout the war according to the "mistake" and other questions, there was some tendency, particularly late in the war (in the Nixon era) for them (but not the well-educated) to move in a more dovish direction on questions of military strategy. This was especially notable in their disproportionate refusal to go along with Nixon's Cambodian invasion of 1970.

[9] On this issue, see John Mueller, "Vietnam Revised," *Armed Forces and Society*, December 1982, pp. 167–73.

[10] There are limited data to afford a comparison with opinion during World War II. That war was unquestionably far more popular than the wars in Korea and Vietnam, but not so popular as one might think. Although the percentage rose later, six months after Pearl Harbor only 53 percent said they felt they had a clear idea of what the war was about, as compared to 48 percent for the Vietnam War (in 1967). Toward the end of the war some 15 or 20 percent expressed a willingness to make peace with Hitler on the basis of the *status quo* — thus leaving him in control of France.

[11] On this issue, see also Lawrence W. Lichty, "Video vs. Print," *The Wilson Quarterly*, Vol. 6, No. 5, pp. 49–57, and Michael Mandelbaum, "Vietnam: The Television War," *Daedalus*, Fall 1982, pp. 157–69.

YEAR-END U.S. TROOP STRENGTH AND BATTLE DEAD IN THE VIETNAM WAR, 1961–1973

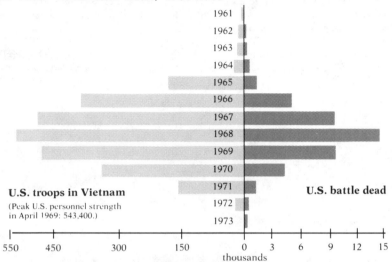

U.S. troops in Vietnam
(Peak U.S. personnel strength in April 1969: 543,400.)

U.S. battle dead

1961
1962
1963
1964
1965
1966
1967
1968
1969
1970
1971
1972
1973

550   450   300   150   0   3   6   9   12   15
thousands

57,717 U.S. servicemen had died by the end of 1973: 47,268 in battle, 10,449 from other causes. Defense spending as a percentage of both the U.S. budget and Gross National Product declined long before the war ended.

DEFENSE SPENDING AS A PERCENTAGE OF FEDERAL BUDGET AND GNP 1961–1975

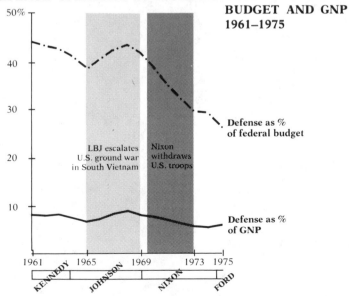

50%
40
30
20
10

LBJ escalates
U.S. ground war
in South Vietnam

Nixon
withdraws
U.S. troops

Defense as %
of federal budget

Defense as %
of GNP

1961   1965   1969   1973   1975

KENNEDY   JOHNSON   NIXON   FORD

POPULAR SUPPORT FOR VIETNAM WAR AND TWO PRESIDENTS

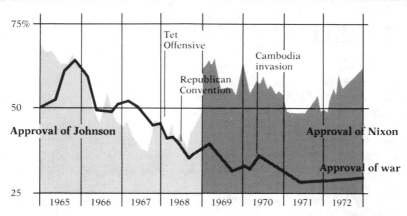

The Gallup poll questions (above) were: "Do you approve or disapprove of the way (the incumbent President) is handling his job?" and "Do you think the United States made a mistake sending troops to fight in Vietnam?" Answers to the "mistake" question do not indicate policy preferences, e.g., escalation or withdrawal. Americans reacted similarly to the Korean War (See WQ, Summer '78). Ironically, the erosion of U.S. popular support coincided with a long decline in enemy battalion-size (400- to 500-man) attacks after the 1968 Tet Offensive. After Tet, the percentage of South Vietnamese in relatively "secure" areas, as measured by (uncertain) U.S. statistics, rose steadily until 1972, when Hanoi launched its Easter Offensive.

COMMUNIST BATTALION-SIZE ATTACKS, 1965–1972

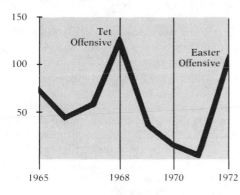

PERCENT OF SOUTH VIETNAM'S POPULATION IN 'SECURE' AREAS, 1967–1972

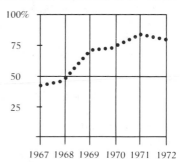

Source: U.S. Department of Defense; *The Budget of the U.S. Government*, 1970 and 1977, Government Printing Office; John E. Mueller, *War, Presidents, and Public Opinion*, 1978; Journal of Defense Research, Series B, Fall 1975.

THE VIETNAM VETERAN

"There is something special about Vietnam veterans," antiwar psychologist Robert Jay Lifton wrote in *Home from the War* (1973). "Everyone who has contact with them seems to agree that they are different from veterans of other wars." U.S. intervention in South Vietnam, Lifton suggested, had produced a deeply troubled Lost Generation. On television and in the movies (*Coming Home, The Deer Hunter*) of the 1970s, the Vietnam GI was regularly portrayed as either victim or psychopath — at war with himself and society. In effect, such stereotypes helped to make the veteran a scapegoat for an unpopular war.

The available facts, drawn from Veterans Administration data and other surveys, supply a different portrait.

Of the 8,744,000 personnel on active duty during the "Vietnam era" (August 5, 1964, to January 27, 1973), 3,403,000 served in the Southeast Asia theater. Roughly 2,594,000 of that number served in South Vietnam; perhaps 40 to 60 percent of them fought in combat, provided close combat support, or were frequently exposed to hostile action.

How well did the U.S. combat soldier and Marine perform during their one-year tours? Most analyses support the conclusion that American officers and men learned fast and fought well against a tenacious, often elusive foe during the 1965–68 period preceding President Nixon's 1969 decision to begin to withdraw. Thereafter, discipline eroded. Recorded "fragging" incidents — assaults by troops upon officers with intent to kill, to injure, or to intimidate — rose from 96 in 1969 to 222 in 1971. Drug abuse reached epidemic proportions; in 1971, 28.5 percent of U.S. soldiers in Vietnam admitted to using narcotics such as heroin and opium. Worldwide Army desertion rates rose from 14.7 per thousand in Fiscal Year (FY) 1966 to 73.5 per thousand in FY 1971.

But U.S. Army desertion rates during World War II were not dissimilar (63 per thousand in 1944). Indeed, most desertions by those who served in Indochina took place *after* they came home and were seldom related to opposition to the war; drugs and insubordination were a worldwide Army phenomenon. Ninety-seven percent of Vietnam-era veterans earned honorable discharges.

The "psychopath" image was equally far-fetched. Despite the war's peculiar strains, the rate of psychological breakdowns ("combat fatigue") among servicemen in Vietnam was below those of Korea and World War II. Yet American servicemen suffered permanently disabling wounds at a far greater rate in Vietnam than in earlier wars — 300 percent higher than in World War II, 70 percent higher than in Korea — partly because of the Viet Cong's use of mines and booby traps. Improved medical care enabled more badly wounded men to survive.

Despite the much-publicized March 1968 massacre of civilians at the hamlet of My Lai by an Army platoon led by Second Lieutenant William L. Calley, few U.S. infantrymen committed atrocities during the Vietnam War; prosecution of offenders tended to be vigorous and punishment harsh.

U.S. troops in Vietnam represented a much broader cross-section of America than is commonly supposed. For example, blacks accounted for no more than 12.5 percent of the total number of Americans killed in the war at a time when blacks constituted 13.5 percent of the total U.S. male population of military age. Only 25 percent of U.S. personnel deployed in Vietnam consisted of *draftees*, versus 66 percent of military personnel during World War II.

The chief inequities were economic. Three-fourths of the troops in Vietnam came from lower-middle- or working-class families (and one-fourth came from families below the poverty level). Compared with their more affluent peers, individuals with lower-income backgrounds faced twice as great a likelihood of serving in the military. (Ivy League college graduates were conspicuously rare in Vietnam.)

Most Vietnam veterans have adapted successfully to civilian life; and 14 are now in Congress (two Senators, 12 Representatives). "Post-traumatic stress disorder," which has afflicted perhaps one-fourth of Vietnam veterans, appears to derive from the common perception among these men that they received a far less friendly reception upon their return than did veterans of other American wars. This perception is not inaccurate. For one thing, neither Lyndon Johnson nor Richard Nixon (nor the nation's college presidents) proposed a "GI Bill" for Vietnam veterans that matched the federal education benefits awarded to earlier generations of ex-servicemen.

Even so, statistics on suicide, divorce, crime, and drug use show that the Vietnam veteran compares favorably on these counts with his nonveteran peer. And in March 1982, despite the economic recession, more than 90 percent of Vietnam veterans held jobs.

BACKGROUND BOOKS: VIETNAM

As the *New York Times'* Fox Butterfield wrote after the Wilson Center's Vietnam history conference last January, "a small group of scholars, journalists, and military specialists. . .have started to look afresh at the war."

In so doing, examining new documentation, they have challenged many of the old claims of the "hawks" and, more notably, of the antiwar "doves" whose views largely prevailed in academe and book publishing and often gained media acceptance during and after the turmoil of the Vietnam years.

Perhaps the first apolitical "revisionist" study was *Tet!* (1971) by *Washington Post* veteran Don Oberdorfer, who concluded, as most historians do now, that the Communists' spectacular 1968 Tet Offensive was a defeat for Hanoi in South Vietnam, even as it demoralized political Washington. In *The Unmaking of a President* (1977), Herbert Schandler, a retired Army colonel and one of the authors of the *Pentagon Papers*, followed up with a scholarly, eye-opening dissection of Washington decision-making during the hectic February—March 1968 period. Another *Post* man, Peter Braestrup, analyzed press and TV performance during the Tet drama; he found that journalists had been overwhelmed by this *Big Story* (1977) and too hastily portrayed what turned out to be a Communist setback as a battlefield disaster for the allies.

A major contribution to understanding how the United States got into Vietnam came from Richard Betts and Leslie Gelb (director of the *Pentagon Papers* project and now a *New York Times*man in Washington). In *The Irony of Vietnam* (1979), Betts and Gelb undercut one widespread notion that the press itself had fostered: that Lyndon Johnson secretly decided on massive escalation in Vietnam even as he seemed to promise the contrary during his 1964 presidential campaign. Working with newly released documents at the LBJ Library in Austin, political scientist Larry Berman followed up with a closer examination of LBJ's decisions and hesitations during the 1965 escalation in *Planning a Tragedy* (1982); he is now working on a sequel covering the 1966–68 period.

American hopes for a negotiated settlement only led to confusion, wrote political scientist Allan Goodman in *The Lost Peace* (1978), a history of U.S. peace "feelers" and peace talks with Hanoi. The North Vietnamese had told Washington from the outset, Goodman added, that there was really "nothing to negotiate"; victory, not the prewar status quo, was the North Vietnamese objective.

Relying partly on newly obtainable military files, Guenter Lewy, a political scientist at the University of Massachusetts, produced a controversial, data-packed study of *America in Vietnam* (1978). Even as he described South Vietnam's long ordeal (including 300,000 civilian deaths), Lewy concluded that Americans did not wage an "immoral" or unusually destructive war in the South, or engage in "terror bombing" of the North, as alleged by the Left.

Memoirs aside, few U.S. military men have dwelt, at book-length, on the lessons of the war. However, Colonel Harry Summers broke the ice in 1981 with *On Strategy*, an attempt to prod his fellow officers (and civilian policy-makers) into re-reading the maxims of Clausewitz as they applied to the U.S. failure in Vietnam.

And a former critic of the war, *Commentary* editor Norman Podhoretz, stirred up a storm in literary Manhattan by exhuming the wartime statements of the New Left and analyzing *Why We Were in Vietnam* (1982). It was not "immoral" to help the South Vietnamese defend themselves against Hanoi, he argued, but it was probably impossible, given the circumstances, to win.

None of these books is the last word. Much territory remains to be explored. Many complex issues need added investigation.

The further study of the conduct of the war (especially after 1968) has been limited by the slow — and slowing — rate of declassification of official U.S. documents, and the reticence of some major figures. Lyndon Johnson, Henry Kissinger, and Richard Nixon have done their memoirs. But none has been forthcoming from Dean Rusk or Robert S. McNamara (who, unlike Rusk, declines even to discuss Vietnam). Moreover, no great enthusiasm has been shown by private foundations or universities for Vietnam studies using the sizable archival resources that now *are* open to scholars.

Even so, research is being done. Political scientist Timothy J. Lomperis will soon publish a critique of the oft-cited "revolutionary" aspects of Hanoi's war in the South, *Vietnam: The War Everyone Lost — and Won.* Editor Robert Manning is shepherding an illustrated multivolume history, *The Vietnam Experience,* for Boston Publishing Company. Newsman Neil Sheehan is finishing a biography of John Paul Vann, the archetypical U.S. adviser in Vietnam.

Keeping track of such efforts — as well as of contemporary affairs — is Douglas Pike. His quarterly *Indochina Chronology* newsletter is available free by writing to Professor Pike, Institute of East Asian Studies, University of California, Berkeley, California 94720.

The armed services have employed by far the largest number of historians devoted to chronicling the Vietnam War, especially U.S. combat experience. The Army published a series of monographs of uneven quality (on the Special Forces, riverine tactics, etc.) during the 1970s; its 16-volume official history of the war will only start appearing later in this decade, in the tradition of its massive, highly regarded accounts of World War II and Korea.

The Marine Corps has published three volumes of its war history (through 1966); the Air Force and Navy have moved more slowly. A "Select Bibliography of Department of Defense Publications of the Southeast Asia Conflict" is available by writing LTC A.G. Traas, Histories Division, U.S. Army Center of Military History, Washington, D.C. 20314.

A lengthy essay on Vietnam books was published in *The Wilson Quarterly* ("Vietnam as History," Spring 1978), too early to include James Webb's *Fields of Fire* and several other first-rate combat novels. However, most of the books listed below were cited in that essay.

From *The Wilson Quarterly*, Summer 1983, with revisions.

A SHORT VIETNAM BOOKLIST

History, Memoirs, Journalism, Polemics, and Fiction

Air War Study Group, Cornell Univ., **The Air War in Indochina** (Beacon, rev. ed., 1972); Michael Arlen, **Living Room War** (Viking, 1969).

Larry Berman, **Planning a Tragedy** (Norton, 1982); Douglas Blaufarb, **The Counter-Insurgency Era: U.S. Doctrine and Performance** (Free Press, 1977); Anthony T. Bouscaren, ed., **All Quiet on the Eastern Front: The Death of South Vietnam** (Devin-Adair, 1976); Richard Boyle, **The Flower of the Dragon: The Breakdown of the U.S. Army in Vietnam** (Ramparts, 1972); Peter Braestrup, **Big Story: How the American Press and Television Reported and Interpreted the Crisis of Tet 1968 in Vietnam and Washington** (Yale, rev. ed., 1983); Jack Broughton, **Thud Ridge** (Lippincott, 1969); C. D. Bryan, **Friendly Fire** (Putnam's, 1976); Josiah Bunting, **The Lionheads** (Braziller, 1972); Joseph L. Buttinger, **Vietnam: A Dragon Embattled** (Praeger, 1967), **Vietnam: The Unforgettable Tragedy** (Horizon, 1976).

Philip Caputo, **A Rumor of War** (Holt, 1977); Michael Charlton and Anthony Moncrieff, **Many Reasons Why: The American Involvement in Vietnam** (Hill & Wang, 1978); Charles Coe, **Young Man in Vietnam** (Four Winds Press, 1968); John L. Cook, **The Advisor** (Dorrance, 1973); Chester L. Cooper, **The Lost Crusade: America in Vietnam** (Dodd, 1970).

William J. Duiker, **The Communist Road to Power in Vietnam** (Westview, 1981); Dennis J. Duncanson, **Government and Revolution in Vietnam** (Oxford, 1968); Van Tien Dung, **Our Great Spring Victory** (Monthly Review, 1977).

Frank Callihan Elkins, **The Heart of a Man** (Norton, 1973); Gloria Emerson, **Winners and Losers** (Random, 1976).

Bernard Fall, **Hell in a Very Small Place: The Siege of Dien Bien Phu** (Lippincott, 1966); **Street Without Joy: Insurgency in Indochina, 1946–63** (Stackpole, rev. ed., 1963), **The Two Vietnams: A Political and Military Analysis** (Praeger, rev. ed., 1964); Frances FitzGerald, **Fire in the Lake: The Vietnamese and the Americans in Vietnam** (Little, Brown, 1972); Charles B. Flood, **The War of the Innocents** (McGraw-Hill, 1970).

Leslie Gelb and Richard Betts, **The Irony of Vietnam: The System Worked** (Brookings, 1979); Allan E. Goodman, **The Lost Peace: America's Search for a Negotiated Settlement of the Vietnam War** (Hoover, 1978), **Politics in War: The Bases of Political Community in South Vietnam** (Harvard, 1973); Zalin Grant, **Survivors** (Norton, 1975); Sen. Mike Gravel, ed., **The Pentagon Papers: The Defense Department History of United States Decisionmaking on Vietnam** (Beacon, 1971).

David Halberstam, **The Best and the Brightest** (Random, 1972), **The Making of a Quagmire** (Random, 1965), **One Very Hot Day** (Houghton, 1967); P. Edward Haley, **Congress and the Fall of South Vietnam and Cambodia** (Assoc. Univ. Presses, 1982); Larry Heinemann, **Close Quarters** (Farrar, 1977); James B. Hendry, **The Small World of Khanh Hau** (Aldine, 1964); Michael Herr, **Dispatches** (Knopf, 1977); George C. Herring, **America's Longest War: The United States and Vietnam, 1950–1975** (Wiley, 1979); Seymour Hersh, **My Lai 4: A Report on the Massacre and Its Aftermath** (Random, 1970); Gerald Hickey, **Village in Vietnam** (Yale, 1964), **Sons of the Mountains** (Yale, 1982), **Free in the Forest** (Yale, 1982); John G. Hubbell et al., **P.O.W.: A Definitive History of the American Prisoner of War Experience in Vietnam, 1964–1973** (Reader's Digest Press, 1976); Ken Hurwitz, **Marching Nowhere** (Norton, 1971).

Lyndon B. Johnson, **The Vantage Point: Perspectives of the Presidency, 1963–69** (Holt, 1971); Ward S. Just, **To What End: Report from Vietnam** (Houghton, 1968).

Doris Kearns, **Lyndon Johnson and the American Dream** (Harper, 1976); Steven Kelman, **Push Comes to Shove: The Escalation of Student Protest** (Houghton, 1970); Douglas Kinnard, **The War Managers** (Univ. Press of New Eng., 1977); Henry A. Kissinger, **White House Years** (Little, Brown, 1979), **Years of Upheaval** (Little, Brown, 1982); Robert W. Komer, **Bureaucracy Does Its Thing: Institutional Constraints on U.S.–GVN Performance in Vietnam** (Rand, 1972); David Kraslow and Stuart Loory, **The Secret Search for Peace in Vietnam** (Random, 1968); Nguyen Cao Ky, **Twenty Years and Twenty Days** (Stein & Day, 1976).

Anthony Lake, ed., **The Vietnam Legacy: The War, American Society and the Future of American Foreign Policy** (N.Y. Univ., 1976); Daniel Lang, **Casualties of War** (McGraw-Hill, 1969); Guenter Lewy, **America in Vietnam** (Oxford, 1978); Don Luce and John Sommer, **Vietnam: The Unheard Voices** (Cornell, 1969).

S.L.A. Marshall, **Ambush** (Cowles, 1969), **Bird** (Cowles, 1968), **The Fields of Bamboo** (Dial, 1971), **West to Cambodia** (Cowles, 1968); John T. McAlister, **Vietnam: The Origins of Revolution** (Knopf, 1969); John T. McAlister and Paul Mus, **The Vietnamese and Their Revolution** (Harper, 1970); Harvey Meyerson, **Vinh Long** (Houghton, 1970); John E. Mueller, **War, Presidents, and Public Opinion** (Wiley, 1973).

Richard M. Nixon, **RN: The Memoirs of Richard Nixon** (Grosset, 1978).

Don Oberdorfer, **Tet!** (Doubleday, 1971); Tim O'Brien, **Going After Cacciato** (Delacorte, 1978), **If I Die in a Combat Zone, Box Me Up and Ship Me Home** (Delacorte, 1973); Robert E. Osgood, **Limited War Revisited** (Westview, 1979).

D. R. Palmer, **Summons of the Trumpet: U.S.–Vietnam in Perspective** (Presidio, 1978); Howard R. Penniman, **Elections in South Vietnam** (American Enterprise Institute, 1973); Douglas Pike, **History of Vietnamese Communism, 1925–1976** (Hoover, 1978), **The Vietcong Strategy of Terror** (U.S. Mission, Saigon, 1970), **War, Peace, and the Viet Cong** (MIT, 1969), **Viet Cong: The Organization and Techniques of the National Liberation Front of South Vietnam** (MIT, 1966); Robert Pisor, **The End of the Line: The Siege of Khe Sanh** (Norton, 1982); Norman Podhoretz, **Why We Were in Vietnam** (Simon & Schuster, 1982); Samuel L. Popkin, **The Rational Peasant: The Political Economy of Rural Society in Vietnam** (Univ. of Calif., 1979); Thomas Powers, **The War at Home: Vietnam and the American People, 1964–1968** (Grossman, 1973).

Jeffrey Race, **War Comes to Long An: Revolutionary Conflict in a Vietnamese Province** (Univ. of Calif., 1971); Walt Rostow, **The Diffusion of Power: An Essay in Recent History** (Macmillan, 1972).

Harrison E. Salisbury, **Behind the Lines: Hanoi, December 23–January 7** (Harper, 1967); Al Santoli, **Everything We Had** (Random, 1981); Herbert Y. Schandler, **The Unmaking of a President: Lyndon Johnson and Vietnam** (Princeton, 1977); Jonathan Schell, **The Military Half: An Account of Destruction in Quang Ngai and Quang Tin** (Knopf, 1968); Robert Shaplen, **The Lost Revolution: The U.S. in Vietnam, 1946–1966** (Harper, rev. ed., 1966), **The Road From War: Vietnam, 1965–1970** (Harper, 1970); U.S.G. Sharp and William C. Westmoreland, **Report on the War in Vietnam** (Government Printing Office, 1969); Susan Sheehan, **Ten Vietnamese** (Knopf, 1967); Frank Snepp, **Decent Interval: An Insider's Account of Saigon's Indecent End Told by the CIA's Chief Strategy Analyst in Vietnam** (Random, 1977); Harry G. Summers, Jr., **On Strategy: A Critical Analysis of the Vietnam War** (Presidio, 1982).

W. Scott Thompson and Donaldson D. Frizzell, eds., **The Lessons of Vietnam** (Crane, Russak, 1977); Robert F. Turner, **Vietnamese Communism: Its Origins and Development** (Hoover, 1975).

Sidney Verba et al., **Vietnam and the Silent Majority: The Dove's Guide** (Harper, 1970); Sandy Vogelgesang, **The Long Dark Night of the Soul: The American Intellectual Left and the Vietnam War** (Harper, 1974).

James Webb, **Fields of Fire** (Prentice-Hall, 1978); F. J. West, **The Village** (Harper, 1972); William C. Westmoreland, **A Soldier Reports** (Doubleday, 1976).

ADDENDUM:

A number of people have suggested additions to the Vietnam book list. These include a detailed report on postwar *Violations of Human Rights in the Socialist Republic of Vietnam, April 30, 1975–April 30, 1983* by Ginetta Sagan and Stephen Denney (Aurora Foundation, 1983); *Chance and Circumstances: the Draft, the War, and the Vietnamese Generation* by L. M. Basker and W. A. Strauss (Knopf, 1978); Archimedes L. A. Patti's memoir/critique of the 1944 – 46 period, *Why Vietnam?* (Univ. of Calif., 1980); *The United States Army in Transition* by Zeb B. Bradford Jr. and Frederic J. Brown (Sage, 1973); *Air Power and the Air Lift Evacuation of Kham Duc* by Alan Gropman (Washington: GPO, 1979); *Without*

Honor by Arnold Isaacs (Johns Hopkins, 1983); and *Vietnam: A History* by Stanley Karnow (Viking, 1983).

New editions are being published of Don Oberdorfer's *Tet!* (DaCapo Press, 1984 forthcoming), and of Herbert Schandler's book under a revised title, *Lyndon Johnson and Vietnam: The Unmaking of a President* (Princeton Univ. Press, 1983).

Reviewing scores of veterans' memoirs and other new Vietnam books is the monthly *Vietnam War Newsletter*, published at $16 per year by Thomas W. Hebert, P.O. Box 122, Collinsville, Conn. 06022.

From **The Wilson Quarterly**/*Autumn 1983, with additions.*
c 1983 *by the* Woodrow Wilson International Center for Scholars.

THE SOUTH VIETNAMESE

By Third World standards, the easygoing Saigon government of 1954–75 was as efficient as most, and far less repressive than many, notably the ruthless regime in Hanoi. Given a peaceful post-colonial decade or two, and some good leadership, the Republic of Vietnam might have developed into a fairly prosperous, stable nation like, say, Malaysia or Thailand.

But there was no peace. And neither Ngo Dinh Diem, the South's first Chief of State (1954–63), nor its last, Nguyen Van Thieu (1965–75), was a bold leader. Each suffered from personal insecurity, caution, and remoteness from ordinary South Vietnamese. Neither was able — or willing — to build broad-based political support outside the French-educated urban middle class. As a result, Army generals, themselves divided by rivalries, were the arbiters of South Vietnam's turbulent politics.

To stay in power, Thieu, himself a general, felt compelled to pick senior commanders on the basis of loyalty first, honesty and competence second. As one ARVN officer told the *New York Times* in 1975, "The generals amassed riches for their families, but the soldiers got nothing and saw no moral sanction in their leadership." In one year (1966), more than one-fifth of ARVN's soldiers deserted — not to the Viet Cong but to go home.

Land reform did not come until 1970. The war ravaged entire districts, notably in Quang Ngai and Hau Nghia provinces; overall, 1.2 million refugees were generated between late 1965 and mid-1967 alone. And each year, the Viet Cong kidnapped or assassinated thousands of village chiefs, schoolteachers, relief workers.

Yet, despite official corruption, lackluster leadership, and severe hardships, the South Vietnamese people never went over en masse to the revolution. No ARVN unit defected to the foe. According to political scientist Samuel Popkin, the Communists' costly 1968 Tet Offensive (and their massacre of civilians in occupied Hue) discredited two Viet Cong propaganda themes: inevitable victory and a happy future under Communist rule. After Tet, Saigon belatedly organized more than two million civilians into local armed self-defense groups. By war's end, more than 220,000 South Vietnamese soldiers and militiamen had died to defend their country.

The massive U.S. presence from 1965 to 1973 both helped and hindered the South Vietnamese. American troops, advisers, and fire-power offset Hanoi's advantages and staved off defeat — but encouraged Saigon's psychological dependence on the Yanks. Washington decried Saigon's shortcomings but did not insist on solutions. The unilateral withdrawal of their powerful but war-weary ally in 1973 — and later U.S. aid cuts — demoralized Thieu, his troops, and his best commanders. Left alone to face the Northerners, the South was fated to succumb.

"We small nations can end up losing high stakes [by counting on U.S. pledges of support]," observed Bui Diem, former Ambassador to Washington, on the 10th anniversary of the Paris peace accords. "You can . . . say 'Well, it is an unhappy chapter [in] American history.' But that is not the same . . . for the South Vietnamese."

From *The Wilson Quarterly*, Summer 1983, with revisions.
© 1983 by the Woodrow Wilson International Center for Scholars.